Through the Land of Fire

Fifty-Six South

Through the Land of Fire

Fifty-Six South

BEN PESTER

SEAFARER BOOKS

SHERIDAN HOUSE

© Ben Pester 2004

First published in the UK by:
Seafarer Books
102 Redwald Road
Rendlesham
Woodbridge
Suffolk IP12 2TE

And in the USA by:
Sheridan House Inc.
145 Palisade Street
Dobbs Ferry
N.Y. 10522

UK   ISBN   0 95427 505 5
USA   ISBN   1 57409 202 2

A catalogue record for this book is available from the British Library

Library of Congress Cataloging-in-Publication Data

Pester, Ben
  Through the land of fire : fifty-six south / by Ben Pester.
    p. cm.
   ISBN 1-57409-202-2 (alk. Paper)
1. Pester, Ben, 1924---Travel. 2. Voyages and travels. 3. Marelle
(Yacht) 4. Atlantic Ocean. 5. Cape Horn (Chile) I. Title.

G540.P47 2004
910′.9167′4—dc22
                                        2004017597

Typesetting and design by Julie Rainford
Cover design by Louis Mackay
Front cover: *Marelle* mirrored in the superbly beautiful
Caleta Olla, Beagle Channel

Illustrations by Rowland Pickerill and Louis Mackay
Maps by Ben Pester
Photographs by crew of *Marelle*

Printed in Finland by WS Bookwell OY

DEDICATION

To Tom, my late father in law, who, also having a love affair with *Marelle*, devoted many hours of his later life to her needs.

THE OBJECTIVE

CABO DE HORNOS
55º 59′ SOUTH 67º 16′ WEST

CONTENTS

PREFACE

This is an account of a voyage made in a small wooden vessel with the express purpose of sailing round the formidable Cape Horn. A complementary objective was to experience cruising through the lonely, dark and beautiful waterways of Tierra del Fuego at the uttermost end of South America.

It was accomplished over nine months spanning the new millennium in my 35-year-old Bermudan sloop *Marelle*, being accompanied throughout by one friend and by a second for the latter part. The aggregate age of the three men in this particular boat was 193 years. The greater part of 18,000 miles flowed under the keel, with the longest passage being ninety days non-stop at sea. The moment of rounding the Horn was the realisation of a boyhood aspiration which was to take all of my seventy-five years to achieve.

The spirit of the cruise was Corinthian in the way sailing was practised earlier by truly amateur yachtsmen. We had no sponsors and were mercifully free of the all-powerful commercialism which controls modern sailing and the lives of those engaged in it, all pursuing fame and fortune. The description 'Hype and High Seas' applied by a television reviewer to a highly publicised event may say it all.

Marelle is a beautiful boat, built to classic traditional form in 1965. Custom-designed by James McGruer of the Clyde for ocean racing, constructed of teak and subsequently converted for cruising to designs by Alan Pape of Cornwall, she is very different to the mass-produced, super-efficient plastic boat of today.

She is a person. With her I have a profound empathy. We are both veterans of many thousands of miles of sailing in different seas around the world. She was to play the pivotal role in this unfolding saga of the trip to the Horn. This is her story as much as mine.

The sea is the consolation of our day, as it has been the consolation of the centuries ... There, on the sea, is a man nearest to his making, and in communion with that from which he came, and to which he shall return. For the men of very long ago have said, and it is true, that out of the salt water all things came.

H. Belloc, *On Sailing the Sea*

ACKNOWLEDGEMENTS

First and foremost to my crew for their invaluable assistance in giving me the benefit of their wide experience, as well as for their generosity of spirit in accommodating a skipper who, although they never said so, must have been at times a trial throughout the long voyage. It was their contribution that made the venture what it was, a success.

Of comparable importance was the participation of our wives. Without their unstinting backup, encouragement and especially the indulgence of their playboys, the trip would never have happened. I am particularly grateful to my wife, Susan, for her practical input and advice not only on the adventure itself but in putting together this book.

An extra thank you is due to Adrie and Jeremy who were particularly helpful in contributing appendices to the book. In its writing Fraser was also a most useful contributor with his record of events, particularly our highs and lows.

I am most grateful for valued assistance from Rear Admiral Alberto Mantellero of the Chilean Navy. His books on pilotage in the waterways of Tierra del Fuego and an excellent reference work on the origins of the names in the channels were sources of most useful information.

Others not mentioned in the text to whom I want to express my appreciation are:

Kim Morgan of Penryn, my friendly shipwright, who right from the beginning of my affair with *Marelle* has worked on her to the highest professional standards. He has I know enjoyed this because in his view she is a real boat, that is made of wood. He is, as he says, 'not a tupperware man'.

Colin Warren, owner of Metal Surgery, Penryn, who with the team spearheaded by Peter, his machine-shop chief, had been involved with *Marelle* from her early days in Falmouth. I came to rely on their expert and almost instantaneous attention to my frequent requests for engineering assistance. Colin was also the generous donor of my spare sextant.

Rowland and Delia Pickerill, who have not only sailed with me for many years but have done a significant amount of work on *Marelle*. It was a big help for them to give their time, coming all the way down from near Nottingham, to render valued assistance prior to the departure for the south. Rowland very kindly did the marine scene sketches.

Amanda Major not only most competently transcribed the manuscript onto disc but remained remarkably cheerful despite my all too frequent amendments. Michael Bradley was a big help with his highly skilled computer graphics.

PERMISSIONS

Quotations on pages 48, 50, 68, 88, 89, 98, 108, 116, 125, 134, 136, 138, 140, 143, 185, 237 have been reproduced from South America Pilot, Vol 2, Africa Pilot, Vol 1, The Mariner's Handbook and Ocean Passages for the World by permission of the Controller of Her Majesty's Stationery Office and the UK Hydrographic Office (www.ukho.gov.uk)

Photograph of *Marelle* in Appendix 5 has been reproduced by permission of Beken Maritime Services

Appendix 5 *Marelle* has been reproduced by kind permission of *Yachting Monthly* where it appeared in August 1965.

INTRODUCTION

Lives there a sailor who would not have made a Cape Horn passage in his own small vessel rather than any other voyage in the world?

Argentinian yachtsman Vito Dumas

'God in heaven, will this wind ever relent and let us get away from here?'

Marelle was at anchor in the depths of the Straits of Magellan with the sodden wind blasting over us, dominating our world, hurling itself at us to shake the boat and tear at mast, rigging and everything on deck. Down below the cabin was warm and dry, the oil lamps softly aglow and the heater spreading its comfort. Snug. The cabin exuded a sense of security but its occupants were not at peace. Tenseness was in the air. The anxiety was a mutual feeling although individually unexpressed. The giveaway was that from time to time one or other of us would silently station himself at a cabin window to peer through the green water sluicing over it, to check on whether our position had changed in relation to the few shore lights visible in the otherwise unrelieved dark nothingness. If those lights had moved it would have confirmed our anchor was on its way, dragging inexorably across the bottom. We inevitably would have ended up ejected into the bay in the black pitch of the night, lashed with driving rain squalls and spray torn off the tops of waves, thence to be subjected to the unimpeded force of the wind. An unpalatable thought.

We were experiencing first-hand the full impact of the weather conditions to be expected as a matter of course in this storm-ravaged region of the world. How was it then that we had voluntarily subjected ourselves to the hostile conditions in which we now found ourselves? For this, I told myself, I could blame, or partly blame at least, my companions. It was a convenient line of thought.

It had been a good lunch. Assisted perhaps by a bottle or two of very palatable wine, the mood of the little party was relaxed. Our hosts were Adrie and Jeremy Burnett, friends since Susan and I had come to dwell amongst the Celts, some ten years before. We had made the pilgrimage to the spiritual home of St Piran from 'Up Country', as the Cornish whimsically refer to the lands north of the Tamar, and had stayed. Falmouth had taken us unto itself as our temporal home.

It was time for the inevitable snapshots to come out of a trip Susan and I had just made down to southern regions embracing the Antarctic Peninsula and a small slice of Tierra del Fuego. This had been enjoyed to the full in a chartered Russian ice-strengthened survey vessel of modest size, carrying forty or so passengers. Full-blown cruise liners are not for us.

It was a marvellous experience and it may have been that some of our enthusiasm had washed off onto our audience. We had been half expecting the glazed look that spreads over the eyes of those compelled with weary resignation to accept guests' offers to show 'our photos'. Apparently not, as out of the blue Jeremy suddenly came up with 'Have you thought of taking *Marelle* down south?' inferring that 'If you have, I will come with you'. His question was to have far-reaching consequences. 'South' meant the uttermost end of South America including Cape Horn.

On completion of our Antarctica excursion Susan and I had stopped over for a few days in Ushuaia, to seize what we thought then would be the once in a lifetime opportunity to see something of that very much off the beaten track area which comprises the Land of Fire, Tierra del Fuego. A mysterious part of the world, a name known to many, but seen by few. Although I did not know it at the time, the Goddess of Fortune was to smile on me and send me back on a return visit.

Ushuaia, on the Argentinian side of the Beagle Channel, lays claim to be the southernmost city in the world. This claim to city status may in part be due to possession of a small, unpretentious yet interesting cathedral, largely of wood. This provides a link with the past. Although today very much part of Argentina, Ushuaia was founded in 1871 by the English missionary Thomas Bridges. Unwittingly that act was to launch the 'Fatal Impact', to quote Alan Moorehead's graphic expression, culminating in the extinction of the Fuegians, the indigenous Indian tribes. It is a terrible tragedy on the human conscience.

The western world's close involvement with the tribes scattered throughout the few liveable parts of Tierra del Fuego stems from Captain FitzRoy's arrival in HMS *Beagle* to undertake the excessively demanding task of charting those forbidding waters. He was a skilled navigator and determined. So much so that his work has lasted through to this day. A humane and devout man in the orthodox pre-Darwinian mode of the day, he was nevertheless afflicted with the same unfortunate belief held by the missionary throughout history that the locals' way of life in remote places had to be changed, totally if needs be, for their own good. The arrogance of the self-appointed purveyor of the only Truth is staggering. The fact that the Fuegians had existed as they were for countless centuries with a lifestyle that had adapted so well to an incredibly hostile environment was of no moment. They had to be saved from themselves! Although FitzRoy's experiment, albeit with the best intentions, of taking three Fuegians back with him to England ended in grim failure, others took up the challenge to get the natives onto the right course. Their nemesis had arrived.

There were an estimated seven to nine thousand Indians inhabiting the region when Bridges set up stall with his mission at Ushuaia. Today there are none. Apart from what is preserved in the tiny museum in the town there is little to indicate they ever existed. Broken spirits, epidemics and a deliberate policy of extermination by incoming settlers did the trick. There are now no more souls to save. Operation complete.

In Thomas Bridges' defence it has to be said he felt civilisation would inevitably overrun the Fuegians and this would be 'either with the Bible, the gin-bottle or the rifle and the first was surely the best way.' He wanted to get in first but in the event the outcome was the same.

The world of course has moved on and not necessarily for the better for all. In Ushuaia there are still tensions and a sense of supposed deprivation. On the seafront promenade there is a memorial to the conflict in the Falklands, or should one say Islas Malvinas, with an ominous legend to the effect that 'We will be back!'

Standing beside this rather sad structure we could look over the harbour and across the full width of the Beagle Channel to the Chilean side. The border, subject in the past to actual conflict, between Chile and Argentina runs along the centre line of the channel at this point. Each country zealously guards its side. There is not much love lost.

Lying alongside a barge in the harbour, which is very exposed, was a British yacht taking something of a beating in the short sea raised by a fresh wind off the channel. She was in a rather inaccessible berth and we did not pursue the thought of paying our respects, instead walking on into town to keep the circulation moving. As it turned out it was an opportunity missed to gain first-hand intelligence on sailing in those waters. As we were subsequently to discover, British-flagged vessels of any sort are a rarity down there. We were only to encounter one other, a yacht.

We had been able to get a feel for this hugely impressive, dark and largely unattainable scenery with its air of bleakness that had so enthralled the young Darwin when with FitzRoy on the latter's second visit. The whole region is riddled with English names, reflecting its pulling power for explorers and adventurers through the ages from Francis Drake onwards. To the west was the snow-covered Cordillera Darwin, the southern extremity of the mighty Andes. To the east to perpetuate the links with the past lay the Sierra Lucas Bridges. Lucas was Thomas's son, born in Ushuaia and witness to the impending demise of the Fuegians.

It appeared that some of the deep impressions left with us of these southern regions had become apparent during lunch to have prompted Jeremy's remarks. No, I hadn't had any thoughts up till then about going south in *Marelle*, but now I did. I let the idea soak in for a couple of days and then rang him. Was he serious? 'Yes I am' came without hesitation. We were on!

Suddenly I could see the fantasy, deep-seated and dormant for so many years, of rounding Cape Horn in my own boat, about to become a reality. Cape Horn! Superstar amongst the capes of the world. As Felix Riesenberg, American master in sail and writer put it, 'Not to have sailed around the Horn is equivalent to not being a sailor. Seldom does the Horn fail to live up to its evil reputation.'

I imagine most, if not all, people harbour in their inner selves a thought, idea or wish to accomplish something special to them in their lives. Sadly of course all too often that something, whatever it is, remains unrequited. But I was about to become one of the blessed.

This would be the third time an opportunity had presented itself for the achievement of that 'something special' in my life. The first was before the war as a schoolboy in New Zealand, in the late thirties. Although they were the last days of commercial sail there was still a significant fleet of big square-rigged sailing ships, mainly four-masted barques, carrying grain from South Australia to Britain and Europe. Their owner was Captain Gustaf Erikson of the Finnish port of Mariehamn in the Baltic. By cutting costs to the bare bones he was able to keep these great ships going. Having no engines their fuel bills were nil and another major expenditure, cost of labour, was helped fortuitously by the seemingly strange desire of young men to sail in Erikson's ships. Although the Age of Sail was dying the romance of it was not. Not only were these young men willing to subject themselves to the hard work and hard living associated with the sailing ship, but they were prepared to pay him for the privilege of working his ships. The arrangement was that the young hopeful would be indentured as an apprentice, for which a premium had to be paid. In return he received what amounted to not much more than pocket money, euphemistically referred to as a wage.

This is what I had set my heart on. As soon as I left school I would join one of these square-rigged vessels across the Tasman in Port Lincoln and thence sail to a European port or perhaps 'Falmouth for orders' by way of Cape Horn. A boy at my school, two years older than I, had done just that and I was quietly confident, as the young are inclined to be, that my parents would come up with the money to indulge their son's obsession. Then Adolf Hitler got in the way.

The fantasy faded only to flare up again some years later. An old New Zealand friend, Peter Mulgrew, who had been in the Antarctic with Edmund Hillary on the combined transpolar expedition with Sir Vivian Fuchs, was looking for a new adventure. He put together a small team to charter in Punta Arenas a Chilean Navy auxiliary sailing cutter which they would sail through the waterways of Tierra del Fuego, double the Horn and terminate back in Punta Arenas. He wrote asking me to join the team. I agonised over the offer but in the end had to give this second opportunity a miss. On this occasion business and family affairs got in the way. But now a good lunch had brought it all to life again and this time I was to make it. To cap it all, it would be in my own boat!

Having decided to go, the question then was where precisely and when. The two objectives were the Horn itself and the associated plan of cruising through the waterways of Tierra del Fuego. Getting there and back would be a secondary mission. Delivery trips in effect. The timing would have to be the southern summer in the latter part of 1999 extending over into the first part of 2000.

This brought into being a third objective. What about the new millennium? How to mark the advent of this milestone in the history of mankind was very much a nationwide talking point. Never mind that in real terms it was a year out. It seemed to be of importance to many that the occasion warranted much more than the usual humdrum high jinks of seeing in a normal new year. Its real significance to mankind was hardly mentioned.

Another question was the mounting hysteria, second only to the BSE scare, over what would happen to the world's high-tech systems when the millennium struck. The prophets of doom were having their field day but not with us. Old *Marelle* brushed all this aside. The world's electronic systems could be consigned to the scrap heap for all she cared. However we did feel the arrival of the great new millennium itself should be given its due mark of respect. That had to be OFF THE HORN!

The major decision having been taken, it was now a matter of getting down to the detailed planning, including getting round the awkward question 'How much will this exercise in self-gratification cost?' There was an important issue here. As Susan would not be coming with me I had to struggle with justifying the spending of a not inconsiderable sum of money on a personal whim, with myself as the sole beneficiary. I need not have worried. It seemed to be her belief that a husband is a better person to live with when pursuing a definite project on which to focus attention. This is particularly so in retirement. Armed with this idea, real or not, I was then able to live with my conscience and get on unreservedly with the project. It had to be assumed that Jeremy had also been cleared for takeoff and it was soon apparent that he was to be the full beneficiary of Adrie's enthusiastic and very constructive involvement. It is not to gainsay all of this to venture the proposition that for many women an occasional break from 'their man' is not always unwelcome. Witness to Adrie 'coming on board' was her immediate volunteering with Jeremy and backup from Susan to pick up the exacting and vital responsibility for catering and storing.

There was however a condition attached to the encouragement by the distaff side for the venture. It was considered that a third crew member was desirable in the event of 'something happening to one of you old chaps' at sea on a long leg. He would also be valuable with the hard work associated with mooring up in the channels of Tierra del Fuego. There was a shortage of candidates willing to embark on such a long and demanding trip. One did join only to prove incompatible and was asked to leave the boat in the Canaries. He was not to be missed, as fortunately we were to be joined by an eminently compatible pair of strong hands, flying down from Cornwall to meet up with us in Argentina.

An immediate issue was to construct the passage plan, of which a vital part was the timetable. For this of course charts, pilots, sailing directions, routeing charts and the like had to be procured. Additionally a study of the writings of those who had been before us would be obviously beneficial. Although I had my own library, the depth of our reading was increased by books Jeremy had, through family links in publishing.

I thought it would be of considerable value to communicate with those who had personal experience of sailing in and around the Horn region. One seafaring author of considerable experience of the far south is the well-known Hal Roth. His book *Two Against Cape Horn* although written some time ago is necessary reading, particularly for me as his *Whisper* had a similarity with *Marelle*. There was to be a further link in that both boats suffered damage in those waters, albeit Roth had a bigger problem resulting from his boat being driven ashore near the Horn. Our damage was relatively minor but in both instances we called on the Chilean Navy with the same response: unstinting friendly help. Roth's exposure to sailing in southern waters, both in summer and winter, with his wife is unique. A little hesitatingly I wrote to him about such things as ground tackle and methods for securing to the shore. These are two issues vital to one's peace of mind in those waters. He came back very promptly with constructive and most useful comments.

Two further valuable contacts were the coauthors of the Royal Cruising Club Pilotage Foundation pilot on Chile. This had been compiled by two husband-and-wife teams, Ian and Maggie Staples with Tony and Coryn Gooch. In establishing contact with them it helped that we were all fellow members of the Ocean Cruising Club. The RCC pilot fortuitously had only just been published and was to be in frequent use as we worked our way through the labyrinths of the Tierra del Fuego canals. We got used to this description. The English word channels is 'canals' or rather *canales* in Spanish. They could not be more different to canals as we know them in Europe. The pilot is remarkable for the detail it contains, with a wide coverage of anchorages suitable for small craft. We were to find only one mistake of any consequence, which was pretty good in the context of the plethora of detail it contained.

Research into available literature on those parts unearthed another worthwhile pilot. The *Yachtsman's Navigator Guide to the Chilean Channels,* edited by Rear Admiral Alberto Mantellero in both Spanish and English, covers a large selection of anchorages in Chilean Patagonia and the *Fueguinos*. Like the RCC pilot it is detailed on where to anchor and importantly where to deploy the highly advisable shore lines. Where, as was frequently the case, both publications covered the same locations there was a good degree of compatibility but with useful variations. As it happened we were to have only one cause for disagreement with its recommendations on anchorages. It was food for thought that most of those who had been there before us had managed without such aids. Joshua Slocum certainly had, with no engine and none of the equipment which the modern sailor cannot conceive of doing without. But then to paraphrase Bill Tilman 'Joshua Slocum was Joshua Slocum'. They don't make 'em like that any more.

I rang the Admiral in his office in Chile. A courteous response with an informative discussion lead to him posting off a copy of his pilot. He wished us well.

Apart from its function as pilot and general compendium, it contains interesting commentaries on sailing those waters. One was a note that when cruising through the 'fascinating channels of Southern Chile' one should always keep in mind 'that the sea although beautiful, does not tolerate ignorance nor stupidity which, at time(s), exact a steep price'. A further stern warning is 'This GUIDE was written for competent and responsible skippers and crews, experience, training, competence and caution are essential. Due to the variety and number of challenges found crossing it is not a place for novices.'

In continuing to work through the guide one comes across gems such as 'These island(s) and channels ... saw the arrival of the first white man ... when Hernando de Magallanes discovered in 1520 the strait that now carries his name. He was followed by other navigators ... as well as pirates and buccaneers like Drake and Cavendish.' Poor old Drake. He is to suffer for ever from a split personality. In Spanish and Latin American eyes he is a villain. In England he is one of her greatest seamen and revered for not standing any nonsense from the Spanish. His impact was so dramatic that even until recent times apparently South American mothers would threaten fractious children with *El Draco.*

Whilst still on the subject of this Chilean pilot it is worthy of note that it was produced under the auspices of the Maritime League of Chile, described as a 'a private, non-profit organisation dedicated to the oceanic destiny of the nation. With its wish to help and foster nautical sports, maritime interest of great national and international importance...' I know of nothing in Britain that comes even close to such a wide-ranging and very laudable agenda.

However in one maritime activity England retains its foremost position: charts and sailing directions. In this field are the incomparable Admiralty *Pilots*. In their own way these are literary masterpieces. The grammatically precise prose is prosaic and temperate in tone but manages when appropriate to be so descriptively dramatic without resorting to hyperbole.

The *Pilots* relevant to where he sailed were a constant source of pleasure to no less a critic than Hilaire Belloc. In his *The Cruise of the Nona* he says 'The unknown authors let themselves out now and then, and write down charming little descriptive sentences praising the wooded heights above the sea, or sounding great notes of warning which have in them a reminiscence of the Odyssey.' He quotes one delight, 'But the mariner will do well to avoid this passage at the approach of the turn of the tide; or if the wind be rising, or darkness falling upon the sea.'

There are seventy-four volumes all told of the *Pilots*, blanketing the world. In them is an extraordinary wealth of detail, the accuracy of which is beyond question. Written with all sizes of vessels in mind, they nevertheless recognise the special needs of small craft and cater for these accordingly. By small craft they mean vessels down to 12 metres. We could with a little push just fit into this definition. Certainly we found the content applicable to our requirements. The volume of particular reference to our route was the *South America Pilot Volume II*, comprising the coasts of southern South America and the Falkland Islands. It was a book kept ready to hand on the bookshelf, as the senior member of our little library of reference books.

Charts were to be something of a problem for the south. Admiralty charts for the Magellan Straits themselves were adequate for our needs but coverage of the waterways south of this, the principal highway, was somewhat lacking. On the few charts that were available there was reference to a comprehensive range of large-scale charts, but unfortunately these were shown as having subsequently been cancelled. When questioned on this the Hydrographic Office was a little coy but implied that these charts had been withdrawn because their accuracy was too suspect for the Hydrographer to apply his endorsement. But how did he know? Why had they not been updated from the current Chilean and Argentinian charts? Something of a mystery. Perhaps with the MOD on his back the Hydrographer was worried about cost, as in all fairness charts for that part of the world would not be bestsellers. We would have to wait until Punta Arenas where I knew there was a Chilean Navy chart depot.

We were now in a position to draw up the overall route plan. In doing so I called on that invaluable guide *Ocean Passages for the World.* Mine was the 1923 edition, which is a little more sailing-vessel oriented than today's. There is a nostalgic note in the front to the effect that it had been published by 'Order of the Lords Commissioners of the Admiralty'. A hark back to more majestic days. Rule Britannia still prevailed.

The route chosen was after leaving Falmouth to take in the Atlantic islands of Madeira, the Canaries and Cape Verdes. Then across the equator and a run down the coasts of Brazil and Uruguay to the Argentinian port of Mar del Plata on the south side of the River Plate estuary. Here we would restock and gear ourselves for the legs in the south. It would then be close along the coast of Patagonia to the eastern end of the Magellan Straits, into Chilean waters and on to Punta Arenas. This would be the launch pad for the cruise through Tierra del Fuego, leading to the other Chilean naval base of Puerto Williams, the southernmost permanently inhabited place on earth. Then the Horn for the millennium as the most southerly point of the voyage. Now homeward bound, stopovers were planned for the Falklands and the Azores before the last leg home to Falmouth. There were 16,000 nautical miles to be sailed. We were in fact to cover more than that distance through the water.

Sailing date was set for 30 August 1999 with an estimated return date around 13 April 2000 in Falmouth. There was a personal significance to 30 August. Forty-six years before on that day I had left Plymouth with one companion to sail my yacht *Tern II*, ex Claud Worth, out to New Zealand. It was to be hoped this forthcoming cruise would be just as successful.

CHAPTER ONE

GENESIS: WE GET IT TOGETHER

You should not try to lug along what you are trying to leave behind.
L. Francis Herreshoff

Herreshoff's words struck a chord. We were in total agreement with the sentiment. Not for us the way it is today, when the miracle electronic products which are part and parcel of urban living are stuffed into yachts and taken to sea with their owners, as life-support machines, into an elemental world in which such devices are alien. As another sage on a similar theme expressed it, 'At sea I learned how little a person needs, not how much.' This was the maxim we followed in our voyage planning. The less we had the less there was to go wrong and the more we could empathise with our surroundings. We did not want shoreside clutter to intrude into the simplicity of life at sea.

It was countdown. With something more than eighteen months to go from the conception of the idea, it was tempting to think there was more than adequate time to get the programme together. Herein lurked danger. We would need to be on our guard about letting time get away from us. What we had to ensure was that we didn't fall into the trap of permitting ourselves the luxury of a flexible sailing date. It was agreed that barring a major mishap to one of our persons and within the constraint of it being reasonable weather at departure time, the date for sailing was sacrosanct. What was not done by then would have to remain undone. From past experience it is always the case of wanting one more day 'just to do this' or that or something else that had suddenly become highly desirable to get done. One could justify not sailing indefinitely.

An overriding consideration in the planning was the expectation that once we left home it would be much more difficult to get work done on the boat as well as being appreciably more expensive. Self-sufficiency was to be the guiding philosophy. This raised the 'spares spectre'. Makers' handbooks available for the major items were perused with religious zeal, with the more enterprising manufacturers helpfully giving a list of recommended spares for extended cruising offshore. The fact that *Marelle* is not a bright young thing bedecked with today's high-fashion accessories (electronically speaking) eased the spares problem.

In turn this obviated the need for manufacturers' technical data which require an intellect at PhD level to comprehend. In this regard, as perhaps there is a relevance to the old adage that 'if all else fails read the instructions', trying to comprehend this data was an activity which we would largely be spared by keeping the degree of sophistication down to a low level. Keep it simple, was the cry. Anyway who wants a load of complicated equipment just to go sailing?

Compiled early on was the 'what if' list to cover the possibility of failure of each item of gear and equipment on board, large or small. This was a thought-provoking exercise on how to cope with dramas ranging from keel bolt fracture and the lead keel falling off, to the toilet seat fracturing due to over-enthusiastic pumping of the vacuum operated heads. As disasters go these would have been of equal status.

The potential for gear failure is considerable for any small craft, ancient or modern, whether it be occasioned by faulty design, material shortcomings or just wear and tear. The latter was particularly relevant to what we would be doing. After all, the forthcoming voyage of nine months or so would entail withstanding the full onslaught of conditions from the tropics to the rigours of the Southern Ocean and be the equivalent of many years of normal cruising in home waters. This would be compounded by the boat not receiving the maintenance given to craft which are normally laid up each year. In our case boat, gear and crew would just have to keep going with the minimum of attention and, as regards the crew, a self-inflicted paucity of tender loving care.

What then of the wisdom of embarking on such an exacting adventure in an ageing wooden boat and her equally ageing skipper? In the early planning stage these little doubts raised themselves usually in the dark middle hours of the night. They were soon disposed of however. In *Marelle* I had complete confidence. Her attributes of inner strength and sea-kindliness have stood out clear and unequivocally over the many miles we have sailed together. I knew her very well and was happy with what I knew. If she had an Achilles heel it was me. However, I was in my turn able to give her a measure of confidence. She accepted my assertion that like all young men I was immortal. Moreover it had to be said that we were not going to be disadvantaged by having with us a companion whom I knew to possess considerable skill and sailing know-how. With Jeremy I had the feeling that here was a man to take most things in his stride and, as was subsequently demonstrated, retain a remarkable degree of equanimity in the face of the most adverse circumstances. My initial feeling was to be fully vindicated. Later we were to be joined by another good man. *Marelle* and I were to be in safe hands. As it turned out, however, there was a viper in the old lady's bosom. Stainless steel. The one failure that did occur was due to this villain.

In readying boat and gear for the trip south we had a flying start in that *Marelle* had been in possession of a Department of Transport Sail

Training Ship certificate complying with its demanding Code of Practice. However, the 'Things to Do' list kept growing inexorably to 'break the ton' and reach 101 items.

I was relaxed about her bodily state of health. I had assumed responsibility for her in 1990. One does not buy, in the sense of acquiring ownership of, a pedigree classic boat. Rather one assumes the role of carer during a period of stewardship. Soon after being elevated into this position I had given her a major refit. The keel was dropped. All the keel bolts which had been in silicon bronze were renewed in aluminium bronze and whilst we were at it most of the through-hull and floor bolts were also replaced. I had given some thought to using stainless steel for the keel bolts, endorsed by the surveyor at the time, but decided against. I distrusted it. Unfortunately I was to be proved right. I also felt that *Marelle* would feel happier with a more traditional material with which she would have a greater empathy. Being of all teak construction she was rot-free. Her laid teak decks, although worn over the years by the countless footsteps of innumerable crews, were tight. Her splined carvel hull remained beautifully fare with no sign of working. Moreover it admitted not a drop of the sea. The old lady was sound in wind and limb and would take us anywhere. I and my fellow travellers were happy to be her companion on the long trip ahead.

The question of who were to be these fellow travellers needed to be addressed. We were looking for a third body. First choice was a friend made from the trip down to the peninsula in Antarctica. Colin Robertson was an orthodontist practising in South Africa. He, like Susan and me, had seen enough of the bottom end of Patagonia to want to see more of it. There were obvious benefits in having on board a dentist. Moreover someone familiar with medical practice would have been valuable and gone a long way to supplementing what I had learned whilst undergoing the Ship Captain's Medical Training Course. The advantages of having an in-house dentist had been demonstrated when we had been in the Antarctic. Colin's services had been called for to attend to a distressed Russian seaman in our ship, suffering from acute toothache. Apparently the man's teeth were in a very bad way due to neglect. The mouths of many of his shipmates were expected also to be in poor shape, a reflection perhaps on modern Russia where the lower-income workers may be unable to pay for services hitherto provided by the state under the previous regime. A benefit of the so called 'certainty of communism'.

Colin with his wife Rosemary came over to stay with us in Falmouth to discuss the programme in detail and to meet Jeremy and Adrie. It soon became apparent, however, there was going to be a stumbling block in his joining us. In his profession he had a commitment to his patients, for whose ongoing treatment he had to make firm bookings for many months ahead. The question was, if he were to join us for the southern part of the passage how sure could we be as to where we would be and when? The answer was of course that in a sailing activity one can never be sure. As it turned out we were to have over a month's overrun. He was keen to join but after full consideration had to give the idea away. It was a pity but understandable. It brought home to me that there are advantages in being retired and not having to work for one's living. He did however make a useful contribution in putting together an emergency dental kit to carry on board, with a guide on its use. As it happened Jeremy lost a filling whilst we were at sea from a troublesome tooth. I was ready to try out my new-found DIY dental knowledge but he didn't seem to share my enthusiasm, stating quite firmly that the tooth was not worrying him. Just as well perhaps. As Colin subsequently pointed out if there was a problem with a professionally applied filling falling out, there would not be a great future for a temporary one that I attempted, bouncing about at sea. I think though that I would like to have had a go, especially as it wasn't my tooth.

As there was no likely candidate from our circle of sailing friends and acquaintances, despite a notice on the board in the Royal Cornwall Yacht Club, it would be necessary to tap the open market. I put advertisements in the Ocean Cruising Club newsletter and the Royal Naval Sailing Association journal.

Additionally I sent a copy down to the Ocean Cruising Club's 'our man' in the Falklands, local Port Officer Carl Freeman, with the request he display it where appropriate at his discretion. The thinking was that one vein to tap would be the armed forces. There could be a serviceman or woman returning to the UK who might be able to persuade their commanding officer to grant special leave for 'adventure team building' or something of the like in today's terminology. I did in fact get a couple of responses from locals, but as it turned out these were not pursued.

The Ocean Cruising Club flyer brought in an interesting lead. Tomas, a Spanish yachtsman, although not an OCC member, had picked up my advertisement on the internet. After an exchange of correspondence he came over to Falmouth to stay with us, met Adrie and Jeremy and had a trial sail. It looked promising. There would be obvious advantages in having a Spanish-speaking person on board when we were in Argentina and Chile. I had undertaken an adult education course in Spanish for the complete beginner which gave me an understanding of the rudiments of the language, but not being a natural linguist I knew that it was going to be hard work trying to converse in Spanish in South America, with the added complication that it is very slightly different to Spanish Spanish. Accordingly the inclusion of Tomas in the crew would have been beneficial on that score at least. It is possible though there could have been a downside to his presence when communicating with South Americans. He gave me the impression that coming from the 'old country' he felt he would be treated with extra respect by the ex-'colonials'. If there was this arrogance it would obviously not be well received. After all, they had been forced to fight bloody wars to free themselves from the Spanish yoke. I might have been imagining things but I was just a little uncomfortable.

It was agreed that he would join us in Las Palmas in the Canaries, then leaving in the Falklands to fly back to Spain on expiry of his leave from work. Unfortunately it was not to work out.

The RNSA approach which was targeting crew for the home run from the Falklands brought in several other enquiries. One of these was from Fraser Currie, who conveniently happened to be living at Malpas up the River Fal. Ex-Royal Navy and now self-employed, he was also a classic boat owner with considerable sailing experience. Another plus feature was that at fifty-two he brought the average age of the crew down dramatically. There was also a hidden agenda, hidden from him that is, that being young and obviously fit and strong he would be just the lad for the expected heavy mooring work in Tierra del Fuego. He wanted to do a long ocean cruise. He was to get one but it was to be more than he expected. He would join us in Stanley. As his timing was flexible and all our home team were comfortable with him joining the seagoing team, I suggested he might like to join earlier in Mar del Plata to do the southern bit, the purpose of the whole exercise. He accepted with alacrity. It proved to be a good move.

Another problem to be tackled was insurance. *Marelle* had for some years been with Haven Knox-Johnston for UK and European waters. However Haven did not want to be in the business for extended ocean cruising. Recognising the problem, Chris Knox-Johnston did volunteer his services should I encounter difficulty in securing an alternative insurer. On a previous extended passage I had gone without cover due to the very high cost. This time there was more at stake and I was particularly concerned about third-party liability.

There was a certain coyness common to all the well-known insurers I approached in entertaining cover for the trip. One did respond eventually but with a proposal that contained an impossible premium and an obscene excess. It was almost a personal insult. If the idea was to turn me off, it was completely successful. To meet the premium I would have had to have sold the boat. I went back to Chris. He arranged an introduction to Robert Holbrook of Admiral Marine who came up trumps.

Although none of the insurers and their fellow conspirators, the underwriters, explained their hesitancy it had to be assumed this was due to a combination of the age of boat and that of the skipper as well as the type of boat. A wooden boat, perceived as a relic of the past, would be viewed more as an item of curiosity than an acceptable insurance risk.

With regard to the skipper's age one could imagine the underwriters as bright young or youngish things in the City, who would view someone of my age as being on the verge of extinction, probably needing a zimmer frame and almost certainly incontinent. However Robert was made of sterner stuff. On receipt of a favourable survey report, which he naturally had requested, and being made aware of the inclusion in *Marelle*'s crew of a younger (and experienced) contingent, he was able to offer an acceptable package with very reasonable premium and excess.

In the meantime work progressed on schedule with the 101 Things to Do list. The boat was hauled out for a very satisfactory survey carried out by Captain Anthony Head of Plymouth. The affront to a lady's dignity of having the very depths of her being 'closely inspected and sounded, and judiciously spiked' was mollified by there being 'no evidence of deterioration'. The Volvo engine was lifted out for servicing and also closely inspected (but not spiked), the gas system changed over to propane, and the storage capacity trebled. The all-important Taylors paraffin cabin heater was given an overhaul and additional spares laid in. I entered into discussion with the makers on the exhaust gas cowl design in anticipation of it having to cope with extremely strong winds in the south. Chillington Marine did not have a special cowl but suggested a 'small tube from a tin can' to surround the mushroom cowl. On being asked if the brand was important, the reply was that any of the fifty-seven varieties would suffice. I have had this trouble before with wind destabilising the burner flame and found a Heinz can of beans, with both ends removed, fitted neatly (without the beans). A more sophisticated design was fabricated in stainless steel and this was to stop blow-back even in the horrendous winds of southern Patagonia.

A vitally important consideration was provision for heavy weather with the associated risk of damage and gear failure. The standing rigging was renewed and the rig stiffened up with the addition of a movable inner forestay for which a staysail was made to measure. Runners were installed to take the pull of this sail and were so positioned that they could provide lateral support in the event of shroud failure. David Carne, a Falmouth personality who did the work, kindly donated spare rigging.

Steering gear and rudder failure can occur to the best of boats and would constitute a major problem offshore. With the help of an old friend, Rowland, a mechanical engineer, the Whitlock steering system was overhauled and relubricated. In the event of total steering failure an emergency steering oar arrangement with mounting brackets was set up. For self-steering on the longer passages, in addition to an Autohelm, a secondhand Aries wind vane was acquired. Nick Franklin, its designer, now living in Penryn and who had manufactured the gear in the first place, overhauled it and was most helpful with the installation.

Possible problems with compass dip in higher southern latitudes emerged, after reading literature supplied by Plastimo on the balancing of compasses for the varying influence of the earth's magnetic field. The message was that we would need a specially adjusted compass, to replace our existing Poseidon pedestal-mounted compass, when sailing in those waters. I sought a second opinion from Kelvin Hughes as I was not enthusiastic about having to change over compasses twice in the course of the voyage. They were most cooperative and put me in touch with the principal compass adjuster in their Dutch company, W. Harbicht, who advised 'Since you are not sailing permanently in southern hemisphere don't worry about a dip of the compass-card. A dip you most probably won't notice.' He was right. We didn't notice.

In preparation for the violent wind conditions to be expected when anchored in the southern regions, we reinforced the ground tackle with extra anchors and chain. Additional octoplait anchor rodes plus hundred-metre polypropylene shore lines in made-to-measure open-top bags, designed for controlled running out when using the dinghy, were put on board. Because of the supreme importance of the latter we carried a spare inflatable. It was to be needed.

An obsession with communication seems to be a predominant feature of living in the contemporary world of today, ashore and afloat, but it was not to be with us. On board was an ICOM VHF set with an oldish Apelco handheld. Both of these gave excellent performance. To complete, rather quaintly perhaps, our on-board communication system was a set of International Code of Signals handmade flags with the Code book. These were a hangover from the days when *Marelle* met the Offshore Racing Council's special regulations for Category O: Trans-Ocean races; the highest category. We did not feel deprived at not having MF and HF transmitting capability or an SSB transceiver, let alone any satellite communication system. It seems compulsive for boats' crews today to have to maintain daily contact with other boats on passage as well as regular ship-to-shore contact. This applies particularly to the hundreds if not thousands of yachts on the North Atlantic and West Indies circuit. If the sea and boat life are so unfulfilling and unsatisfying in themselves that constant contact with others is essential, one wonders why more people don't just fly over to the Caribbean and hire a boat for cruising those waters, thereby avoiding the inconvenience and discomfort of an ocean passage. After all, rallying and partying feature very prominently in today's offshore yachting.

Not having the wherewithal to raise the alarm on the good old MF 2182 kHz wave band in an emergency, we would fall back on our EPIRB. This was a Pains Wessex SOS 406 mHz which we selected as appearing to be the best on offer from the types suitable for small craft. This, with our Lifeguard Forties six-person liferaft, would be our safety net.

Apart from speaking to the occasional passing ship, which would initially have to be picked up visually as we did not have radar, we would remain incommunicado on each passage leg. We were quite content with this and it was to work out very well. The preoccupation with the obligatory PC, email, Inmarsat and the rest is all-pervading. It would seem the laptop has become so essential that no ocean-going yacht can possibly go to sea without one. The rationale escapes me. If we had wanted instant contact with anyone anywhere we might just as well have stayed at home. Jeremy did have a small short-wave radio, with SSB receiving-only capacity, mounted in his boat which we re-installed in *Marelle*. We had no joy with the SSB facility, using the set purely for tuning into the World Service of the BBC. We only did this occasionally. At sea when one's world comprises a flat disc three miles in radius and the celestial dome over one's head, world events of no matter what magnitude shrink to near triviality.

Hooked into all this communication technology is of course the ubiquitous weather fax. This it would seem is another 'must have' in the modern ocean cruiser. Why? I can understand the value to ocean racing greyhounds such as those competing in the long-distance marathons like the Vendée Globe, Whitbread/Volvo and The Race. It would be critical to them to know about the weather systems lying ahead. Their speeds are so incredibly high that they are able to re-position themselves to the best advantage. This does not apply to anywhere near the same extent for the average cruising boat with its more modest speed of advance. What matters to mere mortals like the rest of us is what is going to happen in the more immediate future. The weather fax supplying data for offshore areas cannot cater for the localised scene. It can be argued that it is better not to know what lies ahead if we don't possess the ability to take, if needs be, avoiding action. So why stand the cost and have to accommodate the clobber associated with the fax setup? In *Marelle* we relied on the time-proven aids to weather forecasting, barograph, run of the sea, appearance of the sky, behaviour of the wind etc. At the end of the day however, it frequently probably doesn't really matter. One puts up with what one gets when it hits.

To find our way across a world of our own we carried a Furuno GPS Navigator as a concession to the modern technological world. It was excellent. Easy to read with a wealth of features which I am sure would have been of inestimable value, if we had been able to master the handbook. That it was an extremely convenient and remarkably accurate navigational tool goes without saying, but it was to reveal its true worth when we were experiencing later on some difficulty in the Straits of Magellan. Even though Jeremy brought along his battery-powered handheld GPS I did not want to put total reliance on this electronic marvel. Accordingly I had on board my tried and true old Plath sextant. Additionally I had been loaned a younger, beautiful little Smith which very generously was subsequently donated. During the trip it was my intention to keep my celestial navigation hand in, particularly on stars. I carry on board a star globe. More specifically, though, I was keen to have a go at picking up Venus in daylight hours to cross this with the sun, to give possibly the most accurate fix of all in astronomical navigation. Sadly the flesh was not to be as willing as the will. Such is the seductive power of the satellite.

The work list began to shrink. Adrie was progressing well with the store ship programme. Essentially she was putting on board the basic provisions for the whole voyage, which meant she was going to purloin every nook and cranny down below. This, combined with all the rest of the extra gear, was putting us very much in the proverbial 'quart into a pint pot' situation. The extra pint pots could only be found by stowage on the coachroof, giving a camel-like appearance, as well as utilising the cockpit and the least exposed positions on deck. *Marelle* started complaining as her waistline, always an area for concern for a lady, vanished below sea level. But what could we do? We could only reassure her that as we ate our way through the foodstocks she would regain her trim. Health and dental checks were attended to, wills updated and passage planning finalised. We would meet the sailing date.

The Horn was calling!

I ask the ladies where I call,
'Your husbands, are they here or gone?'
And get this answer from them all –
'Round Cape Horn.'

Anon, *Round Cape Horn*

CHAPTER TWO

ATLANTIC ISLAND HOPPING

*We who adventure upon the sea, however humbly, cannot but feel we are
more fortunate than ordinary people.*
Claud Worth, *Yacht Cruising*

When men come to like a sea life, they are not fit to live on land.
Dr Samuel Johnson

Sailing day – tumultuous crowds – shakedown – murder unlikely –
Madeira m'dear – warmth of Porto Santo – acceleration zone lesson –
night arrival Gran Canaria – Tomas joins – salutary lesson over dinghy –
hurricane season hang-up – happy to leave – trade wind sailing –
unpleasant ride – Cape Verdes arrival – Porto Grande no change – funny
old birthday – we are rooked – Tomas asked to leave – sail

There was a sensuous feel to the sea as it slowly rose and fell, its surface
a speckled sheen, glistening in the sun. It was seductively beckoning us
to venture out onto itself, inviting us to get on our way south. South to
the Horn.

The great sweep of the North Atlantic spread itself out before us as we
cleared Lizard Point. The weather can be distinctly unpleasant off this
geologically unique, serpentine mineral-based Cornish headland, with sea
conditions decidedly dangerous when a strong wind opposes the fast-
running tidal streams. But not today. We were favoured with the
conditions associated with a 'light breeze', Force 2, the sea state for
which is depicted as 'small wavelets, … crests have a glassy appearance
but do not break' in the measured prose of Admiral Beaufort when
composing his ever-enduring Wind Scale table. Compiled in 1806, it is
quite remarkably still universally used into the present day. On shore, he
goes on, 'the wind is felt on the face: leaves rustle: (wind) vanes move in
the wind.' At sea, the wind is 'that in which a man-o'-war with all sail set
could go from 1–2 knots.' For us it was gentle sailing.

Astern was the Lizard lighthouse with its small complex of attendant
buildings, all brightly white in the sun. As the distance between us
became greater they gradually blended into the backdrop of the land
behind, until all passed beyond our vision. With the sun going down and
the land already gone, the awareness of being alone enveloped us. How
many sailors over the centuries, outward bound like us, have felt the
same as they passed through these waters? Although around us were

ships going about their business and sharing the sea with us, it was so evident they were complete 'islands unto themselves'. Their very presence only served to increase our feeling of isolation.

The Lizard has a status of great significance in the history of marine navigation as one of the world's most prominent sea marks. It is the most southerly promontory on mainland Britain and constitutes the northern gatepost at the entrance to the English Channel. Together with its opposite number, the southern gatepost of Ushant, it marks the line of dramatic transition from the confined and protected coastal waters of the Channel to the usually stern ocean conditions of the Atlantic.

Countless deep-sea sailing ships at the end of a long ocean voyage have made, or all too often failed to make, with fatal results, their landfall on the Lizard. It was then on to 'make their number' to the signal station for onward reporting to Lloyds; before sailing on to anchor in Falmouth Bay 'for orders' or running on up Channel. When westward bound, it had been for so many ships the last sight of home, as they thrashed to windward down Channel, standing close into the land, on their way out into the open deep water.

Happily the Lizard's time-hallowed links with deep-water sailing have not died with the passing of commercial sail. Because of its prominent geographical position defining the eastern boundary of the North Atlantic, it constitutes the logical finishing line for transatlantic ocean yacht races. The parade of sail still continues past its rock-bound base, right through to our technologically advanced day and age.

Departure day for us had arrived undramatically and with no occurrence of any last-minute hitch to warrant deferring, even if we had wanted to, the fateful moment. Perhaps secretly though we might have welcomed an excuse for a delay, as it may be common to us all to have a reluctance to leap out of the security of the familiar. But the weather forecast was promising and apart from the last-minute fresh provisions we were fully stored, watered and fuelled. Private intimate farewells had been made. We could go!

Falmouth has seen sailings beyond number and ours would be just another one, but each departure would always be intensely personal. The same question always comes up at this moment. Unless the need to earn a living is involved why would anyone voluntarily leave the comfort and warmth, physical and emotional, of one's home? I don't know why, but here Jeremy and I, presumably sound of mind, were of our own free will launching ourselves on a very long journey up and down two oceans with all the uncertainties that would involve, not to mention the discomfort and inconvenience. Looking back through my journal it was a philosophical question to which I was to return throughout our time away but never with any resolution. Others have thought the same:

He who goes to sea for pleasure would go to hell for a pastime.
                                                                 Samuel Johnson

Marelle was on a club mooring off the Royal Cornwall Yacht Club in Falmouth harbour where I had been able to see her from our bedroom window. She looked as though she wanted to get going. It was time to join her.

Accompanied by members of our extended family who had come from up country to see us off, Susan and I walked down to the landing in front of the club for Jeremy and me to be taken out in the club launch. With us went Adrie, bringing her last-minute fresh stocks plus the first few nights' dinners prepared by Susan. She always did this for the start of a passage.

Fraser came close alongside in his well-presented boat *Havssula*, ready to escort us out into Falmouth Bay. He must have been wondering when and if we would ever meet again. Several other boats were also getting into position to come out with us and see us on our way. We appreciated the gesture.

Adrie went ashore. We waved to the folks on shore, hoisted the mainsail and sailed. Well not quite. Due to a hang-up on the foredeck in letting go the mooring pendant we sailed around the buoy doing a complete turn. This untoward manoeuvre was to cause some confusion in the ranks of the shore party who thought we had set off, only to see us apparently sailing back again. They may have thought that Jeremy and I had come to blows already. I hoped that the impression given was that we were doing some final fine-tuning of the rig. The second attempt was successful and we were away.

Accompanied by our little fleet we sailed in the light wind slowly out of the harbour entrance and past Pendennis Point, on which by now our farewelling party, reinforced by other friends, had repositioned themselves. Behind them was quite a crowd of well-wishers all waving gaily. It was evident that the news about our trip had spread afar and a fair slice of Falmouth had turned out to see us off. Rather gratifying, we felt. We subsequently heard that this crowd was assembled there for some unrelated event or other on the water, but, having picked up why our people were there, they joined in the farewell waving bit. But for us it did not do our morale any harm.

One of our escort called out to enquire 'When do you expect to see your waterline again?' A pertinent point. The poor old girl felt sluggish. She was so deep in the water and certainly not her usual jaunty self.

We continued to wave to our little group and they also kept waving until we could no longer distinguish them. It was a deeply felt occasion, the memory of which stayed with us. Our escorts one by one peeled off, with *Havssula* the last to go. Now feeling very much alone we faced up to adjusting to a sea routine that was to become ingrained in our way of life for the next nine months.

The course had been laid off on the chart for Madeira about 1,250 nautical miles ahead, more or less on a rhumb line. A slight dogleg would be needed to give a comfortable offing on Cabo Finisterre at the north-western tip of Spain. A waypoint 50 miles west of the cape would keep us well clear of the Traffic Separation Scheme but not too far out to make a measurable increase to the distance. Closer in to the land at this point can be a source of headaches. On an earlier trip some years ago we had been much nearer the cape, cutting the corner to save miles, and had paid for our sins. Fog. Finisterre does not enjoy a good press on this hazard, as well as the promontory being guilty of upsetting the wind patterns in its adjacent area in this region of the eastern Atlantic. Localised gales are a feature but on that occasion we got the other treatment. No wind and nil visibility. We had shared a small patch of sea with a continuous parade past us of ships heading both north and south as they bent their tracks to squeeze around our adjacent headland. With little fuel and no radar we had that helpless feeling in the midst of the cacophony of sound from ships' horns. In those days the principles of traffic control had not been devised. It was an experience I was not keen to repeat. 50 miles would keep us clear of the Finisterre version of Piccadilly Circus but not too far out to lose the benefits of the Portuguese Trades. These are fresh to strong winds that predominate on this coast between May and September blowing from between north-east and north-west but principally northerly. This was one of the factors that had determined our departure from England by end of August. From September these so-called trade winds work round to the south. This obviously was undesirable, particularly as the proportion of south-westers putting us hard on the wind would increase significantly.

We took our departure from the Manacles Buoy at 1300, read the log and set up the Aries self-steering gear. The adventure had begun, and we were only too well aware of the 16,000 miles by chart that lay ahead of us. We were alone and felt alone as we cleared the southern extremity of Falmouth Bay and all that had been home to us. The note in my journal reads 'In perfect sailing conditions Jeremy and I settled down to our watches and were off', adding rather pathetically 'All this so I can get home again.' I wondered how Jeremy was feeling but he kept his thoughts to himself.

Without the need for any debate we were agreed twenty-four hour vigilance would be kept, with someone always on deck. We would not succumb to the temptation of leaving the Aries to get on with it whilst we saw our watch out, snug and warm in the depths of our sleeping bags. Because of their self-imposed situation that is what single-handers do and in the main get away with it, cheerfully ignoring in the process the bedrock of the International Regulations for Preventing Collisions at Sea, Rule 5. This is the one that brings all on the sea to heel with its solemn intonation 'Every vessel shall at all times maintain a proper look-out by sight and hearing.' How the lone sailor and his or her insurer, be there one, reach an accord on this one I know not. Personally speaking, as skipper and bearing the awesome responsibility for the vessel and all who sail in her, I did not relish the prospect of trying to answer some awkward questions from my maker, let alone a coroner, should something horrible go wrong. We were to adhere to this good lookout resolution throughout the whole voyage.

We further agreed on a straight three-hour watch system as the best compromise arrangement for two people. I have tried the standard four-hour stint, time-honoured over the centuries, as well as two hours, but have always come back to three hours. Four hours is too much like hard work if on the helm and certainly too long to keep alert if not actively engaged in steering. Two hours does not give one long enough in the pit. In fact it is only an hour and a bit by the time one has got one's gear on and off, gone to the heads and generally fiddled around.

A vital item on the agenda was how best to arrange the routine for cooking and clearing up afterwards to sit comfortably within the watchkeeping system. High on the priority scale was how to fit in a 'happy hour'. Normally in *Marelle* I have followed a no-alcohol regime at sea but I suspected Jeremy would not accept this measure of pomposity. Some time together at the end of the day before the sun went down seemed a good idea. In fact it was more than that. Almost a necessity, as an occasion to voice one's inner thoughts in a relaxed social setting. We were to follow this as long as the grog stocks lasted.

Our three-hour watch system started at midday, 1200, taking it in turns to cook and following the rule that the cook did not do the washing up and clearing away. It worked out well. Towards the end of the afternoon as 1800 approached, the watch below, having had his kip, would bring the drinks up into the cockpit. This practice was only thrown if we were having to hand-steer or the weather was being unkind, as it was most of the time in the Southern Ocean and South Atlantic, there being then a marked disinclination to share the misery of the watch on deck. After the socialising the evening meal was served and tidied up comfortably before the changeover for the first watch at 2100. A minor drawback was that the off-watch man missed out on most of his rest time. However, we were getting an adequate amount of sleep and it was not too exhausting when on watch, seated comfortably in the corner of the cockpit under the sprayhood watching the Aries beavering away. This routine became very much part of our lives particularly the avoidance of hand-steering. When preparing to come on watch the first thing to look for was whether the watch on deck was under the sprayhood or withstanding the elements standing dejectedly at the wheel. When on Aries it was a snug feeling to watch lumps of ocean being flung over the wheel and reflect that a helmsman would have been taking the lot.

The weather remained kind to us as the day progressed. We were being smiled on from on high as we carried with us a world that was bright and cheerful. The sun beamed down, enveloping all around us, and with it we had a gentle fair breeze indulging us as we reacclimatised to our new existence.

I do not suffer from seasickness but Jeremy needed to take something to help him adjust to sea conditions and would need a day or two to 'feel himself'. This was to happen, it appeared, every time we started on a new leg but being Jeremy he never complained. I admired the way he coped and respected his stoicism.

We continued to be spoilt with a pleasant night's sail under a vivid moon and steady progress, with Ushant bearing 125° at 0515. We were under all plain sail but the wind was dropping and veering. With wind coming more astern it was becoming difficult to keep the genoa from collapsing behind the mainsail. However, the wind's gentleness meant we could enjoy our evening drink in peace and help Jeremy on the road to recovery. We were being broken in gently.

For supper we enjoyed the remaining half of the leek and turkey crumble Susan had prepared. This was complemented with boiled potatoes and carrots, all cooked in Channel water and eaten at the table. Luxurious living!

1 September, Wednesday, my journal entry reads 'Very difficult to remember what has gone past. The days are full with sleeping (as much as possible to hold back the ever-present enemy of tiredness), preparing and eating meals, routine maintenance and working out how best to keep

up boat performance with the need to protect the gear from the heavy wear and tear that is always present ... However we are progressing and all in all we have had a good passage.'

Food, its availability and preparation, had from departure day plus two begun to emerge in our world as perhaps the major factor. This developed from the time that Jeremy was reappearing from his being a near gastronomic recluse. It soon became apparent that he was a skilled cook and moreover interested in the art, becoming my guide and mentor – subsequently even more so for Fraser. Throughout the voyage a voice would be heard floating up from the galley, 'Jeremy! what do I do about this?' His bread making, which he had worked at before we left, was a success story in itself. Fresh bread at sea is a delight that defies description.

That night we had the last of Susan's pre-cooked dinners. A beef in beer concoction. Jeremy, not given to hyperbole, lavished it with praise. I joined in the chorus of appreciation. Contentedly resting on well-fed stomachs we had one of those memorable night sails, all too rare, with a moonlit-dappled sea and a kindly wind pushing us steadily on course under a huge vividly orange moon. We were running parallel to the southbound lane leading into the Traffic Separation Scheme off Finisterre, and very evident on our beam was a never-ending procession of ships marching south. Six hundred are reported as passing round this turning mark each day.

The wind kept veering to east of north and continuing to ease. It was a question of what was the best sail configuration with the breeze now well aft. The obvious answer was main and spinnaker or, failing that, goosewinged genoa. Offering up the excuse of age and a desire for a quiet life we settled on the genoa, which is quite large, sheeted out through a block on the main boom end which was squared off under control of preventer and main sheet, the mainsail being down on the boom. It was a relaxed sort of rig, giving a somewhat pedestrian speed of advance.

That evening was for me to be the culinary moment of truth. I was duty cook and tackled one of my four standard dishes. Beef chowder. During the run-up to our departure I had assiduously practised my repertoire. The dish was voted a success but something was missing. It was a pity about the peas. I had broken them out of the ready-use locker but with all my faculties concentrated on the chowder I had forgotten to cook them. A milestone in the cruise had been passed, but another event of importance in its progression was about to occur.

The wind was veering further and continued to do so until it ended up in the south-east. This put us on a reach, involving a sail change back to mainsail and taking the genoa off the boom end. I affected this during my forenoon watch with Jeremy resting below on his bunk. With all this going on and with the knowledge of how sound is greatly magnified below decks, I was surprised that he did not surface to offer to lend a hand. The moment passed and it was not until some time later that the truth came out during our happy hour. He revealed that he had been feeling a little put out that at times I struggled to do too much on my own without involving him, which rather relegated him to passenger status. It was a very pertinent point. It was good it had been aired. It could well be a disease common to all skippers that they feel there is only one way to accomplish any task in their boat. Their way.

The wind went back into the northerly quarter and was to stay there with benign strength apart from half a day when it got up to Force 7, bringing with it a confused sea. This was throwing our stern around, creating a problem for Mr Franklin as the Aries had become known. We were still on a learning curve about how to treat him, so gritting our teeth we went back to hand-steering. Jeremy seemed to have more of an artistic flair on the treatment of the gear than I displayed, being it would seem rather a slow learner. Mr Franklin had by now become the established third member of the crew and we were to exploit him dreadfully without any feeling of guilt whatsoever.

Back to more gentle conditions over the remaining distance to Madeira we were able to use to good advantage our twin headsail rig. This comprised taking the roller genoa out on one spinnaker boom and another genoa of comparable size out on the other side on the other spinnaker pole. This little-used sail was from the original wardrobe and was fitted with hanks which we clipped to the outer of the moveable forestays. Of these there were two. The forward one ran from the masthead just below the roller genoa attachment down to the stemhead immediately abaft the roller gear. The inner led from a point above the crosstrees down to a position midway between the mast and the stem, the deck being suitably strengthened to take the loading. On these portable stays we could set an array of hanked headsails, sailing the boat as a cutter at will. These stays acted also as preventers in the event the genoa furling gear carried away. It was to do just that when we were in the south. As *Marelle* liked to dress to suit the occasion we had quite an extensive headsail wardrobe. In addition to the working genoa on the South Coast Rod Rigging roller furling gear there were two genoas, working jib, storm jib and heavy-duty staysail, all fitted with hanks. We also carried a spinnaker, trysail and assorted spare sails.

During these latter days we virtually had the ocean to ourselves. One ship was to pass close by at night heading north. She slid down our side without a sound, a black bulk with no lights on deck and no sign of life, merging into the darkness of the night astern. A ship manned by dead men. Later, in daylight, a largish yacht crossed our stern under mainsail alone, apparently tacking down wind. She informed us on the radio she was under charter and bound also for Porto Santo. We pledged to meet up on arrival, but never did. Apart from the paucity of human life in our world, marine life was also not abounding. One whale was blowing and a pod of dolphins which after a brief visit lost interest and vanished ahead. We were too slow for them.

It was about this time Jeremy spontaneously came out with 'I am enjoying myself!' I did not want to analyse my own feelings but yes it had been an easy ride and enjoyable. I think this was largely because we had been in home waters, so to speak, with a friendly, welcome-on-the-mat feel about them. I was to remember this as we got south. There the seas felt distinctly alien. They were to make us aware they were not our waters.

At breakfast time on Friday 10 September we had the high landscape of Ilha de Porto Santo fully in view. We had chosen to stop over here rather than Madeira itself as from all accounts Funchal was not so suited to yachts. Although we had not come very far in distance within the context of the whole voyage and what lay ahead of us, we felt the inner glow of achievement. Although far from being for either of us a first ocean landfall we savoured the moment as being rather special. The passage had fulfilled its purpose as a trial run. Nothing had surfaced to indicate there was anything of any consequence wrong with boat or gear. Adrie's provisioning was working out well. Moreover I felt Jeremy and I had settled down well together and the odds were definitely against murder on the high seas.

At midday we passed the breakwater guarding this manmade harbour and entered Porto Santo.

Further in is a stub wall jutting out from the breakwater protecting a small marina. Lying alongside the wall were a couple of quite large yachts looking rather the worse for wear from storm damage. We secured to them whilst we had lunch and a beer before tackling the harbour authorities. Some girding of loins was a prerequisite to tackling the expected tortuous route through the bureaucratic process. We had had no success on the radio in trying to raise the marina office but need not have worried, as down came a young man on a bicycle to reveal all. All smiles, he introduced himself as Miguel the manager of the marina 'complex'. This was to turn out to be more than the small boat area but took in a boatyard and ship repair facilities. With his excellent English, courtesy and friendliness he set the tone for what was to be a pleasant interlude in our journey south. Moreover he was full of information about whom to see and where to smooth our entry into the country. With him we drew up a programme to get fuel and go out to a mooring in the harbour. Not only would this be cheaper but more hassle-free than persuading *Marelle* to behave herself when manoeuvring under power in the narrow confines of the rather crowded marina. When she was built marinas were not around and engines were something of an add-on. She was designed for sailing and that was that. Consequently her propeller and rudder configuration do not favour tricky footwork in restricted space which is so easy with the modern boat. Getting in and out of marinas under power for us is always an adventure.

I went ashore first to tackle the port entry administration and then to procure phone cards to call home. The former exercise was painless, the officials being pleasant and cooperative. As they would not want to make their task any more onerous than need be, it did not take long to get all the required stamps on our documentation. I was to look back with nostalgia to this occasion when locked in combat later on with the administration in parts of South America. The second operation was much more complicated. Yes, cards were available but always from the office next door. In the last one I found its sole occupant painting the ceiling. I addressed his lower extremities. He called down to say his office was also out of cards but new ones were being printed. However he didn't know when. Perhaps I might be lucky if I went into the town. I was lukewarm about this, it being blazing hot outside (mixed metaphors perhaps) and the town some way off. Half an hour's walk, I was told, and I was tired. But as so often happens when struggling with a difficult situation abroad a local saviour appears. In this case it was an affluent looking gentleman, impeccably dressed in a smart suit and with perfect English. 'Can I be of any assistance?' Yes he could, especially as he had a large air-conditioned Mercedes. He took me into the town, delivering me to the post office where he informed me cards could be procured. He brushed aside my words of thanks and drove back from where we had come. In addition to having rendered this service he had usefully brought me up to date on the local politics. Inside the post office, courtesy to a stranger was continued. On learning what I wanted a staff member directed me to the head of a long queue, which quite happily moved back one step to let me in.

Would one encounter such old-world courtesy back home in Britain? Rarely, I suspect. But then Porto Santo is old world, as an outpost of Portugal, whereas Britain today does not seem to know what world to inhabit.

I reported back on board flushed with success and the heat to be greeted with 'Where have you been?' The whole operation had been more protracted than I had realised. On the yacht next door it was all go as the young men were fighting with the engine to get it to start. They wanted to get to Portugal and we wondered about that. It would be an unenviable passage against wind and current. They took time off to make their long hose available so we could water ship. It was then ashore to call the folks at home, and into the local seafood bar at the water's edge for a tasty and well-lubricated supper, enjoyed all the more as it had been cooked by someone else. We went back on board for a long undisturbed night's sleep, relaxed and contented, particularly having been once again in contact with home. Next morning it was around next door to refuel, and right on schedule Miguel turned up in his runabout. He escorted us out to the yacht anchorage and secured us to a swinging mooring, where it was pleasantly cool away from the stifling heat in the inner harbour. We enjoyed our evening drink.

We gave ourselves a few days to relax, tidy up the inevitable small jobs on board, reprovision and absorb what is Porto Santo and its interesting past.

It is believed to have been first discovered as far back as early in the fourteenth century by an Englishman, Robert Machin. In the following century it was to be re-discovered by the Portuguese. Prince Henry, a son of John I, King of Portugal, and who was to go down in history as Henry the Navigator, was possessed of an insatiable curiosity about what might lie beyond the shores of his native country. To help satisfy this obsession he despatched in 1418 a venturesome local gentleman, Juan Gonsalvo Zarco, into the path of the setting sun to find what was out there. In bad weather he stumbled on Porto Santo and later Madeira itself, given that name 'on account of the great quantity of wood found on it'. He brought back to Henry glowing reports on what he had found. Islands, uninhabited and ripe for colonisation. This the Portuguese did, led by Gonsalvo complete with family. This was a rare occasion when colonisation did not entail subjection and absorption of the existing inhabitants. The acquisitive Spanish always had their eye on it but apart from a brief tenancy at the end of the sixteenth century the archipelago has remained in Portuguese hands. It was in British interests for it to remain so. With this in mind an English garrison was stationed on the main island, Ilha da Madeira, in the early nineteenth century to discourage the Spanish.

As it was for us, the group has been a convenient staging post between England and all points south and west. It was here that Commodore Anson in 1740 thankfully anchored his fleet to catch his breath. This was in the course of what was to be the first circumnavigation by an English sailor involving a doubling of Cape Horn. It was to be a remarkable voyage accomplished against almost overwhelming odds. When fighting to round the Horn his fleet was virtually destroyed in appalling weather by 'the blind horn's hate', to quote Kipling. His crews were then decimated by scurvy before arriving home with one remaining ship, but with a fortune in her hold.

For many of his men the stopover in Madeira was in fact to be their last breath. To make up crew numbers before he left Spihead the Admiralty had put on board almost anyone they could find still taking a breath, including invalid pensioners from Chelsea Hospital, some of whom were carried on board on stretchers. They were all to die. We had an affinity with Anson. His ship *Centurion* and our *Marelle* both carried pensioners, but fortunately those in the latter vessel did not meet the same fate as those who sailed with Anson. After restoring and reassuring himself he had eluded a Spanish fleet on a seek-and-destroy mission, Anson sailed into maritime history books as well as great wealth.

He was in no doubt about why he was on that voyage. His instructions from the Admiralty were clear and to the point. He was to make as much mischief as he could for the Spanish in what they considered to be their private lake, the Pacific Ocean, or as they knew it the Great South Sea. In the words of Their Lordships 'You are to do your best to annoy and distress the Spaniards ... by taking, sinking, burning or otherwise destroying all their ships.' One notes the word *all*. No half measures here. In particular he was charged with taking the 'Prize of All the Oceans', the fabulous, treasure-laden galleon, with the appropriately ponderous name of *Nuestra Señora de Covadonga*, which made an annual run from Acapulco in Mexico to Manila. Take her he did, and Anson's share of the prize money was more than enough to ensure he lived in considerable comfort for the rest of his life and the one after that.

George Anson was an achiever, becoming Admiral of the Fleet Lord Anson. During two terms as First Lord of the Admiralty he established the Royal Marines and did much to improve the efficiency of the Navy. Under his guidance the Royal Navy became the unchallengeable force it was to be for another two centuries. But he did not stop there. Being a humane man, or, as we would say today, a caring person, he was concerned about welfare and did much to improve the lot of the sailor on the lower deck. *The Oxford Companion to Ships and the Sea* has this to say about him: 'His predominant characteristic was a rational calm which no adverse circumstances could shake.' How many amongst us would like to have that said about us?

Around thirty years later Captain Cook called at the islands in the course of his first two voyages. Apart from their benefit as a source of very welcome fresh fruit and provisions, he seems to have enjoyed his stay and appreciated the hospitality. Although not in the same league as these greats, we also found our part of Madeira a pleasant place to catch our breath.

At anchor near us was a pretty little wooden boat. It was to a Harrison Butler design, self-built by a young German couple on board and known to Jeremy through the Harrison Butler Association. They came over for a drink and we enjoyed their interesting company. Their English was near perfect with barely any trace of an accent. They were on their way to somewhere but did not know where that somewhere was, perhaps the West Indies, perhaps not.

'We enjoy our life,' she said but added 'I am always sick, you know, the whole time at sea from when we first leave!'

I have wondered since what happened to them and whether she was able to continue to live with that destructive affliction. They were true ocean roamers.

It was time for us to be away again. We had a schedule to maintain, with Tomas arriving soon in Las Palmas in the Canaries. Early next day we were ashore in the dinghy and the walk into the town. We wrote our last cards drinking coffee under an umbrella in a shady little square, then visited the home of Christopher Columbus just round the corner. He had lived there in and around 1480. The island is no doubt proud of its famous resident, one of the most celebrated names in the world. We made our last stores purchases and walked back along the edge of the main tourist attraction in Porto Santo, a truly beautiful beach with its long expanse of golden sand. Still largely unspoilt – but how long before it is loomed over by ghastly tower blocks of holiday flats, with the sand buried under beach umbrellas and acres of red bare flesh?

I called in at the marina office to settle our dues with the highly efficient and most attractive young lady. I kept trying to find excuses to prolong the conversation. She was not however able to produce any mail for us. What on earth had happened to it? I left a forwarding address but was not too hopeful. I had to go back on board rather despondent but shortly afterwards Miguel came out at his usual high speed in his runabout waving in triumph our long-awaited mail. We could now leave.

Tuesday 14 September. After a very blowy night with vicious squalls whistling down the valley opposite we got under way, escorted out by Miguel. He sped us our way with a cheery farewell, which left us with a good feeling about Porto Santo. Under genoa before a Force 4 plus and lumpy sea at an unpretentious six knots we started to eat into the 300 miles to the Canaries. During a beautiful afternoon we left the outlying island of Deserta Grande astern and hauled down the courtesy flag, severing our last link with Madeira.

I was duty cook that night and tried a corned beef and onion fry-up with the now familiar boiled potatoes, carrots and peas. Jeremy was impressed by the effort in view of the sea conditions, but made no comment on the cuisine itself. As a chef I am fortunately not temperamental. It was a quiet night with fishing boats causing a problem and all around us. Parallel with us we had the lights of a sailing vessel but come the dawn she was nowhere to be seen. Possibly she was Lanzarote-bound. The wind had been steady from the east, a whole sail breeze, but now it was slowly dying and for company we had a whale blowing out on the beam, also it would appear going to Lanzarote.

A distinctive feature of these islands is the Acceleration Zone phenomenon. We were about to experience this. The wind built up from the north, well aft, and I had been watching a turtle swimming near us, when in a matter of minutes the wind was up to gale-force proportions. Under full main we were creaming along, bolt upright on the calm sea. It was great sailing but we had far too much sail up and I started to get nervous. I called Jeremy. We clawed down the main and rolled up the genoa. Under bare poles we were still tramping along. The wind then died as quickly as it had come. These winds, following the Bernoulli venturi principle, are funnelled down between the islands with a dramatic increase in speed.

We were left with a damp, dreary night to pick up the lights on the north side of Gran Canaria and proceed down the coast to the entrance to Puerto de la Luz, the port of Las Palmas. We marked time to let a large freighter pass round the breakwater ahead of us and made our way through the channel buoys flashing over the black still water in the approach to the yacht harbour. At 0030 we let go in the anchorage on the north side of the new breakwater protecting the marina. Against the glare of the lights on the foreshore it had been a little difficult to judge distances but we ended up comfortably in the midst of a small fleet of yachts who were anchored out there, presumably either to avoid paying marina fees or because there were no berths. Certainly in the night light the marina looked fairly full. We preferred to anchor rather than crashing around in the middle of the night not knowing where we were going. As it turned out it was fresher and cooler where we were, outside the claustrophobic confines inside.

Our intention was to be in Las Palmas for the shortest possible time. We had to pick up Tomas, and go through the usual routine of refuelling, watering and topping up stores, but the latter would have to be comprehensive as supplies in the Cape Verdes are limited. We would then get on our way. Las Palmas is not everyone's idea of a gift from God and certainly not mine. This was my third visit, the first being way back in 1953 when we were the only yacht there, with the anchorage to ourselves. There was no marina of course. At that time the port was infamous for filthy harbour water and pronounced waterfront thievery. On the other hand it was famous for the beauty of its women and quality of its fruit. Things have changed since then. The marina has brought the boats in because to have a pontoon berth is a 'must have' today. The quality of the fruit is still good although I am not sure about the other feature, but perhaps that is because I am older.

There was a little problem on timing that I was keeping in mind. In August and September the occasional hurricane can originate in the vicinity of the Cape Verdes before tracking across to the West Indies. Ideally we should wait until comfortably into October before going down there. It was a factor tempering my desire to complete our business in the Canaries and get on our way south. It would seem to be a seaman-like precaution to cool (if that is the word) our heels in Las Palmas a little longer.

Next morning after a leisurely breakfast we got our anchor and moved into the marina alongside the Texaco fuelling berth. In its own way this spot has become well-known in the yachting scene as either a place to get things or to find out where to get them. Its rather special place in that scene is due to Pedro who runs it. A friendly and most helpful man, he made us feel welcome. He gave us our diesel and on our behalf called up the harbour authority office. No, there were no spare berths in the marina due to a local sailing event. There seemed to be plenty of vacant places to me, but we were quite happy to go back out to our spot in the anchorage. A little rolly perhaps but we were saving our coppers.

As it would be a couple of days before Tomas was due to arrive from Spain I thought a little break from the boat by taking myself off for the day might be a good idea. It would also give Jeremy a break from me and give him some time to himself. Accordingly I took the bus round to Puerto de Mogan on the south-western part of the island. I had been there before and had liked it. A little harbour full of yachts but attractive. I also wanted to say hello to an English girl, Maya Holleyhead, who was part-owner of a local chandlery, Sunshine Maritime. Before we left Falmouth I had been in touch with her. She had taken the trouble to go to Las Palmas to sketch the latest developments in and around the yacht harbour. This was for a Royal Cruising Club pilot and she sent the details to me with follow-up information over the phone. Her buoyage notes had been useful when we had come into the harbour in the dark. I wanted to tell her about this and also to get some items of gear for the boat.

The bus ride is an hour or two on a perilously winding road, much of which has been cut out of the hillside and hangs over a sheer drop to the rocks far below. Not a road for the faint-hearted, the driver swinging round the bends with great aplomb and a certain disregard for the normal rules of self-preservation.

A feature of the drive is a view of the stark tower blocks of holiday flats which extend down the coast. They dominate the foreshore and crowd out the beaches which are crammed, like seats in a cinema, with ordered rows of deckchairs. I personally could not imagine a worse way to spend a holiday but millions do, year on year. An enormous industry has served and successfully promoted all this, as witnessed by the endless march down the coast of new blocks of these monoliths. I was disappointed to find the chandlery closed on reaching Mogan. I had forgotten about half-day closing on Saturday. However it was pleasant to stroll through the streets, enjoying in due course a light lunch overlooking the little clean harbour. My waitress was a charming young woman and I lingered on. It was more appealing being here than in Las Palmas but I strengthened my resolve and faced up to the return adventure. On arriving back I made yet another attempt to legitimate ourselves in our berth, but again no one was at home in the port office. It would seem we could sail to suit ourselves and no one would be any the wiser or care.

A note in my journal for the next day reads 'Our way of life is expected to change today with the arrival of Tomas.' Change it did. Jeremy went into the marina in the dinghy to pick him up. I viewed with dismay on their return the mountain of kit he had with him. The entry continues 'Storage space is now at a premium and will be exacerbated in Mar del Plata with Fraser coming on board. However I expect we will manage.' The plan for the following day was the stores top-up, Jeremy taking Tomas with him. They would use the dinghy to ferry them out.

This was not to be. I was down below when the quartermaster and assistant came alongside. 'We are sinking!' and so they were. The port-side sponson on the Narwhal was giving up, deflating before our eyes. A quick unload of the stores and up on deck with the dinghy. There was a long split halfway along and obviously beyond our on-board repair capability. So up anchor, back to the Texaco jetty and Pedro. He found us a berth nearby alongside the wall where we could conveniently get the dinghy ashore. We carried a spare Avon Redcrest inflatable as a spare but as a dinghy would be so critical in the south we didn't want to write one off at this stage. From the Royal Cruising Club pilot for the Atlantic Islands, an excellent publication edited by Anne Hammick, we tracked down the address of a liferaft and inflatable service centre. Tomas and I took the poor sorry object to the centre to receive from the owner, rather surprisingly from South Korea, a stern lecture on over-inflation. What we had done was now only too clear. It had been fully inflated in the cool of the morning before breakfast, only to become overblown during the heat of the day, splitting the seam. The question was, what other mischief had been done? Although there was a mountain of work lying around he would obligingly get it done in a couple of days as well as checking the rest of the dinghy as best he could. I noted at the time all of this had been transacted without Tomas, despite my awful Spanish and the owner speaking no English. The centre was rather fun. Ongoing communication was through the boss's delightful daughter Muya who ran the business.

'I lived in Cardiff for five years,' she told me. 'I loved Wales so much I am going back next year.' Pity Susan, who is Welsh, wasn't there. She would have lapped it up.

Sure enough two days later we heard a voice hailing us from the quay side: '*Marelle* your dinghy is ready.' In his inimitable way Pedro had walked round to give us the news first-hand. We went immediately in a taxi to pick it up, received another lecture on our misdeeds, paid the very modest bill, left something in the staff Christmas fund or whatever is the Korean equivalent, and said farewell to Muya. She was one of those people one would like to meet again but never do.

We could now sail. Tomas had earlier found the harbour office open and had checked us in. I went round to get our clearance for the Cape Verdes and settle our account. I ran into a slight problem. Officialdom in places like this is most particular about the paperwork. I completed the exit details under the close scrutiny of two eyes and a large moustache. Their owner pounced on a discrepancy. *Marelle* had grown during our stay! Tomas, typically perhaps but no doubt with the best of intentions, had shortened her overall length on the entry form, thereby reducing the berthing charge. I had now blown it. However as officialdom was on the winning side the issue was not pursued.

We secured for sea, had an indifferent meal ashore and turned in for an early night. We didn't sleep too well. Tomas had arrived with a bad cold and had given this to us. He was up and down throughout the night taking his various pills and miracle cures. Like many of his kind he took his health very seriously, carrying with him a portable pharmacy to keep things in order. I even had to get up and change over the hinges on the skylight to prop it up the other way to keep the draft off him, thereby resulting in a marked rise in cabin temperature.

Friday 24 September. 'Sailed at 0945. No wind and under engine. We have been here a week! Settled the watchkeeping routine. I will be relieved by Tomas which will enable me, before dropping off to sleep, to check on how he is managing.' The wind built up and we ended up with a rather wild night under a magnificent full moon and the slowly vanishing lights strung out along the coast of Gran Canaria. I noted 'Would not be too unhappy to be there and not here. A holiday flat in one of those tower blocks could have its attractions.' It would seem we had picked up the full weight of the north-east trades early on.

The passage to São Vicente, our target in the Cape Verde Islands, is only about 850 miles. It is a rhumb-line course and with the wind likely to be in the north-easterly quarter and of good strength, a straightforward passage could be expected. Moreover one enjoys the benefit of the Canary Current sweeping south-west. It should have been a good settling-in run for Tomas. But I was beginning to have doubts about him. He was very quiet. I told myself that this was understandable for the first few days at sea. Although we were making good progress it was not comfortable. The skies were grey and the sea around us cold and unfriendly. A problem with the wind astern was it was bringing dampness into the accommodation below. This meant keeping the cabin doors closed, the shut-up atmosphere not helping if the watch below were not feeling too well.

I took this into account when assessing Tomas. He was keeping his watch without complaining but did nothing else. Just slept. Here was the big difference. Jeremy I knew would also not be feeling his best at this early stage in the passage but he did not let it affect him. He got on with what needed doing. Tomas off watch was the complete passenger.

However, the ship's routine carried on. It was my turn again as duty cook, a more onerous role with the rolling that accompanies downwind sailing. Constraining dishes, despite the use of fiddles, really required cooks with three arms. However I thought I would try one of my standard dishes. Yvonne's Tuna Curry on rice. Who Yvonne was I never discovered but her recipe was a good way to give tuna a lift in life. It needs all the help it can get, we all agreed. It was not a success. Jeremy made a brave attempt but gave up. Tomas didn't even try. I ate mine but had to admit something had gone horribly wrong. It hit me. I had cooked the rice in unadulterated sea water. It was too much for any palate.

We continued to push south and it was getting appreciably warmer. My watch that night was a sheer delight. Quite beautiful with a full moon and the inky black dome full of stars. They were standing out so intensely from it. Orion and Sirius were on full parade, now well above the horizon and being joined by the brilliant, gorgeous Venus. The stars were to become our friends and we were to look forward every night to their companionship. They helped to offset the feeling that the waters around us were hostile. The earlier sense of familiarity had been lost. One wonders how the navigators of old felt as they left what they knew so well and plunged into the complete unknown. We at least knew what lay ahead of us.

Tomas continued to concern me. When it was his turn to prepare supper nothing happened. Jeremy stepped in. Tomas quite simply had climbed into his bunk. I spoke to him later about this but got not much more than a blank response. I was starting to ask myself 'Do we need him?' The value we were getting for the space he and his belongings occupied was low.

The following day was the halfway mark. Tomas joined me in the cockpit during my watch to announce 'I am worried about the next long distance we have to sail.' I waited for him to reveal what he was thinking, but I knew what I wanted him to say. He continued 'I do not feel this life is right for me.' I in turn said that if he did get off at the next stop no one would think the worse of him. I was being chicken. I wanted him to take the step, not me. He then advanced the idea that he could perhaps fly to Mar del Plata to join us there and do the southern leg. I had to tell him this was not on; we were not a cruise ship. Later I told Jeremy of this conversation. He maintained a neutral stance, leaving the decision, as it had to be, with me.

Flying fish were now all around us with one or two lying in the waterways each morning but the hands before the mast did not fancy them. The wind was annoyingly erratic in direction and strength, which meant frequent adjustments to our twin headsail trade-wind rig. We had alternative versions of this. One was the working roller genoa out on its pole and the other genoa goosewinged on the outer moveable forestay on the other side. The other option was to replace this second genoa with the smaller staysail held out on a bearing-out spar. This was an easier arrangement to play with in a wind change, albeit with some loss in speed, but they were comfortable rigs and free from the dangers of an accidental gybe should we have had the mainsail set. With the main set we would have gone faster but there would have been the chafe problem on the lee shrouds and spreader.

Friday 1 October brought the total distance to date to 2,200 miles by log. It was also a perfect day which did wonders for the morale of all hands. The wind had steadied into the north-east and more in trade-wind mode. Off watch it was uncomfortable though. Hot and clammy, it was difficult to rest in one's bunk with the quite erratic movement. However we were rapidly closing the northern part of the Archipelago de Cabo Verde as it so described on the chart. We were heading for Porto Grande on Ilha de São Vicente. As we entered the channel between this island and its neighbour to the west we experienced the marked acceleration in wind speed which is an almost permanent feature of this channel. We took one of the twins off and rather prematurely took the boom off the other. The sea was turbulent in the brisk wind, causing steering difficulties. Jeremy was aiming to keep the apparent wind on the quarter but seemed to be letting the stern swing through the wind, causing the genoa to gybe. It then filled with a shuddering crack. This irritated me and I was having to bite my tongue. Shortly after he had to go below and I relieved him, only to do precisely the same myself with the genoa. There wasn't much I could say.

We entered harbour at 1230, letting go in four metres off the town, Mindelo, and veered a generous thirty-five metres of cable. Nothing much had changed since I had last been here in 1996. It was still blowing very hard and the scenery was as bleak as ever. The wind is a permanent problem, with the fresh trade wind reinforced by gusts rushing off the land up to gale force.

The *Africa Pilot*, which includes the island, refers to frequent squalls and advises 'Vessels should be prepared with second anchors in case of parting their cables or dragging.' Pretty serious stuff. Even with the amount of chain we had out it was being pulled up clear of the water in the gusts.

The only thing that seemed to have changed was inshore, where there was a pontoon arrangement secured to an old moored vessel with two or three yachts alongside. We took the dinghy in to investigate on our way inshore to phone home. It turned out the pontoon 'complex' was a venture set up by a German using a converted Rhine river craft to provide basic facilities for charter vessels and yachts passing through. We received a cordial welcome from the young man in charge, Julius. He opined it was not worth worrying about customs, immigration or the maritime police as it was Saturday afternoon. Monday would be fine. We asked about fresh water but there was a problem here. The hose bringing it from shore was leaking; but not to worry, he could do our laundry. Somehow there was apparently water to do this, but we should have smelt a rat. We did so later. Of the German owner we never saw a sign. Back on board I continued to wrestle with the Tomas problem but slept well that night with a cooling draft through the boat and no bouncing about. I was also relaxed about the hurricane risk when we left here, as we were now into October.

AT ANCHOR OFF MINDELO

Next day, Sunday, was not a rest day, with all hands turned to cleaning ship. I grabbed the moral high ground by insisting on doing the heads and environs. Tomas went ashore to explore the town to be joined later by Jeremy for a meal, leaving me happily on my own to guard the ship. We had a policy of never leaving her unattended. I became aware that something else was different. No one was offering to look after the boat or pressing their services on us to satisfy any of our needs, however diverse. Last time even before the anchor had hit the bottom we had boats around us and even hopefuls swimming out. What had happened to them? It remained an unsolved mystery. Either the police had been over-zealous or the sharks had played a part. The *Pilot* warns 'Sharks frequent the bay,' adding helpfully 'boat sailing is dangerous owing to the heavy squalls off the high ground.' There no doubt was a linkage.

Monday was an action-packed day with a call first-off on the Policia Maritime who, after completion of the formalities, retained *Marelle*'s 'blue book'. The blue book provides proof of the boat's registration, her ownership and her personal details. Without it we could not slip away and avoid paying our harbour charges. Sadly the blue book, officially the Certificate of British Registry, is now a relic of the past, a casualty of Treasury avarice and the political imperative to 'modernise' everything, particularly if it works. The book is in itself a work of art, produced on high-quality parchment and folded into a hardback cover. It is filled out in neat handwriting giving precise, detailed information about the boat with a particularly useful record of all her past owners. Some of the section headings might seem of limited relevance to the twenty-first-century amateur sailor, but the entries have an old-world charm about them. 'Whether a Sailing, Steam or Motor Ship' and 'Depth in hold from tonnage deck to ceiling amidships' and even more importantly 'Number of Seamen or Apprentices for whom accommodation is certified' are just some of the questions posed by the blue book. The modern certificate aims at nothing more ambitious than an encapsulated data sheet, cheap and basic with no hint of romance about it. Whereas the blue book was for life, the way marriage certificates used to be, and incurred only a one-off charge when it was first created, the new certificate has to be renewed every five years with of course a fee.

The official at the Policia Maritime had been smiling and friendly with good English. With the police, however, we had some difficulty. I had taken Tomas ashore for a purpose. Language. The officers we spoke to had no English and Tomas turned out to be of little use. He tried them with Spanish and Portuguese to no avail, complaining that our particular official spoke too slowly! I had difficulty with this. In the end pidgin English and gesticulation bore fruit. In the meantime Jeremy had got on with the stocking-up programme. He had assumed permanently the role of quartermaster, taking charge of the stores and organising all the purchasing. And a thorough job he did too. We lived well and I had no worries.

During two visits to the island I found much of interest, one attraction being the complete lack of tourists. It is certainly not a place for a family holiday. It is not known when the archipelago, consisting of fourteen islands, was first known about but its discovery has been attributed to another one of Henry the Navigator's enterprises in the fifteenth century. Colonisation followed in the beginning of the next century with no shortage of labour. Slaves from West Africa. This racial characteristic is dominant today. The inhabitants are now an interesting blend of the African stock and European, speaking an equally interesting language mix of Portuguese, a local Creole-type dialect and some spread of English as well as other European languages. I liked the place and its people.

They have had their problems over the centuries. Drake paid two visits and left his mark. In 1577 at the start of his circumnavigation, a Portuguese cargo vessel had the misfortune to fall in with his squadron off the island of Santiago in the east and which housed the capital. Not only did the ship give up its cargo but also its pilot, the highly experienced Nuñez da Silva. He remained a 'guest' of Drake's during the Straits of Magellan transit. He was impressed by Drake's competency and rendered outstandingly valuable assistance. In fact a lot of what we know about that part of the voyage is due to his log.

The fate that ultimately befell da Silva was a revealing example of Drake's utter ruthlessness in the way he dealt with people, and the inhumanity displayed when it suited his purpose. Having created havoc amongst the Spanish on the western shores of Nova Hispania and achieved his treasure-grabbing objectives, Drake needed to pursue his exit strategy whilst he was still in front. Off the Mexican coast he had captured a Spanish merchantman and, having looted her, saw the opportunity for putting his pursuers off the scent by confusing them on where he would go next. It was to be a masterly exercise in disseminating misinformation. In the course of his everyday discourse with da Silva he fed him a series of false clues. Then without warning the unfortunate pilot, now of no further use to Drake and despite the friendship that had built up between them, was put aboard the Spanish ship, which was then freed to proceed on her interrupted passage. Drake surmised, correctly as it turned out, that da Silva would be delivered into the tender care of the Inquisition. Under torture he would give the false intelligence to the

Spanish authorities, desperately anxious to know the future marauding plans of Captain Francesco Draquez on the shores of Central America. Drake in fact was heading west, confident he would be free to do so, unmolested.

It so happened that included in the loot taken from the ship into which da Silva had been deposited was a young black girl, a comely lass called Maria, who was carried on board *Golden Hind* over to the Spice Islands in the Portuguese-dominated part of the East Indies. Working her passage, as it were, she became heavily pregnant in the course of the long time at sea. As it was impossible to determine the father-to-be – the contenders could have been any one from the Captain down – Drake was presented with a problem. Not only were they ill-equipped to cope with the complex situation of having a child born on board but there would be a delicate public relations exercise to handle on arrival back home. Drake solved the problem in his inimitable way. He marooned her with a couple of other unwanteds on an out-of-the-way deserted location with only the bare minimum of provisions. Drake was thus confident Maria would not come back to haunt him. But in fact she did. Subsequently in a widely publicised history of the events, Drake was lambasted for his gross inhumanity. However, any opprobrium that might have resulted from this did not dent his status as a national hero in the eyes of the adoring public.

Drake was to have another go at Santiago, returning to the Cape Verdes in 1585 when he put ashore a surprisingly massive force of soldiers numbering nearly one thousand at Cidade Velba, which was then the capital. Disappointed at not finding any loot, they sacked it. That disappointment was the seed of mutiny. The soldiers Drake had throughout his fleet were mercenaries, recruited with promises of the rich rewards that would be theirs for the taking. The expedition, like all before it, had been assembled to plunder the Spanish in the New World but with the added incentive of picking up spoils on the way. The first setback was missing off the Iberian Peninsula by just a few days the arrival home of the Spanish treasure fleet, this piece of unpalatable news being passed to them by a passing French ship. On top of this came the Cape Verdes disappointment.

Drake's hold over the troops was at best tenuous. They were not part of a regular army and subject to the rigid discipline associated with such a structure. One did not exist in the England of the day and was not to come into existence for another couple of centuries. The Duke of Wellington was likewise to have problems with his unruly foot soldiers in the Peninsular Wars. Such men were prepared to fight with great vigour but only if they could enjoy the spoils of victory, which they considered was their right. With nothing coming their way, Drake's soldiers were getting restless. From the experience of an earlier voyage when confronted with a major disciplinary problem, he knew that what was demanded was to orchestrate a highly visible demonstration of his authority. This was vital if he were to keep control and stop the whole venture falling apart. An occasion for him to put his stamp of authority on the situation then conveniently presented itself.

A steward in one of the ships was accused of having committed sodomy with a couple of the ship's boys. Drake convened a court and the steward was put on trial. He confessed and was summarily executed on the spot. The message was not lost on the soldiers as well as the sailors, that Drake had the power of death over life and was prepared to exercise that power. He was for all to see the ultimate authority. He then ordered the fleet to sea and laid off the course for the West Indies.

Distinguished visitors to the Cape Verdes since then include Captain Cook in the course of his second voyage in 1772. In line with what had become standard practice with outward-bound East Indiamen he took in water and fresh provisions. In 1832 no less a person than Charles Darwin spent some time botanising over the hills of Santiago, having landed from HMS *Beagle*. A more permanent British interest developed when the activity centre shifted to Mindelo, which emerged as a steamship bunkering port and an important link in submarine cable communications. Long gone are the tennis courts and golf courses of the Brits. Gone they may be but not forgotten. During my earlier visit to Porto Grande we had moved the yacht into the inner basin, home to the fishing fleet, to get fuel and water. We secured alongside one of the fleet whose owner took our lines and entered into a discourse. He bore a resemblance to Nelson Mandela with the same dignified manner and an almost equal command of English. There was something on his mind, as witnessed by constant glances at our ensign. The owner of our yacht was a member of the Royal Cornwall Yacht Club and as a consequence we were wearing the defaced blue ensign with its special emblem in the fly. The Club's patron is the Prince of Wales and the emblem is his plume comprising three large, white ornamental feathers. It was becoming evident that our fisherman was fascinated by this, but in the reserved, polite way of the Cape Verdes islanders, was hesitant to speak out. Eventually however he did.

'Please can you tell me why you have ice cream cones on your flag?'

'Actually, they are not ice creams, but the feathers in the crest of the Prince of Wales.'

His face lit up. 'Ah! Princess Di!'

Such is her fame that she was a byword in this out-of-the-way backwater, buried in the depths of the Atlantic. She no doubt would have been gratified, but, without being uncharitable, the feeling would not possibly have been shared to the same extent by the owner of the ice creams.

Despite the views expressed by the *Pilot* there is an attraction to the harbour. The anchorage is uncluttered and unregimented. So unlike yacht marinas which are the complete opposite. Confined, controlled, regulated with the occupants all on top of each other. Perhaps because of this difference the Cape Verdes attract a special type of yachtsperson. Alongside the German's barge was another German in a small boat who, from time to time, would cruise around the islands or go off tramping over the hills. He was deciding whether to cross the Atlantic to see if he would like a long ocean passage on his own. If not, what then? No idea. In the meantime he just sat around in his cockpit all day. He was in no hurry.

Another lone ranger was an English woman Jeremy had met ashore. Having given up on her husband who wasn't into sailing, Eleanor had set off single-handed across to the West Indies, then ending up back here in Porto Grande. She was living in her boat up on the slipway in a boatyard having an osmosis outbreak rectified. She also did not know what she would do next. Another true ocean wanderer. People like her and the German are at home in the relaxed, basic lifestyle of places like the Cape Verdes.

Back in our little world the moment of decision about Tomas was nigh. He sensed I was not happy about him and turned to Jeremy for company, feeling his innate kindliness. On the night of my birthday, of all days, they went ashore for a meal, accepting an invitation from Julius on the German's barge to a special meal of local cuisine. It was a funny old birthday but I was happy to be on my own to think it all through. It was the right thing for me to take the decision first and then tell Jeremy. Earlier in the day I had spoken to Sue, Fraser's wife, in Falmouth, to confirm he was still on line and she said he was. He was out at the time. He would as arranged be flying down to Mar del Plata to await our arrival. This cleared the way. Early next morning I spoke to Tomas and asked him to leave the boat there and then, doing my best to explain the reasons why. He took it very well and I think deep down he was relieved that the decision had been made for him. He was a proud man and conducted himself with dignity. I wondered how he would explain it all to his family and friends on his premature return. I wondered also what role I would play in his memory and in his account of events.

I told Jeremy and I felt he was also relieved and in agreement. Within the hour Tomas was ashore with his gear and had organised a midnight flight to Lisbon.

I cleared with the police and immigration people, collected the all-important blue book and settled our harbour dues. The equivalent of £3 for six days! We were ready to sail. Jeremy had completed his storing but we needed water. Anchored next to us was a big Dutch topsail schooner whose skipper had also been to the special Julius dinner party ashore where he had chatted with Jeremy. He had very kindly suggested we fill our cans from his tanks. This we did. It was not a problem for him he said as he would be going into the commercial docks to water ship in advance of his next charter party. He said he would take in about 8 tonnes! With carefree charterers on board he would probably need all of that.

OUR DUTCH SCHOONER IN PORTO GRANDE

We went ashore, posted our mail and made the last phone calls. Back on board the mood was relaxed. I sat with my drink, wreathed in the delicious smells wafting up from one of Jeremy's special concoctions.

CHAPTER THREE

SOUTH TO THE TROPICS

The Sun's rim dips; the Stars rush out:
At one stride comes the Dark.
S. T. Coleridge, *The Rime of the Ancient Mariner*

Sea routine – run out of trade winds – speak our first ship – Doldrums tedium – beneficial difference in temperaments – south-east trades – pernickety about crossing the Line – Brazilian coast – perfect nights – star-struck – Jeremy needs the NHS – torrid time off Cabo Frio – lecture on the error of our ways – wonder why we are here – River Plate – tricky entering Mar del Plata – experience Argentinian bureaucracy – we must be criminals

'Lash up and stow!' The time-honoured morning call in the Navy to get the hands moving. For us it was also very much time to get moving. Departure day from the Cape Verdes had arrived. I noted with a twinge of concern that the day being Friday 8 October we were now five days behind the plan but I told myself we stood a fair chance of making this up in view of the long passage ahead of us. The deadline we now had to meet was to get to Mar del Plata to pick up Fraser. He would be planning his flight to Buenos Aires to arrive in the second week of November and we didn't want him exposed for too long to the temptations of South America. The precise calculated distance in following the route recommended in *Ocean Passages for the World* was 3,810 nautical miles. The passage plan speed was a very modest one of a hundred miles per day. Somewhat pedestrian, but it gave a generous allowance for everything from gales on the nose to spells of no wind, to be expected in the Doldrums and the Variables. It would be largely under sail as the assistance we could expect to get from the engine would not be great due to severe fuel limitations.

Ahead lay an interesting mix of weather systems. We hoped to carry the north-east trades for a few days after leaving the Cape Verdes before the wind started to haul southwards and become erratic as we approached the Doldrums. Having negotiated these we could expect a moderate southerly, putting us on the wind until getting into the south-east trade winds, just north of the equator. We could rely on these to take us down the coast of Brazil until a little north of the latitude of Rio de Janeiro. By this time the wind would have backed into the north-east. It would then be a step to crossing the tropic of Capricorn and leaving the tropics for sterner stuff. In the last thousand miles to the River Plate and across it to Mar del Plata the wind could be anywhere. In the main what we expected was what we got. In looking ahead we had the comforting anticipation of nothing above a Force 6 until we got down to Cabo de São Tome lying to the north-east of Rio. The South Atlantic routeing chart did not show a gale Force 8 until another three hundred miles further on. Apart from the irritation of the Doldrums, and they were to prove a real irritation, the period ahead of us was to see the best sailing of the whole voyage. The sure knowledge of fair winds and an absence of gales relaxes the mind wonderfully.

With everything lashed up and stowed and a good breakfast under our belts we tackled the task of recovering the long scope of chain out on the anchor. This took time and had its problems but finally, with the anchor firmly lashed in its chocks on the foredeck, we were away on the longest leg of the voyage if one excluded the marathon ahead of us from the Falklands to Azores.

As we got our anchor we noted our friends in the topsail schooner were also having difficulty in recovering theirs. She had been riding to two anchors but in a rare shift of the wind the cables had become twisted. They had what mariners call a 'foul hawse' and it was causing them considerable difficulty in sorting out the tangle. The ship's mate, a young Dutch girl, was on the wheel and working the engine controls, standing on a box so she could see over the deck house. The skipper with his small paid crew was struggling on the forecastle using language which probably had previously been unknown to these local men. Earlier I had met the mate. She had been getting practical sea experience in the schooner and was about to return to Holland to go to a maritime college to study for her Master's certificate.

IN COMPANY WITH OUR DUTCH FRIEND OFF MINDELO

We sailed. No one noticed. So different to the last time when in a Canadian yacht *White Trillium*. Then there had been an anchorage full of boats and we had received a farewell fanfare of foghorn blasts. It had been quite a moving experience and something of a ritual involving every boat in the harbour. I had been crewing for friends, Rosemary and David Whitten, on passage to Antigua in the West Indies.

Out in the channel the wind, although not of the strength it had been when we came in, was enough to get us on our way. I noted in my journal 'I fear it is going to be a long and rather tiring passage'. We were then on the threshold of the very purpose of all that we had set out to do. That night I lay in my bunk reviewing the lessons we had learned since leaving Falmouth. How well prepared were we for what lay ahead? The conclusion drawn was to leave me reasonably confident although there would always be nagging in the back of my mind. 'If only I had done this or some other thing!' Too late now.

We had in fact encountered a deficiency, totally unexpected, in the gear, which was to cause some irritation later in the south. When we had been weighing anchor with the hand-operated windlass in Porto Grande the chain every now and then would slip a few links off the gipsy. Before we had left home I had beefed up the chain size, ordering a new gipsy to suit. Having been assured this would fit I had not tested it under load but it was evident there was in fact an annoying mismatch. Now miles on our way there was not much we could do about it.

The next few days on passage were quiet going as we continued to carry the trades, now much more subdued and their days numbered. The wind was inexorably veering into the east as it worked its way southwards and lightened. Three nights out it gave up altogether during my watch below. The slatting of the sails and banging of the gear woke me. After putting up with it for some time I began complaining until, finally snapping, I leapt up into the cockpit to confront Jeremy.

'Don't keep on about it! There is not much we can do,' was the rather testy but not unreasonable response.

I digested this and thought there are advantages in having a more phlegmatic attitude to life. It must help in coping with adverse situations, particularly when only limited action can be taken to alleviate them. The differences in our natures rather than generating relationship problems created, I believe, a good working amalgam. We offset each other.

Now well down into the tropics, our environment was changing. Evidence of this was as we forged southwards on a close reach we were treated in the night to a blindingly vivid display of 'sheet' lightning illuminating whole areas of the horizon as though it were daylight. The impact of each dazzling burst of light was overwhelming. Then came a rapidly rising wind bringing with it heavy rain. I seized the opportunity to wash my hair and felt so much better as a result. It is quite surprising how such small things can affect one's wellbeing. Later Jeremy had a similar experience in his watch. However he displayed more initiative by taking a shower under the boom gooseneck, from which water was gushing as rainwater cascaded off the mainsail. When he told me about it I admired his fortitude as it must have been pretty damn cold.

The weather pattern continued to change with the wind shifting into the south-east. This raised something of a quandary. We had to get into the best position to handle the southerly winds certain to be lying ahead of us to ensure we crossed the equator at the chosen point. A major consideration was the width of the Doldrums belt lying just to the north of the Line. The narrowest part of the belt and its location vary seasonally. For our time of the year the crossing should be between 24°W and 29°W and the further east the better. Because of having to beat against the southerly our bible the *Ocean Passages for the World* advised further we should cross the latitude of 5°N close to 20°W. As we were then in 25°W we needed to head south-east. Fortunately the wind kept veering further southward, allowing us to point in the right direction hard on the starboard tack. This changed our lifestyle. In one way it was a pleasant change from the incessant rolling associated with downwind sailing, but now we had a rocking-horse action as we punched into a head sea. Whereas before the decks had been bone dry, now they were running water continuously. To go onto the foredeck was to invite a soaking. It also meant we could not risk opening the skylight to get badly needed air into the cabin. True to form the wind then failed completely. Back to the banging and slatting again. The cacophony of sound went right through one's very being. We ran the engine in the hope that the wind might be shamed into doing something. It wasn't. After a while we stopped the engine. Nothing, still no wind. Back to the old routine of gear torture.

'What the jerking to and fro is doing to the mainsail stitching is anyone's guess!' my journal laments.

It was at this moment that a little lightness came into our lives. During the night we were passed very close to by a large vessel. We called her up on the VHF to be greeted almost immediately by the captain coming on to the radio. Very pleasant and very friendly. Yes, he would pass on any messages we had to Falmouth Coastguard, MRCC, the Maritime Rescue Co-ordinating Centre. This he did by telex.

Please be advised that our vessel sailed past the good yatch [*sic*] '*Marelle*' in position Lat 11° 10′ N, Long 023° 49′ W. Our vessel is en route from Gibraltar to Sepetiba in Brazil. We enquired with skipper if we could render any services, wherein he requested us to contact MRCC Falmouth and request you to contact their families and advise them that all is OK and that they are in good health. The weather at the moment is calm sea, with no wind at all. There were two persons on the yatch [*sic*]. Pls pass on above to their families.

Thanks N best regards
Capt. S. Crasto
Master

M.V. *MINERAL ZULU*

After wishing us a good voyage she swung on her way, leaving us to ourselves and a warm feeling. I thought to myself there is so much good in the world why do we hear so much that is bad? Before leaving Falmouth I had logged with the Coastguard *Marelle*'s particulars with the complete passage plan. On receipt of this message the Coastguard rang Susan, passed on the content and invited her to come round to collect a copy of the text. This procedure was to be followed whenever it was appropriate to speak a ship. Invariably the response was friendly and fully cooperative. Equally so was the Coastguard who went out of their way to field these calls and pass them on so promptly to Susan. No ship failed to pass on a message and not one went astray.

The ocean suddenly became crowded. Next morning I heard Jeremy calling at the same time as there were two prolonged blasts on a ship's horn. A big, high-sided freighter *Progress* was close alongside. She was also carrying passengers, as a small group was assembled on the superstructure waving their arms off. She had altered course to close us. I wished them good morning on the radio. A deep Russian-sounding voice responded. He also wanted to know if we wanted anything. We wished each other a good voyage. She turned back onto her original course, the little crowd waving farewell. I felt strangely sad and lonely. Like the contact last night it had been a moving moment. In a sentimental rush of feeling I noted 'Yes, people on the whole are good.'

The wind arrived. With it came the rain clouds. Dense, heavy cumulonimbus, dark and threatening, closing in on us from all around. The routine was becoming established. Shorten sail, then soap and towels at the ready. The first downpour hit us but surprisingly not too cold. We soaped ourselves all over and I lathered my hair. The rain stopped. The sun came out. There was now no option but to use precious fresh water to wash down before the soap baked on.

The clouds came back, forming up into a massive black bank marshalling themselves for the next onslaught. The squall hit us. Gale force with a tearing, roaring explosion of sound streaking the sea with long bands of ragged spume. *Marelle* stood up to it under reefed main and took off as we wound up the flogging genoa. The viciousness dissipated but the rain stayed with us all night with remorseless persistence.

We had entered the Equatorial Trough more famously known as the Doldrums. Although this belt of unstable air moves with the seasons and varies in depth it is always there. A permanent feature constituting a permanent, major obstacle to the vessel under sail whether going north or south. It is a 'bridge of sighs' stretching from Africa to South America and cannot be avoided. It was going to give us a hard time.

For the sailing vessel of today the obvious answer is a powerful engine and plenty of fuel. Force on under power when there is no wind with the simple objective of getting as painlessly as possible from one trade wind belt to the other. We wished we had been able to enjoy that luxury.

Our diesel tank held well under twenty gallons of usable fuel, complemented by some jerry cans. Of the fuel available a significant quantity was untouchable, being reserved for battery charging. This had to be by the engine as we had no other charging systems such as wind generators, solar panels or towed impellers. Life would certainly have been easier with one or other of these. Consequently we had to maintain a tight regime for controlling electrical power consumption. But all we needed really was power for the GPS and the compass light. Everything else was switched off. Navigation lights, a major drain on the battery, were only switched on when we had other ships' lights in sight and closing us. I became somewhat obsessive about energy conservation, which I think was a minor irritation to Jeremy, but he seemed to live with it.

In pursuit of the Holy Grail of keeping power consumption to the absolute minimum it helped that we did not have energy-guzzlers like fridges, deep freezers, microwave ovens and video recorders, not to mention SSB transceivers, PCs and the rest of the paraphernalia seemingly essential to twentieth and now twenty first century ocean voyaging.

Actually when it came to the point we didn't need any battery power at all at sea, or even the engine itself for that matter. We were after all a sailing vessel. For lighting in the cabin we had oil lamps. For navigation the GPS although immensely convenient was far from essential. In an earlier trip extending over 12,000 miles I had used a sextant on average twice a day and thought little of it. It became routine. The principal problem would have been the compass light, ironically the smallest power user of all. The need for it was when we could not call on Mr Franklin or the Autohelm and when there was 'no star to steer her by'. I had tried unsuccessfully to lay hands on a traditional brass binnacle cover complete with oil lamp. As it was to turn out we had need of one later in the passage.

With a severe limitation on fuel we were to experience to the full the frustrations associated with traversing the region largely under sail. Character-building, perhaps, and what did come out were the differences in temperament between Jeremy and me. Except in the often quite violent rain squalls the wind was from light to nothing. This was when Jeremy excelled. He would spend his watch seated behind the wheel concentrating on keeping the boat moving, almost with no discernible feel to the wind. Constantly playing with the sheets, *Marelle* would inch forward. Bubbles on the sea surface drifted past and then dawdled their way astern. His patience was inexhaustible. Infinitely more than I could muster.

'Give it away Jeremy! We are going nowhere.'

'No. Every foot we make is one foot further south and nearer finding wind.'

It was the thrashing that the gear was taking that was wearing my nerves and destroying my patience. There was always movement on the surface of the sea regardless of wind strength. In the aftermath of a squall it would be disturbed, throwing *Marelle* around. In the long periods of calm there would still be an irregular swell. With not enough wind to keep the mainsail quiet it would lurch violently to and fro as she rolled. This would jerk the slides along the foot, causing them to clatter loudly in the track along the length of the boom. This constant snatching was what I found so hard to accept. It was evidently not worrying Jeremy anywhere near as much and I told myself that this was because poor suffering *Marelle* was not his. I was taking personally what she was taking. I suspect though in reality his nature was more resilient and he was able to bear the stress better than I.

The squalls continued to build up around the circumference of our world, awesome in their black menace. Because we were such a small speck on the ocean most of them would miss us or dissipate before they arrived. When they did hit us the effect was violent until they passed on, carrying the wind with them and leaving nothing apart from the rain. Quite frequently this would last through the night. Listening to this depressing downpour we felt guilty at not attempting to catch drinking water but the flesh was woefully weak. It was comfortable, warm and dry in the cabin. Too much so. On deck the helmsman was preoccupied, sitting behind the wheel, trying to keep on course. It would probably be hand-steering for most of the time as there was insufficient water flow over the rudder to allow either Mr Franklin or the Autohelm to function. It was then when completely fed up we would throw the fuel conservation resolutions over the side and crank up the engine. 'What the hell! We can only use the fuel once. When it's gone it's gone!' Anything to get us out of this hole in which it seemed we would be stuck forever. But we were about to become unstuck.

Monday 18 October brought wind from ahead, where it should be. We were back hard on the wind again and it was uncomfortable. She was pitching into the short seas, ladling water over the weather bow, sluicing it down the decks and over the coachroof. I noted 'Jeremy is not feeling a hundred percent. From his odd comments he is obviously not enjoying it at all. I suspect he wishes himself anywhere but here. So do I. But we plug on. We are getting there!'

Apart from the progress we were making the day was memorable in that we had a social hour to finish off the last of the vino tinto even though we had to add water to make a decent drink. We commented on it still being drinkable after all the throwing about, but I suppose one will drink anything at sea.

We rounded the occasion off with a rare tune-in to the World Service. The Commonwealth was being tough on Pakistan. Our Prime Minister had been embracing the Chinese head of state during a visit to the UK but we were assured by R. Cook Esq that 'Human rights would be raised.' Were they? We can't bully China the way we can a country the size of Chile over Pinochet. To us in the middle of the ocean, where we were fully integrated into the environment and the natural world around us, it all seemed so irrelevant. All-important to us was what the wind was going to do and what the barograph was telling us.

Next morning as I arrived in the cockpit I was greeted with 'I think we have cracked it! Looks like trade-wind weather.'

The wind was holding and had backed further to east of south. We were now holding 210° True and with enough easting now at 21°W we could lay the chosen point for crossing the line. The only blemish in our new-found paradise was Jeremy complaining about his underwear. He had been using the laundry that had been done for him by Julius on the barge in Porto Santo. It was uncomfortable to wear, damp and sticky. The penny dropped. It must have been washed in salt water, it was so hygroscopic. We remembered now Julius mentioning the problem in getting fresh water from shore. He had been a bit of a rascal, washing the clothes in water out of the harbour. He had overlooked telling Jeremy of this but had not forgotten to charge the full quoted rate. I felt a little smug as I had done my dhobeying on board *Marelle*.

On Friday 22 October at 1056 we crossed the Line at 23° 39′ W, a little further to the east than I had intended but all to the good. This would give us a slightly broader slant across the south-east trade as we went down the coast of Brazil. From now on we would be on a reach with the wind in the south-easterly quadrant at a healthy Force 5. The big fear the square-rigger captain had was to cross the Line too far to the west. He could then end up to the north of Cabo de São Roque at the north eastern tip of Brazil. His ship would then be faced with the almost impossible task of beating back against the trades to get round the corner to head south. The problem for him and us was the south equatorial current sweeping west at over a knot and getting stronger. Although we were very comfortably to the east I was nevertheless only to feel completely relaxed when we were below the latitude of the cape and well on our way southward.

The problem of Brazil inconveniently jutting out into the South Atlantic with the west-flowing ocean current setting vessels down onto it had been well-known to the early navigators. The difficulty was to determine how much to allow for this current and hence avoid hitting South America. It was not until Cook went south equipped with a reliable timepiece that an accurate estimate could be made for the first time of the rate of change of longitude and hence a measurement of the strength of the current.

On both his second and third voyages the Admiralty had placed on board *Resolution* the world's first accurate instrument for recording time at sea in the form of Larcum Kendall's watch K-1, the progeny of John Harrison's triumphant horological labours. As an illustration of the potency of the new technology, when in 8°S, Cook found there was a 29-mile discrepancy between his observed and estimated positions, from which he was able to deduce precisely the current's drift.

The first visible evidence of the wear and tear *Marelle* had been subjected to was a seam opening up near the head of the genoa. We rolled up the sail past the weak point and because of the reduced sail area set the staysail under it. We were now a cutter – the first time we had tried this rig. It worked well, lifting our speed a knot. It was however to lead to a personality 'clash'. I had spent the rest of my watch fiddling with Mr Franklin to retune him to the changed sail plan. As I was to learn later, this was exasperating Jeremy as he considered my efforts were unwarranted. It lead to a 'frank exchange of views', as the politicians say, on our respective temperaments. He felt my tendency to worry overly about things was irritating and frequently achieved little. I had to agree that perhaps he had a point. On his part he conceded his relaxed attitude could also be irritating. We had cleared the air. At least it stopped me continuing to interfere with Mr Franklin even though he was still, in my private view, not at his peak performance.

Our ordered way of life continued. That night I noted 'Had grilled ham, beans and fried eggs for dinner. Hopefully the maggots were well done when under the grill.' It was also 'another beautiful evening'. A major Burnett contribution had been a large ham on the bone. Put on board in Falmouth, we had been living off it ever since. Being able to carve off a slice of meat was a welcome relief from the tinned variety but later on wildlife moved in and was starting to enjoy it as well. Maggots. Jeremy tackled them from time to time but could never be sure of complete removal. When cutting off slices for consumption it was wise not to look too closely.

On a quiet morning we hauled the damaged genoa down and Jeremy restitched the seam. Working under difficulties he did a good job. I had always suspected he was a better marlinespike seaman than I. The sail was an old one and I was using it to see us through the Doldrums and the tropics, keeping the working genoa for the sterner stuff in the south. We were now very much in the tropics and the ultraviolet degradation was taking its toll of the sail cloth. I wished I had bent on the spare mainsail for this leg to have preserved the working main. As we went down the coast of Brazil it was becoming unbearably hot. Thirty-five degrees in the cabin entrance and appreciably more down on our bunks. It was making it very difficult to sleep at night. We couldn't risk cracking open the skylight because of rogue dollops of cold sea water landing on the coachroof and down into the ear of the occupant of the bunk below. On deck though the nights were lovely, their pleasure only being spoiled by the occasional rain squall building up even though all too frequently they were to dissipate before reaching us. It was the same performance we had experienced quite often in the north.

My journal records 'We reefed down and got out the soap and shampoo. Zilch! I can't smell Jeremy. Hopefully it is the same with him.'

On watch during the day it was just as uncomfortable in the heat. With sun at a declination of 12° south it was remorselessly beating down into the cockpit with all the heat of its tropics fire. There was no shade and no escape until the evening when it went behind the mainsail. The relief was enormous. We could enjoy the evening drink, albeit the social hour had shrunk in time in the all too brief twilight before the night swept over us.

It was a simple life but there were times when the constraints of our existence engendered a certain tedium. This would raise within us the question, never to be adequately answered, 'Why are we here?' Jeremy had, it would appear, been struggling with that very question when he remarked, it being Saturday midday, that possibly our wives were at the yacht club with offers of lunch accompanied by 'Where are those idiots now?' as the enquirer sipped a cold beer. The idiots had forgotten what one tasted like.

Despite this negative attitude, the nights remained heaven and the sailing the best I can ever recall. We looked forward with real pleasure when coming on watch to meeting our friends the stars, filling the heavens with their unbelievable brightness. They were always there and we knew they would always be there, for ever and ever. Adding to the sublimity of these magic nights was an enormous full moon bathing us in its soft light. Looking up at it I could actually see moonbeams spearing down to me. It didn't matter what was happening in the rest of the world. This was ours!

The nearest human beings were on the shores of Brazil, a hundred miles under our lee, away to the west and of no relevance to our enclosed world. The discordant clamour of people could not intrude into our privacy. *Marelle* was snoring along under Mr Franklin's steady guiding hand, with nothing demanded of me. High above my head, darkly outlined against the brilliance of the stars, the sails, full of the warm trade wind, were quietly playing their part. Half turning, I could see below the black, silent void that was the cabin, knowing Jeremy was there sleeping peacefully. There was togetherness but each to ourselves. A great peace was all-enveloping. My thoughts were of home and all that is good in the world.

But the weather was changing as we got down to the latitude of Rio de Janeiro. The trades had gone. The winds were now varying in strength and direction, frequently strong with rough water and leaden skies. The decks were running water almost continuously, taking it solidly over the foredeck. I was proud of dear old *Marelle*. Under a scrap of genoa and close-reefed main she was eating her way up to windward, pushing aside the head seas thrown up by the very strong wind contrary to the south-flowing Brazil Current.

We were approaching our waypoint off Cabo Frio, east of Rio, and ran into a spot of bother. Just before daybreak I heard Jeremy calling me. He was having difficulty in sorting out the movements of two quite large vessels displaying very bright lights. Switching on the radio I called them up on channel 16. An American voice came back, friendly in tone and very polite, saying they had been trying to contact us without success. They wanted to break the news that they were seismic survey vessels part of an oil exploration programme, and what's more towing sweep wires stretching four miles astern of them. We were where they wanted to be! We were given a gentle lecture on the error of our ways. We were on their pad but because of lack of action on our part they had been forced, sweep wires and all, to keep dodging us. In future would we please maintain an adequate radio watch and be prepared to take avoiding action. There were others of their kind around! They wished us a pleasant voyage. It was encouraging they had picked us up on their radar at eight miles. This reflected well, as one might say, on our Firdell Blipper.

The Mariner's Handbook, another worthy publication by the Hydrographic Office, is something of a nautical version of *Pears Cyclopaedia* and like it, full of intriguing bits and pieces of information. It has this to say about vessels engaged in seismic surveys: "They often keep radio silence to avoid interference with registering equipment. Vessels called by light by a seismic survey vessel should, therefore, answer by the same means, and not by radio." It may have been that our friends had tried to call us up by signalling lamp and then in frustration resorted to radio. Just as well, as the prospects for carrying on a meaningful discourse on our part in Morse Code by flashing light were not promising, unless Jeremy had a hidden light under his bushel. Sadly another traditional skill largely lost in the yachting world as we know it.

As the day wore on it was becoming increasingly evident we were in for some unfriendly weather. The wind was hauling into the north-east and building. Wispy cirrus with long tortured streamers was spreading over the heavens and an enormous halo forming around the sun. The barograph trace was sliding steeply downwards. We dropped everything and changed to the storm jib set on the inner forestay before it got dark. Through the night we ran south of west before a full gale, pitch dark and driving sheets of icy rain. Cabo Frio is rightly named. The steep seas were building up fast and beginning to override the self steering gear. Crouched behind the wheel we could hear them roaring up on the quarter then breaking with an explosion of foaming crests, as they snarled menacingly past on either side and disappeared into the blackness ahead. To help the evening along the compass light gave up. This was when I regretted not having that cowl over the compass with its oil lamp. We had of necessity to go back to basics and steer by the wind. Overhead was the ensign, black in the night, streaming downwind and aligned with the course which could be checked from time to time with a torch on the compass card. It was much more positive than an electronic wind indicator with its little pointer. Ours was the way Moitessier thought boats should be steered.

With the dawn the conditions eased and we were back to boat and crew being thrown about in the all too familiar scenario of too little wind and too much sea. It was the prelude to the next slice of drama.

In the early hours I was woken by 'Ben! I have had something of a mishap.' I stumbled up into the cockpit to be greeted by a Jeremy with one side of his face a sheet of blood. It was pouring over the front of his oilskins and seemed to be everywhere. He had been thrown off his perch under the sprayhood and had hit his forehead on a corner of the entrance into the companionway. Fortunately head wounds can look worse than they are and once I had cleaned him up and dressed the open wound everything was looking better. I consulted our other bible, *The Ship Captain's Medical Guide*, on suturing. The wound was so wide open that I thought perhaps it should be stitched. However rather to my relief the good book advised 'If in doubt don't.' Unpractised hands on a very unstable platform might not have been a good idea. I was able to pull the opening together with strip plasters and made him turn in. He was in slight shock and needed sleep. Later I recleaned the wound and applied self-adhesive dressing pads which were brilliant in coping with a very wide and deep opening.

Our adventures in this wretched area and our attempts to shake Cabo Frio off our heels were not yet over. We had another encounter with a survey vessel, French this time. She suddenly appeared mid-morning from over the horizon, sending over her high-speed tender to ask us in the politest terms to get the hell out of it. They were wanting to stream their seismic sweeps, advising there would be eight cables each with a large float on the end. The cables would be more than four miles long and spread out like an enormous fan. Her captain volunteered the information that the Brazilian government had only just issued oil prospecting licenses, which explained why there was nothing on our chart about this being a restricted area. In sight was a very large oil drilling platform and we marvelled at how it was possible to anchor such a structure in these deep waters. We were to read later that the rig suffered a major mishap, suggesting the rig owners had been a little too confident. With little or no wind we wearily cranked up the engine and plugged on south. The

French captain passed on a weather forecast from the Brazilian air force giving a gale warning with particular mention of very high seas in an area centred on 25° south. Depressing as this was, it being only about seventy miles or so ahead of us, it was more inviting than staying where we were, even though we had had enough of gales for a while. In the event when we got there this one had left the scene.

We were not the first to have problems in the vicinity of Cabo Frio. That honour lies with Ferdinand Magellan, who, almost to the month 480 years before us, had rounded the cape and anchored his fleet off what is now Rio de Janeiro. The respective problems were different. Ours were survey vessels and unfriendly weather. His were a little more exotic. Mutineers and young maidens. Culprits responsible for internecine class warfare within the fleet were clapped in irons. The maidens were more of a problem. The young girls from nearby villages had soon caught on that they had something of value to the seamen. The word spread and the maidens from outlying villages joined in, such that in no time at all the market was fully satisfied, literally. So much so that Magellan was having a problem in getting any work out of his mariners. He, like us, resolved his difficulties by getting clear of the area and sailing south. In the variables belt our progress down the southern Brazilian coast and then that of Uruguay was subject to sailing conditions ranging from the beautiful to the decidedly unpleasant. But we progressed, having on 15 November a celebratory dinner to mark the 500 miles to go point.

We had been keeping close in, to continue to carry the current still flowing south and avoid the contrary Falklands Current spreading out north-east. Leaving Rio Grande astern at the bottom of Brazil, we passed into Uruguayan waters. Now sailing gently under twin headsails we made a peaceful entry into the River Plate estuary. The moon was up and our friends the stars, bright and cheerful as ever. Moreover there were no nasties around. For these the estuary has a tarnished reputation. Sudden, vicious and highly dangerous local winds each having its own behavioural pattern but with the shared characteristic of being particularly nasty. The *Zonda* comes in from the north, the *Sudestada* hits from off the sea and the *Pampero* strikes from off the pampas. We thought we had escaped their attentions, only to be hit later when further south by the third one in this unholy trinity.

There is an air of romance about Rio de la Plata but it does not make much of an effort to foster this image. It is a wide expanse, the best part of 130 miles at the entrance, of silt-laden discoloured water and shallows. Being shallow, very unpleasant seas can be thrown up by the thundery weather and strong, violent winds to which it is subject. It is difficult to understand how it could have been described as a sheet of silver by the Portuguese John de Solis who, like his fellow-countryman Magellan, was seeking the gateway to the Pacific. Both were to give their lives in this quest, de Solis being the more unfortunate in that he was eaten before he found that gateway.

The estuary was in a benign mood when we crossed it. That night I wrote 'Long, rather boring middle watch. Desperately hungry. Found some raisins and then thought of the Dutch cheese which we had recently broken out of its locker. Full of maggots! Ditched.' With under 200 miles to go we started thinking about hot showers and Argentinian steaks, only a couple of nights away, so could live with the demise of the cheese.

But we had counted our chickens too soon. Like all fair winds ours started to head us, forcing us up the estuary and over to the Argentinian shore to be confronted by a rather remarkable sight. As though growing in the sea were row upon row of high-rise buildings, very tall and narrow. They had suddenly appeared with dramatic effect. The land was so low that we sailed on for some time before the shoreline appeared. It transpired these grand structures were owned by the wealthy residents of Buenos Aires for their summer relaxation. As we were to discover in Mar del Plata it is a country very much split into those with and those without.

It was to take us another day to beat down to Mar del Plata, entering the small marina at 2000 on Sunday evening 21 November. An event not without its moments. Engine trouble. Ever since we had left the Cape Verdes it had been prone to intermittent sulky fits. It would miss a beat now and then, occasionally nearly petering out before recovering its composure. There was evidently a fuel supply problem and although exploring various possibilities I had been unable to come up with any real solution as to what was making it unhappy.

Now, as we approached the quite narrow entrance into the marina, the engine decided enough was enough and stopped. Although it was persuaded to start again it kept stopping, so we proceeded in a series of fits and starts into the pontoon area to look for a berth. Over to one side we could see what appeared to be the only clear space in a row of boats lying along the length of a pontoon. As we made our final approach and at the point of no return we suddenly lost power, with no time to try to restart the engine. Immediately ahead of us was a smart-looking yacht secured alongside the pontoon. Just as it looked as though we were about to get to know that boat very well indeed a figure was seen running down the pontoon shouting out in good English, 'Señor, give me your line!' This we did. He took a turn and brought us to a graceful stop right in position. Our saviour then vanished before we could render him the thanks that were his due. To the casual onlooker from a distance it was no doubt a well-planned and consummately executed seamanlike manoeuvre. We needed a drink.

Whilst the palpitations subsided we planned our immediate future. Ashore for a meal! We had not allowed for the all-embracing dead hand of Argentinian bureaucracy. Down the pontoon it came in the form of two policemen. Running. Holding their caps on with one hand and with the other, clasping their pistols, they arrived breathless alongside *Marelle*. They spoke no English. Slowly we caught on that the pleasure of our company was sought at the police station. Like now, they indicated. We indicated we had a different idea. Like a hard-earned meal in the town. The exchange of viewpoints was shortlived and not as the politicians would say 'constructive'. Taking us in their four-wheel-drive we arrived at the offices of the Prefectura, the maritime police and coastguard, for a two-hour interrogation and form-filling exercise. The police had been friendly enough even driving us around to a telephone bureau and waiting whilst we called home.

We were somewhat bemused by the extent of the interest shown in our arrival. Either Jeremy had a criminal look about him, or it may have been that the sight of the red ensign had inflamed their passions. The memory of the Falklands conflict, we were to gather later, still seemed to be alive.

Filling out the forms was extraordinarily painstaking and tedious. Multiple copies of the many different forms had to be completed individually as the immigration official did not have a photocopier. Fortunately Jeremy was on hand to restrain my impulse to express my mounting irritation. At midnight we had our fish and chips.

Now fill up your glasses, and say 'Fare you well',
Away-ay Rio
To the pretty young lasses who loved you too well
For we are bound for the Rio Grande.

Sea shanty, *Rio Grande*

CHAPTER FOUR

THE ARGENTINIAN CONNECTION

The estuary (River Plate) is noted for its sudden and violent weather changes, ... for sudestadas, zondas and Pamperos, each of which has its own particular unpleasantness.

H.W. Tilman, *Mischief in Patagonia*

Fraser joins – engineering problem – our friend the 'Admiral' – Mr Fixit – storeship – fellow yachties – discos to dawn – dining out – more bureaucracy – we sail – ill-founded French intelligence – bit by *Pampero* – back to Mar del Plata – we lick our wounds – Argentines are nice people – yet more bureaucracy – we say farewell for last time

Fiesta Nacional. With Mar del Plata enjoying a public holiday on Monday, our first day in harbour, we voted ourselves one as well. We both felt quite washed up and I had a decided wobbliness in my legs. Being the Argentinian equivalent of our bank holiday we had a welcome respite from grappling with bureaucracy. The immigration formalities on Sunday evening had been only the first hurdle to get over. There were more to come. Customs and Health. They were a treat in store for Tuesday. We had to hope that the holiday for the officials concerned was not being spoilt by worrying about the smuggled goods we were landing and the diseases we were introducing into Argentina whilst we remained unchecked.

In the meantime we needed to make contact with Fraser. The fact that he had arrived was evident from the number of messages left scattered around in the marina. He had apparently been coming down each day hoping to see us but with nothing in sight had left information with everyone who happened to be around on how to contact him. Included in the information package was a photo of *Marelle*. One of the recipients of a Fraser billet-doux dutifully came down the pontoon and passed on the details. Jeremy rang the place where Fraser was staying, breaking the news that we had finally made it. The owner, by now a friend, passed on the glad tidings with 'Fraser! This is what you have been waiting to hear.' Almost before the sound of his words had died away Fraser was down to the marina and on board. It was agreed he would do his farewells with his friends, the hoteliers, and repair on board next day, which in turn would give us time to sort ourselves out. During the days waiting for us he had experienced a unique exposure to the grass-roots end of the Argentinian social structure. This had given him a unique, illuminating insight into the lives and attitudes of ordinary people struggling to make a living in a society where a gross inequality in wealth distribution was endemic. It would seem change in the order of things had to happen. It was evident that Fraser had developed a profound sympathy for the lot of the lower-echelon Argentinian. But let him speak for himself.

'On arriving in Mar del Plata I found a small family-run hotel. The owner, Manuel, was in his thirties as was his wife who was a school teacher. Both spoke basic but adequate English. Manuel had worked in the USA for two years.

When I had been there long enough for him to realise I was not a threat as an informant we would sit and talk about what was happening in Argentina. I had noticed a burnt-out car outside my bedroom window which Manuel informed me belonged to his wife but had been burnt by the local police for her refusal to pay protection money.

The nearby restaurants and laundrettes were reputedly owned by members of the local police. I was taken for a drive through the nearby suburbs, comprising large numbers of houses many of which were surrounded by burnt-out cars. These were really no-go areas run by Eastern European immigrants.

The hotel was very much a centre for young trekkers and even a group of young men travelling Argentina hang-gliding. They were the sons of wealthy businessmen from Buenos Aires.

We talked until the early hours and they told me about the widespread corruption with officials receiving large amounts of money. I presumed this information came from their fathers. They were very keen to tell me all about it. It almost seemed they were hoping that I had the wherewithal to break this news outside. Not many English go there. Manuel's wife told me that her salary was paid fifty percent by cheque and the other half in cash so she would only have pension rights on the half paid by cheque. Generally there was an underlying feeling of mistrust and suspicion in talking about social problems.'

In the light of the economic upheaval that occurred subsequent to our return home we could only hope that the existence of those we came to know and like was not too devastated by what happened.

We were lucky to have Fraser with us. Arriving without a return ticket and no address, it took him two hours to win over the officials and be allowed to stay in Argentina.

'Señor! Why do you only have a single air ticket?'

'Because I will be leaving by boat.'

'Where is that boat?'

'I don't know. Somewhere at sea.'

'When will this boat of yours arrive?'

'Don't know. Sometime.'

A prolonged silence developed, accompanied by a long searching look directed at Fraser. The prospect of him being put on the next flight back to England was now a distinct possibility. Fraser played his ace. A photograph of *Marelle*. She saved the day.

First priority for Jeremy and me was a shower in the yacht club's ablutions block at the head of our pontoon. The club had not yet opened for the summer season but made its facilities available. I was mildly surprised at the decor in my cubicle and also at some of the fittings provided. All rather different to the marinas with which I was familiar. On emerging I met Jeremy coming out of his cubicle who remarked 'Any particular reason why you used the Ladies?'

It was ashore that night for the long-awaited Argentinian steak. Close to the harbour was a restaurant complex comprising a large square surrounded by eating places, each vying for custom. Outside would be a vocal man or woman encouraging patronage for their particular establishment. In front of one we were gracefully accosted by a striking young woman dressed in a way difficult to ignore. We went into her place. My concern was how resistant to Latin American charms was Jeremy? The indications were that we would be henceforth eating every night in this particular restaurant. The steak was excellent.

Next morning we were ready to tackle the agenda for our stopover. Fraser came on board and immediately attacked the galley area. Everything was out and ruthlessly scrubbed. It was evident his standards were on a higher plane. Jeremy launched himself into his quartermaster's role and set about the re-storing programme. He was the keeper of the stores list, which he maintained with the zealotry of the National Archivist. This list was a family affair. It had been initially compiled by Adrie when first storing ship, detailing exactly what we had on board and where. It was handed over to Jeremy and was the basis for his restoring programme, keeping THE LIST under his bunk for safety. Fraser and I did not get involved. If on passage we were to perish through starvation we would know whom to blame.

Fraser slipped easily into the boat's routine, albeit there was a period of familiarisation with the new crew member's likes and dislikes. 'How do you like your coffee, Fraser?'

'Hot, black and strong.'

'Like your women?'

He gave my remark the treatment it deserved. He ignored it.

My first task was to tackle Customs and Health, but to my surprise and heartfelt relief these hurdles were of foot stool dimensions compared to those of Grand National proportions we had encountered at Immigration. Health seemed to be primarily interested in the $10 fee. Customs were a little more exacting. I was asked if I spoke Spanish. I replied rather ambitiously '*un poco*' (a little). A mistake. Encouraged by this, the official launched into a long explanation in Spanish of the intricacies of Argentinian customs procedures. On completion he asked me if I understood it all. 'No.' 'What! not a word?' 'No, nothing!' We finally got there with some help from Jeremy's French. However it was all very cordial and I was now of the opinion that the Argentines are nice people. They were as much the victims of the system as were we.

Back at the yacht club the marina staff suggested that we would make life easier for ourselves if we were to engage the services of a local man who knew where to get whatever we wanted and equally importantly what to pay for it. It so happened, by happy coincidence, that they knew of someone who they were sure would be immediately available to fulfil such a role. Our Mr Fixit. Sounded like a good idea. Like a genie out of a bottle, Jimmy, whose real name we never got to grips with, was alongside *Marelle*. When asked what would be his charges for any running around we might call on him to do he replied he had nothing in mind. It would be entirely up to us to put a value on his services. Whatever that value was he would accept it without question. He was to honour this undertaking. The problem for us of course was we had no feel for local market values, but that was something for the future. It transpired that Jimmy, a young man of pleasant demeanour, had lived in California for eight years. Henceforth communication was conducted in fluent American.

Top of my list of things to get done before we headed south was to get to grips with the engine problem. Having run out of ideas myself I felt the need to call for professional advice. Could Jimmy help? Yes, he could. He knew a man who knew a good engineer.

He was to be found in another yacht club next door. Where we were berthed was something of a complex. Our club was the Yacht Club Argentino. On one side of it was a motor boat club which appeared to be predominantly a social club. Its activities in this direction were to become very evident later in our stay. On the other side of the yacht harbour lay the rather grand Club Nautico. Very much a private club, members only, giving the impression one needed a deep pocket, of diamond-mine proportions, to belong. 'Our' club was more for the likes of us. Even so apparently its joining fee was $20,000! It was to the deluxe club next door that Jimmy took me.

As we went through the impressive entrance into the plush foyer I was half expecting, dressed as I was a little informally in my sailing attire, to be directed to the tradesmen's entrance. However Jimmy, with the insouciance of youth, swept through with me in tow. We tracked down his contact, to whom Jimmy, in Spanish, explained my problem. I was greeted with 'Mornin', I'm Norman, Norman Jenkins.' adding a little superfluously that I would appreciate with that name he was Welsh. He wasn't really, but near enough. His grandparents had emigrated from Wales. Although very much integrated into Argentina the family had maintained a tradition of passing the name on unchanged into perpetuity. It seems to be a pronounced predilection of the Welsh to hang on to their nationality.

After a bit of a chat he said the club engineer was good, knew about Volvo engines and he, Norman, would arrange for him to come round to *Marelle* that afternoon. This he did.

The problem with the engine, it appeared to me, centred on an intermittent interruption to the fuel supply. I kept swinging around like a weathercock from one likely cause of this to another. At first I blamed dirty fuel when filling the jerry cans in Falmouth just before we left. Accordingly I changed all the filters to no avail. Then I came up with the rather exotic idea that in the tropics the rise in air temperature in the enclosed engine compartment and consequential loss of density was upsetting the fuel/air mix. Running with the lid off made no difference. This rather far-fetched idea was replaced with the thought that when the boat was heeled and diesel tank fairly full the inclined fuel level was closing off the air vent thus interfering with the flow to the pump. Trying to diagnose the cause and then putting the possible solution to the test was not helped by being at sea and the boat jumping around.

When the engineer appeared I tried each of my bright ideas out on him but I wasn't too sure how much was going in. He spoke no English and the technicalities were way beyond my Spanish. He nodded politely and then set about working through his own agenda. Found nothing. The supposed invalid was enjoying rude health. The engineer was, I thought, looking at me with rather a quizzical expression. A sea trial was indicated.

Having not come up with anything positive, and with vivid memories of what happened when we came in, I was less than enthusiastic about crashing around in the harbour approaches again. It is largely a manmade port with a narrow entrance between two long breakwaters thrusting out into the South Atlantic. If you keep on going it is next stop Africa. Half the entrance is a no-go area referred to on our chart as 'shoaling and extending'. In a fresh onshore wind, which is what we were having, the remaining navigable half suffers from a short confused sea, exacerbated by an energetic surge being thrown back from the breakwater. We pushed out through this lot only to encounter a swarm of fishing boats in a never-ending stream crowding in through the entrance, riding the surge. If the engine failed we were in trouble, it being almost impossible to have handled her under sail. As luck would have it there were no problems but it was one of the most tense moments of the whole trip. It was back to our berth, none the wiser, with a few more grey hairs. I gave the engineer something for his trouble and called it a day, at least for the time being.

With days slipping past we were becoming integrated into life in Mar del Plata, or Mardel as it is known locally. The city started life as an unpretentious little town with a pier in the early eighteen hundreds but underwent a transformation when a developer took charge of its destiny in 1874. Becoming the summer retreat for the wealthy elite of Buenos Aires it enjoyed the sobriquet 'Pearl of the Atlantic'. Now in a more egalitarian society its appeal is to middle class *portenos*. From December onwards they flock to modern Mardel for its beaches and relative coolness, swelling the population of half a million more than threefold. We were fortunate to have been there before this invasion. It also meant that the marina was quiet, as in the season it would be overcrowded. Sailing is very popular in the region. The yacht club we knew was an offshoot of the parent in Buenos Aires which no doubt was the home of large and impossibly expensive boats about to relocate themselves in Mardel.

We noted the absence of foreign yachts. There was certainly no British boat, this being a rare sight in these waters. For company we had only two French boats. With one of these, *Enez*, we were to become chummy in Punta Arenas. The other, *Acka!*, was in trouble with structural failure around the centreplate case. I admired the way the delightful young couple, Didier and Josette, were coping with this setback. The only repair facility was a very limited yard for the fishing fleet, which was mainly of either wood or steel construction. *Acka!* was of aluminium. As no one knew how to weld this Didier had got himself a textbook on the subject. With the boat up on the slipway he was instructing the local welders on how to tackle the work.

Benefiting from the marina not being full we were receiving all the attention we could wish for from the staff. Although the yacht club itself was not fully functioning yet, one of its senior members had taken it upon himself to keep an eye on things. We were down below when we heard in excellent English 'Hello *Marelle*. Welcome. Do you need anything?' On the pontoon was a large, urbane and rather impressive figure. He became known to us as the Admiral. If he wasn't he should have been. He was wanting to help. He was to prove useful when conversing with the staff, whose English was almost nonexistent. Could he help with how we should recompense Jimmy? This was in danger of becoming of rather disproportionate importance but we wanted to get it right. We had become aware of the enormous gap between the strata of society and income levels. Strangely the Admiral did not have any ideas on the subject but would confer with some of his colleagues. In due course he was back with the not unexpected comment that 'It was whatever we thought appropriate.'

By now we had been here a week. It was time we were away. We set sailing day for the following Tuesday. This would be 30 November. On the original programme we should have left on the 16th. The Horn–millennium linkage was starting to look shaky, and we certainly could not afford any further time slippage. However, we viewed with confidence the certainty that in a few days we would be tramping south with Punta Arenas in our sights. We should have known better! In anticipation of our departure on Sunday, Fraser went off to say goodbye to his friends the hoteliers whilst Jeremy and I went up to the yacht club premises for a beer and stayed for lunch. It looked so enticing. Although still closed in the week the dining room was open for lunch at the weekend. It was a perfect day. Sunny and warm with just the merest hint of a breeze. We sat in the shade of a tree on the club lawn overlooking the harbour, drinking good Argentinian red wine and probably too much of it, eating a superb fish salad impeccably served on a snow-white tablecloth. The thought of England in winter took a back seat.

That night it was back to the disco! Saturday night had been sleepless for Fraser and Jeremy with the fun on full volume at the Motor Yacht Club. It was evidently a birthday party. The 'Happy Birthday To You' routine is as familiar in Spanish as in English. This was the well-to-do pampered youth of the town at play, the final whistle not going till well after dawn. Sunday night was a replay. This time I joined the insomniacs on board.

Monday was wrap-up day for departure next day which meant the dreaded visit to the Prefectura for immigration clearance. It turned out to be hassle-free. The officer in charge of the station personally took control of proceedings, helping with completing the forms and applying oil to the wheels. A charming man with whom I felt a decided empathy. There is a human side to bureaucracy after all.

We could go, but walking back to the boat I began to feel uncomfortable. On our papers Fraser was a non-person. He did not appear anywhere. When Jeremy and I had been before the Inquisition on our arrival Fraser was not a member of the crew. Now he was. What would happen when we checked in at the next port of call. The paperwork would not line up. Apart from this I felt in some way I was betraying the trust and friendliness demonstrated by that officer in the Prefectura. Strange, as it is not the norm to feel this way about a bureaucrat! There was no problem. On presenting a Fraser as flesh and blood his name was simply inserted on the bottom of the forms and for the second time it was 'Have a good navigation.'

Tuesday came and the port was promptly closed to all shipping. A hefty easterly was piling rolling surf in through the entrance. During this enforced idleness I had a chat with Jimmy whilst settling up with him. Suddenly he started talking about what he referred to as the murder of young soldiers on both sides during the Malvinas conflict. What he was saying was perhaps predictable but it had a particular significance coming from an Argentine. How unnecessary and wrong it had all been. For us it has largely gone into history but from his vehemence it was apparent that the episode was still very much to the fore with many people in Argentina. The Falklands question will never go away. He talked about the callousness of his own leaders in sending young soldiers with no training and hopelessly inadequate equipment. He felt deeply about this because he knew personally some of those who were sent to their deaths against highly trained professional soldiers. As he lamented, there could only be one outcome. When he had unloaded his bitterness I gave him an envelope containing our best guess. He did not look at it before putting it in his pocket. Saying farewell, he walked off. To what, I wondered.

We remained shut in for another couple of days, which had unfortunate ramifications. Our clearance had expired. Back to the Prefectura. My attendance there was becoming something of a cross between a permanent quiz show and a non-stop stage production, with my lines well rehearsed and honed to perfection. But each performance was different. This time after the now horribly familiar form-filling bit, on which I was now an expert, I was taken under armed guard across the yard to the Prefectura's operational nerve centre. Here were serious young men gazing at large plots used for monitoring all shipping movements on the coast. I was then grilled by a non-English-speaking staff member on our passage plan. How much diesel on board? How much water? *Marelle*'s personal details, and so on. Somehow my homespun Spanish coped. After being sternly admonished about keeping them advised on our progress south I was given the traditional farewell about having 'a good navigation'. I was free to go. I vowed this would definitely be my last performance. Or so I thought. We sailed that afternoon.

The weather forecast given by the Prefectura in English looked reasonable, which gave us confidence in getting us comfortably across the wide bay that is Bahia Blanca lying to the south-west of Mardel. After that that it should be all plain sailing down the Patagonian coast. The Admiral had said we should carry the westerlies all the way down to the Magellan Straits, but it was not to prove quite as simple as that. I suspect the Admiral had not actually sailed in those waters. However the main thing was we were off. We cleared the harbour and headed south, but not without a heart-stopping moment or two. The engine, having lulled us into a sense of false security with its impeccable performance on the previous trial run, started faltering but there was no question of turning back. We would have to live with it, warts and all.

That first night was noteworthy in that it gave us the welcome experience of over five hours uninterrupted sleep when off watch. What a difference the extra body made!

A gentle wind and calm sea ushered in the following day. After breakfast we spoke MV *Palmshead*, French, heading in the opposite direction. They were they said on passage from Punta Arenas to Buenos Aires. The officer of the watch was very chatty, remarking he had recently been working in London and was un-Gallic enough to say how much he liked England. He gave us a weather forecast 'Light north-easterly winds with possibility of rain.' That should help us on our way. It was now 1000. As the Frenchman vanished astern the wind started to pick up and progressively back into the south-west. All the portents suddenly became unfavourable. We close-reefed the main and set the storm jib on the inner forestay, rolling in at the same time a few turns of the genoa. At 1200 it was a bare two hours since that all set fair forecast from *Palmshead*. There was a menacing feeling all around us. The wind was now building up very fast indeed and up to windward an enormous dense black cloud, threatening and full of evil, was enveloping the sky from the horizon and up over our heads. There was no time to lose. We clawed the mainsail down and only just before a gale-force blast hit us with the impact of a pile-driver. With it came a rapidly roughening sea surface and driving rain. At least that part of the Frenchman's prediction was somewhere near the truth.

With the wind now at gale force and a sea becoming more ugly by the minute we turned and ran before it, heading north-east from whence we had come. The barograph had dropped sharply but was now on its way up again. My journal entry comments 'Should be over soon and hopefully we won't lose too much ground.'

'Long foretold, long last. Short notice, soon past.' It wasn't.

Conditions were steadily deteriorating and we estimated we had a storm Force 10 on our hands. Our wind speed indicator reads up to 48 knots. The needle had gone hard onto the stop and remained there. The speed with which the sea had built up was quite remarkable. Part of the reason was we had been heading into the Bahia Blanca with its relatively shallow water and possibly a counter-flow from the Falklands Current sweeping round against the wind. The seas by now were alarmingly high, steep-fronted and irregular with foaming breaking crests. They would be quite unmanageable if trying to work up to windward against them. They had a viciousness about them worse than I could recall having seen before from a small vessel. Mr Franklin was struggling manfully but it was a case of having to revert to hand-steering to ensure we kept stern to the wave fronts. *Marelle* was tracking beautifully and we did not need the storm jib to keep her steady. It was tending to gybe frequently and as we did not want the extra speed in the wrong direction we dropped it. We were now running dead before the wind under bare poles making six or seven knots at times. Although we were heading in a direction in which we did not want to go it was no option attempting to heave to or lie a-hull. Even if we had carried a sea anchor I would not have deployed it. Lying a-hull or hove-to she would have taken too much of a battering as she fell down to leeward off those abrupt seas and been under such a welter of water it would have been dangerous. The safest and easiest ride for boat and crew was to run downwind before the sea. We were clearing the bulge of the land ahead so a lee shore was not something that had to be considered.

It was with enduring wonder that I watched *Marelle* handle these seas. As we slid down into a trough the preceding wave front would well upwards with a rush, to be silhouetted against the dark sky. The rapidly advancing crest would start to curl over, carrying with it a crown of boiling white broken water towering over us until poised to smash down and bury us. Just when it seemed there could be no escape her stern at the very last moment would lift with quite amazing speed until it was at wave-top level. She would then hurtle forward, surfing down the front of the wave, immersed above deck level in a mass of foaming water spread out around us, filling the side decks up to the cockpit coaming. The sequence would then start all over again. Her speed slowing she would fall back once again into the trough of the next wave formation. It was frightening and fascinating all at the same time.

I recalled an earlier discussion with Jeremy on the respective merits of different after-body designs. His boat has a canoe stern, which has always been considered good for handling following seas, dividing the water flow and thereby diverting the seas from breaking over the stern or being 'pooped'. *Marelle* has a sawn-off counter, and watching her performance it was evident the buoyancy in her quarters, greater than that in the canoe stern, was giving her the lift to ride up the wave front to meet the crest. A canoe stern or worse the broad, flat transom stern would, I felt, have caused serious problems in those seas. It would not be confidence-building to dwell for long on the performance of the fashionable scoop stern common on modern boats. This design would seem to have the accommodation of a bathing ladder more in mind than handling a seaway.

In like manner we went through the night. There was no easing of the wind and if anything the sea state was worsening to the extent *Marelle* took a couple of breakers over the stern, filling the cockpit. Not too dangerous in themselves but unfriendly to those sitting in the cockpit as the water level was high enough to spill over the tops of their sea boots and fill them. Throughout it all was the overwhelming roar of wind and sea, dominating one's senses.

It was rough and tough on deck but warm, dry and quiet down below. The cabin doors were shutting out most of the incredible howl of the wind and roar of the surf. I tried to persuade the unemployed helmsman to go below but both Jeremy and Fraser were not feeling their best. They preferred to sit it out in the open and be part of the action. *Marelle* was driving on sweet as a nut and steady enough so that something hot could be prepared on the stove. Fraser did eventually come down. He was wet through and cold with morale at rock bottom. He was quite simply exhausted. I made him get out of his wet gear and turn in. He had to get warm again and gain some rest. Unlike Jeremy and me he had not had time to adjust to ocean conditions. He needed a breather to become acclimatised. Jeremy and I shared the remaining night hours, one hour on and one off. All told I managed about one hour's sleep but felt surprisingly alive and alert. Jeremy, always the stoic, coped in his usual uncomplaining way.

In the forenoon on the following day the wind began to ease slightly and backed further into the south. It was then the screaming hail storms started, soon after I took over the watch. I could see the build-up on the horizon astern with an awful impenetrable blackness. They would arrive, roaring, with hail lashing down and building up in the cockpit and under the sprayhood acting like a scoop. It was agony on hands and any exposed part of the face. God knows what was the wind strength. It took the tops of the waves and just flattened the sea, overlaying it with a dense, white sheet of foam and horizontally driven spray. Then they were gone, racing ahead at great speed.

With a rag of genoa set in between squalls we were on course for Mardel and I decided we would make for it to get some essential rest, a dry-out and a spot of crew morale restoration.

We were getting something of a lee with the wind now more off the land as we made our approach to the harbour entrance. We were following along astern of a freighter when she suddenly sheared off and headed back offshore. The reason, we subsequently discovered, was because the harbour was closed due to the weather conditions. She presumably had reported her arrival and been given the glad tidings. Fortunately our ignorance was bliss. We passed close by the northern breakwater in the dark, coming in on its light for guidance to keep well clear of the shoal area. Of the southern breakwater light we saw no sign. Even in the shelter of the harbour the wind strength was still considerable as we came to anchor off the entrance to the marina. She swung to her cable and was still. The sense of relief in being out of all that tearing wind and angry sea was overwhelming. I called up my friends the Prefectura to make their day by advising we were back, at anchor inside the harbour and suggesting I front up in the morning. A little to my surprise they were relaxed about this, not demanding my presence there and then. They must have been getting soft. It was sheer luck that we had not called them up before we had entered, when we would almost certainly have been refused entry. Another night at sea would have been decidedly unwelcome. I then joined Fraser in a state of semi-torpor. Not Jeremy, who immediately set to and produced one of his inimitable nosh-ups into which everything is thrown. Washed down with a bottle of wine and in a boat at rest it was a moment to savour. We then slept and slept.

Next morning Fraser and I were into the marina in the dinghy and were immediately taken into care by the Admiral. He marked out a berth for the easiest access for us in the wind, which was showing no signs of abating, and then took us out to *Marelle* in the club's inflatable. We weighed and followed him in to our berth. On the pontoon the marina staff were waiting to take our lines, jumping on board to secure us. They departed brushing aside our thanks. It was then a day of relaxation. The staff said not to worry about the Prefectura. They could wait until tomorrow. After all as they pointed out we were now part of the scene.

During our sojourn away the yacht harbour had become crowded. *Acka!* had completed her repairs and was waiting to head south. She was planning to cruise leisurely down the coast and eventually end up in Antarctica. Also there were two large yachts from River Plate stopovers who had come in shortly after our earlier departure, one German and the other Swiss, *Atmos II*. We were to see more of her in the south. Additionally there was a French Canadian single-hander, Roger, who had been leisurely working his way south from Brazil and was now about to head off for Ushuaia via Le Maire Strait He didn't fancy the Magellan Strait. This mixed bag was rounded off by a Canadian, Ray, who came in a day or so after us from the Falklands, having spent the previous year in Tierra del Fuego. He had been through the southern fringe of the same blow we had just experienced and had suffered a major knockdown. It was generally agreed amongst the locals that we had enjoyed a late season *Pampero*. The name is derived from the Spanish word *pampa* for the vast, treeless grasslands which are Patagonia. The *Pampero* originates at the Andes and accelerating eastwards across the *pampas* hurtles from a south-west direction out into the South Atlantic. It becomes violent during the passage of a cold front associated with a low-pressure system. This was what was being recorded on our barograph trace. We were surprised at the suddenness and violence of the wind's arrival but with hindsight it was evident that trace had been giving us advance notice of what was about to hit us.

Vito Dumas was leaving Argentina at the outset of his ground-breaking solo round the world voyage when he was 'blooded' by a *pampero*, describing his experience of that decidedly unfriendly phenonomen thus:

'I was surprised by a *pampero* squall blowing at between 60 and 70 knots … It was in the evening. I was making myself some chocolate and hoped to spend as pleasant a night as possible. The wind outside was so violent that a sail had been blown to ribbons and the raging seas were something to shudder at. I was hove to close to the wind. Suddenly there was a terrific crash. I followed the motion of the boat and found myself sitting on the ceiling of the cabin. This was it.' It wasn't. His *Lehg II* righted herself and 'with that movement of the boat hope came back.' A *pampero* is an experience one does not forget.

That evening we gave a little cocktail party on board *Marelle*, inviting the Admiral with Didier and Josette from *Acka!* This was when we learned more about each other. The *Ackas* were young professionals from Brittany on a year's sabbatical. The Admiral it turned out was a beef baron who, it became apparent as the evening progressed, enjoyed his whisky but entertainingly so. He issued an invitation to visit with him an up-country hacienda and sample beef in the real way. Unfortunately we didn't think we could spare the time to take up this offer. It is something I have regretted ever since.

Our party had also been a thank-you one. The Admiral had been most helpful and had made us welcome. I presented to him for his club my faded and rather tattered Royal Cornwall Yacht Club burgee. In return he gave me the burgee of the Yacht Club Argentino, our host club. It was interesting to compare the two burgees. Mine was of traditional bunting whereas his was very New World, shiny and of manmade fibre. Didier had also been a valuable contact. He had a good selection of charts for the regions to the south. Many of them he had acquired from other French voyagers who had been passing through. In turn he loaned to us the ones we wanted for us to have photocopies made. An efficient operation in Mar del Plata ran off good-quality full-size copies at modest cost. These extra charts filled out my library. Some of them were of French origin and of a larger scale than I had been able to obtain back home. French chart coverage is outstanding. Photocopying of charts is normally frowned upon but under the circumstances I was not going to pass up on Didier's offer.

Everybody was waiting for the weather to come right, which it did the next day. With the exception of Ray, the Canadian going north to Uruguay, the whole fleet, but without us, sailed for the south. All were headed for Puerto Madryn located in northern Patagonia. This enormous region, the boundaries of which are rather vaguely defined, starts at about the latitude of our old friend Bahia Blanca and takes in the southern areas of Argentina and Chile down to the Straits of Magellan. It embraces the snows of the mighty Andes and sweeps down to encompass the endless, arid plains of the *pampas*. Patagonia had gripped the imagination of Darwin and was about to affect us in the same way as we followed in his wake.

We had opted for another day to collect ourselves, hoping that the benevolent northeaster that had set in would be patient enough to stay around long enough for us to get clear away next day. In my mind's eye I could see Didier and the rest tramping south before that fair wind and wondered whether we had made a mistake in staying put, but we really did need that extra day of rest.

It was then back to the Prefectura for yet another form-filling marathon but this time there was a little more flexibility in the system because of our history with them. Then some whisky and a note of thanks to the marina staff, receiving in return a warm farewell. At 1400 we slipped from the pontoon heading out through the all-too-familiar harbour entrance into a choppy easterly. The engine did not miss a beat. We followed the formalities and reported our departure to the Prefectura. We were once again on our way and this time for ever.

I was glad we had made that Argentinian connection.

CHAPTER FIVE

PATAGONIA

Why then ... have these arid wastes taken so firm a hold on my memory?
Charles Darwin

The Prefectura again – Golfo Nuevo – Welsh connection – the flesh weakens – Santa Elena – guanaco – shades of James Weddell – Caleta Sara – difficult time off Cabo Blanco – Puerto Deseado – Cavendish and Davis – Penguin Island – Puerto San Julian – ghosts of Magellan and Drake – Rio Santa Cruz – Darwin and FitzRoy – Xmas Day – right whale spectacular – Rio Gallegos – Butch Cassidy connection – Cabo Virgenes – Magellan's dream

South! Patagonia beckoned. This was the coast of high adventure down which the early navigators had worked on their way to the rich pickings of the great South Seas. The greatest of them was arguably Magellan himself. He knew not what lay before him. Fear of the unknown was to test his resolve and courage to the limit. With the awesome responsibility of command imposing on him the immense burden of sustaining that same courage in each member of his ships' companies there was demanded of him the qualities of a true leader.

The adventurers who followed him – Drake, Cavendish, Davis and the like – although facing dangers and vicissitudes no less than Magellan's, at least knew the way ahead and that a successful outcome was possible in pursuing that route. They had something more to offer their men than just hope and blind faith, the principal weapons in Magellan's staff-relations armoury.

We were about to follow in the wake of those adventurers but with different motivations. Theirs were to gain fame and fortune, principally the latter. Ours were probably more complex, but in essence we wanted to experience those waters if only 'because they were there'. We just wanted to sail them.

Our track down that southern Argentinian coast was very close to Magellan's. He kept the shoreline constantly in view, looking for that elusive opening which would take him through to the 'silver ocean', the Pacific. We followed the same tactics but our objective was to make life easier for ourselves.

That most useful of books *Ocean Passages* is strong on keeping close in, with its exhortation in somewhat lyrical tones that 'the land be kept topping on the horizon until the entrance of Magellan Strait be passed', the reasoning being 'the water will be smooth and more sail can be carried than if farther out'. The assumption was that the wind would be predominantly from the west. In fact it was to be our experience that, close in, land and sea breezes were to play a large part, presumably due to the heat-sink effect of the bare and almost treeless *pampas* baking in the sun during the day and rapidly cooling at night. In retrospect it raises the thought that we might have had steadier winds if we had stayed a little further out in the path of the square-riggers, but then we would have missed out on much that Patagonia had to offer.

Having cleared the River Plate, Magellan skirted the bump projecting out into the South Atlantic on which perches Mar del Plata and then headed south-west into our old friend Bahia Blanca. This was to be our route once again and our second attempt at crossing this wide indentation at the root of the Patagonian coast, south of Buenos Aires. This time the weather was kind to us and we got across in benign conditions. I noted 'the perfect weather continues. Gentle breeze, just off close-hauled, flat sea and bright sun in a cloudless sky. What a difference to a week ago!'

During the crossing we were visited by a Prefectura patrol boat, *Martin Garcia,* asking strange questions about us but friendly enough. Possibly bored and wanting to practise their English, the questions went on interminably until with much cheery waving they drove off at high speed. These contacts were always disturbing as they left us so aware of being alone and far from home. They would be tucked up in bed tonight. Secure. Their weather prediction was we would get a moderate northerly. They were correct, and we pushed south, crossing the fortieth parallel under the faithful twin-headsail rig. However our onboard Met. Office was trying to tell us something, reminding us that we were now in the Roaring Forties. The sky became a riot of torn and twisted mares' tails with the barograph embarking on a slow steady decline. We were now to the east of the narrow entrance to Golfo Nuevo, a large enclosed bay at the head of which is Puerto Madryn. This was a place we had intended to visit but we had given up the idea as we were so far behind schedule. There was a personal interest factor here because of a Welsh connection. Susan is of that extraction. In 1865 a group of poor and disaffected Welsh men and women numbering 153 landed here to create a new home to get away from a miserable life, for which they inevitably blamed the English. They were given land by the Argentinian government and settled in a valley a couple of days march south of Puerto Madryn. I would like to have observed what it is today but had the impression the scene in and around the harbour has changed, and not for the better, in recent years with the advent of sightseers coming to view the wildlife. A colony of sea elephants and another of sea lions are permanent residents, obligingly providing a tourist attraction. High-speed launches cater for whale watchers heading out offshore in the hope that right whales and orcas (killer whales) will be equally obliging. We didn't feel any overriding urge to be part of all that activity. The other off-putter was we understood there was a complication with re-entering the country as the Prefectura in Mardel had to be involved. I didn't feel I had the stamina to face up to any complication to a system which I knew to my cost was already complicated enough.

A very early distinguished visitor to Golfo Neuvo, in effect one could say the first *turista*, was Magellan who, maintaining his practice of coastal kerb-crawling, would have had his heart uplifted on sighting the entrance to the gulf with a wide expanse of water opening up. Alas once again his hopes, literally of a breakthrough, were to be dashed.

Puerto Madryn took its name from the manor house of Madryn, a stately pile near to Porthmadoc in North Wales. It is still there in another role. The honoured lord of the manor who had to live with the exotic name of Love Parry Jones Parry was a wealthy Liberal Member of Parliament and well-known benefactor, being known as the 'poor man's friend'. Recognising something had to be done to alleviate the desperate poverty of the locals he made a trip with two of them to Argentina to look for a location where they could all start a new life. The result was that the brig *Mimosa* was in due course chartered to take the aspiring colonists to their new home, exchanging their fertile homeland for the arid land of Patagonia; but they survived.

The Welsh presence in the area has been diluted to the point of near-extinction. Younger generations now prefer to speak Spanish but apparently there has been an attempt recently to revive the Welsh language and with some success, helped by teachers from Wales going out on yearly contracts. Although full marks must be awarded to those Welsh traditionalists for their perseverance in furthering, to good effect, the cause of their ancient tongue, an impartial observer has to ask the question: 'What is the real benefit to the individual in Patagonia or in Wales itself?'

With the weather portents giving us a clear warning message we closed the gulf entrance as a possible bolt hole should the threatening gale materialise. The weather didn't disappoint us. That evening the wind began to build from the south-west, backing to the south as the front went through. We had got accustomed to the weather patterns being the opposite of what we were used to in the North Atlantic. We saw the night out lying close into the long, low and very dark shoreline, hove-to under storm jib. We were more or less holding position off the Golfo Nuevo heads. In a Force 7, touching 8, *Marelle* was comfortable and we were relaxed.

With the return next day of pleasant weather we were once more on our way southwards, bringing up that night the lights of Puerto Rawson very clear on the beam in bright moonlight and a gentle sea. Keeping close in was having its rewards as regards our comfort at least. Rawson is a modest town with a fishing harbour and the name, one would surmise, a further reminder of past widespread English interests in Argentina. Not so. It was the Welsh colonists spreading south from Puerto Madryn who founded the town on land granted by the Argentinian government. They named it Rawson to honour the official who had facilitated the grant. There could be the makings of a good story here on how it was that an Argentinian *funcionario* landed up with a name like Rawson.

Ten miles or so to the west of Rawson lies Trelew, the main town in the region. It was another Welsh pioneering initiative and founded as a railway junction, its name being made up of *Tre*, Celtic for town, and *lew*, short for Lewis Jones, the driving force behind the railway. In turn this led to the swamping of the founding fathers (and mothers) with waves of variegated immigrants. Growth from the eighty locals to 80,000 was however not without its moments.

Thirty years ago the town received unwanted international attention, as did the country as a whole, over a brutal incident putting the spotlight on the ruling regime. Another in the bloody history of Patagonia. Political prisoners incarcerated in the local gaol staged a breakout, only to have their short spell of freedom terminated in massacre.

This was good time sailing with a satisfactory rate of progress in benign conditions, but a siren voice was about to lure us off the straight and narrow. Close ahead was Puerto Santa Elena. On the chart she looked enticing, small and well protected. She would be nice to know. We glanced at each other. Why not? So in we went, anchoring as it got dark and the brisk breeze dying to the gentlest of murmurs. The thought of a quiet supper and a long night's rest in a motionless boat was irresistible.

The anchorage was totally deserted with no sign anyone had ever been there except for a strange little navigation mark with a pathetically small light perched on it. Its purpose was certainly not evident, except perhaps to boast that on this coast of unrelieved nothingness here was a refuge.

But how many would ever use it? The total quiet and absolute isolation of the place enveloped us. I sat in the cockpit alone after supper, my soul at peace, recording in my journal 'the moonlit, windless calm of a deserted and enchanting piece of Argentina. Marvelling at our very special situation. Unique in my personal world.' If it had not been for that little edifice it was easy to imagine we were the first white people to have been there. In fact it possibly was Captain James Weddell who had that honour. Made redundant from the Royal Navy after the Napoleonic Wars, he became a sealer. In 1822 he anchored where we were now lying, in his 75-foot brig *Jane*, to repair a serious leak in the rudder trunk. A veteran of early Antarctic exploration, he was on his way south on a sealing expedition with his consort, the cutter *Beaufoy*. His name lives on to this day in the Weddell Sea, the scene of Shackleton's disaster in *Endurance*. He is also commemorated in the form of the Weddell seal, the deepest-diving of all seals, as well as various bays and islands. Christmas Day was spent in Santa Elena by Weddell and his men partaking of guanaco, the indigenous mammal looking something like a deer, shot for the pot and tasting like mutton, as the revellers recorded. After the festivities *Jane* was hove down by the bow and the rudder removed to get at the leak. Whilst the work was in progress Weddell, cast in the Cook mould, was surveying our bay and constructing a harbour plan. The shoreline on which we looked would have been what he saw. It is likely to have changed little. The leak repaired, they sailed on below the Southern Ocean convergence to the still largely unknown wastes of the Antarctic region, not only to hunt seals but for Weddell to pursue his devotion to survey work. We were very much in his footsteps on this part of the coast. He had first attempted without success to get into Golfo Nuevo but its strong tides and shoals were too daunting. Working south, and rather anxiously looking for a more accessible place to affect repairs, they stumbled on Santa Elena. Secluded and sheltered anchorages on that exposed, windswept coast are rare so it was with relief and delight that our bay opened up for them. We had rather the same feelings.

We woke next morning after a blissful whole night's sleep to brilliant sunshine and a very strong wind from the south-west. Last night's sunset had been dramatic, wild with tortured clouds on fire. The barograph was rising fast and the wind with it. The unanimous decision was we were better off where we were. Although this unplanned stopover was putting us further behind our schedule it was worth it to enjoy this beautiful spot, free of people.

Jeremy, being something of a naturalist, took a lead from Darwin and went ashore in the dinghy to investigate the wildlife. One could imagine the young Darwin revelling in being here, leaping ashore full of enthusiasm to see what this part of Patagonia had for him. So it was with Jeremy.

The following day with a convenient wind shift we tore ourselves away for a day's sail across the Bahia Camarones to Caleta Sara. This tiny dimple hardly features on the chart but we had been assured by Didier of *Acka!* in Mardel that it was possible to anchor in it. It was a must to visit. He had passed on to us a hand-drawn plan which had been given to him by another French yachtsman who had actually been in there. Written on this plan was '*Paradis*' adding '*Meilleure place de toute la côte Argentina*'. We had to go. Also we were developing a taste for all night in our bunks. Close by Sara is another equally small inlet. Caleta Carolina. We had to wonder who were these girls, particularly as Sara features in several other places in those waters. We were to meet one of them again in the Magellan Straits.

We made our approach with the wind right astern and fresh. It was a dead lee shore and with no sign of an entrance we were rapidly closing that rock-strewn foreshore. Fraser was on the foredeck anxiously trying to pick out the opening. He kept looking back with his eyebrows up to his hairline. 'Do you know what you are doing?' was the message as we passed the point of no return. The answer had to be NO! Suddenly the entrance opened up and we shot in. The Frenchman's sketch was right on. But we still had a problem. Cluttering up the minute anchorage were several fishing boats rafted up to a buoy with stern lines to the shore to stop them swinging. There was just room for us to let go and swing clear of them and the shore, but only just.

Sara was a fun place adding to our Argentinian experience. Jeremy remarked that I could well be the first British skipper to have called there. If so the heroic age of exploration was not yet dead. Certainly the absence of British yachts was quite remarkable throughout our trip. After leaving the Canaries we were to see only one other until we arrived in the Falklands. In southern waters a wide range of flags was on show but the red ensign, or blue for that matter, was nowhere evident.

On Sara's shore were a couple of unpretentious buildings, not much more than shacks, one of which bore a large sign announcing it was the *Club Nautico*. The fishing boats were registered in Puerto Rawson and presumably, being regular visitors in view of their buoy, their crews were paid-up members of the club. If my Spanish had only been up to it I would love to have joined those fishermen for a drink and to have learned what Argentina was all about, something akin to Fraser's experience.

Apart from those few buildings there was nothing. The low hills around the pool in which we sat were brown and bare with no vegetation. As in Santa Elena, small groups of guanaco and rhea were evident. Just standing. Apart from a little muted activity on the fishing boats it was an exercise in still life. There was no wind and the water still. At peace with the world we turned in but I had a small nag in the back of my mind. When we had come in it was near the top of the tide. What would be revealed at low water? If there was a wind during the night and we swung on the tide would we still be clear of the rocks on the foreshore around us? The nag woke me and in the early hours just before daybreak I reluctantly dragged myself out of my sleeping bag, got dressed and went on deck. Sure enough she had swung and as I appeared I was met by the awful sound of the rudder graunching on rocks astern. I started the engine and drove ahead with the team now on deck shortening in cable. We were clear for the time being. Later with a new combination of wind and tide we re-anchored. The fishermen apparently recognising we had a problem offered to share their buoy, some of their number having departed. We declined with thanks and shortly afterwards got under way ourselves. Sara had been another experience I was glad had come our way. Next stop the Magellan Straits! A beautiful day and with the breeze filling in from the north-east we were sailing fast. Something over four hundred miles to go. Would the weather last? It didn't.

Ahead of us lay the broad expanse of the Golfo San Jorge, at the southern end of which lies Cabo Blanco. There is some moment to this Cape. It is the point at which the great square-riggers closed the land on their way south to Le Maire Straits, at the south-eastern tip of South America, and thence on to doubling the Horn. Halfway down this stretch of the coast you pass from the Roaring Forties into the Furious Fifties. Keeping close in, thereby gaining the maximum protection from the ferocious westerlies, has a decidedly beneficial effect on one's enjoyment of life.

The cape also marks the beginning of a stretch of coast which was the stage for some of the great dramas played out by the earliest European voyagers, most with the common objective of becoming millionaires, in modern terms. Portuguese, Spanish, English, French and Dutch made up the cast. For us it was the beginning of the 350-mile run to Cabo Virgenes, the Virgins, the northern arm of the eastern entrance to Estrecho de Magallanes. The Virgins were about to become our immediate and obsessive goal.

Our arrival off Cabo Blanco was celebrated with a full gale from the south-west, hove to as the night came down, under storm jib with the wheel lashed down. It had been an exacting passage and I was ordered by Jeremy to turn in; a command to which I must admit I mounted a somewhat limited resistance. He put together a scratch and as usual tasty meal, serving mine to me in my bunk! Words are inadequate on such occasions. We stayed like that until the early hours, lying comfortably and slowly forereaching to clear the headland.

The weather changes rapidly in those waters, and the next night was another world. Reaching in a light wind and calm sea we were close inshore, just over a mile off with the light from a full moon giving way to daylight. We had just had the longest day and it never really gets dark down there at that time of the year. We were in the inner passage as recommended by the *Pilot* and close outside of us south of Cabo Blanco was a line of shoals, one of which was marked on the chart Banco Byron. We wondered who had given it that name. Certainly John Byron, the future grandfather of poet Lord Byron had been down here sailing as a midshipman in HMS *Wager*, one of Anson's circumnavigational fleet. Having weathered the Horn she was fated to be wrecked on an outer island on the unbelievably unfriendly western seaboard of Tierra del Fuego in the winter of 1741. The experience of the castaways is an unmitigated horror story. Death through hunger, exposure and murder, coupled with mutiny in appalling weather conditions, brought out all that is best and worst in men in adversity. The survivors, pitifully few in number, split into two groups. One made a remarkable open-boat journey back through the Magellan Straits and up to Rio Grande in Brazil where they were taken into care by the Portuguese and returned to England only to face a court martial as mutineers. The other party, including the captain and Byron, struggled north on foot, eventually being placed in benevolent custody by the Spanish governor in Santiago, a city of 'extravagance, vice and folly' and beautiful women. Here Byron, having regained his wellbeing, apparently enjoyed himself. So much so that he was a reluctant passenger in a French ship sailing from Valparaiso, his passage having been arranged by the governor. On returning to service in the Royal Navy he was known henceforth throughout the fleet as 'Foulweather Jack.'

Byron in fact was a lucky young man. Instead of being returned home by courtesy of the Spanish governor he could well have still been in Valparaiso, incarcerated, one could imagine, in a not too comfortable prison. After all, Spain and England were at war. The fact that he had been treated so indulgently was due to Anson.

Leaving Falmouth
with escorts, we
plunge into
the unknown.
Havssula ahead.

Trade-wind rig.
Our twin-headsail
power house.

Jeremy on watch,
but perhaps not quite
what the authors
of the Collision
Regulations had
in mind.

Mar del Plata.
Fishing fleet
and all very
active. No EU
interference here.

Santa Elena.
Jeremy sets foot
in Patagonia
in Darwin's
footsteps.

Santa Claus
at Santa Cruz.

The Virgins. Entrance to the Magellan straits, where Ferdinand Magellan's prayers were answered.

Segunda Angostura in Magellan Straits. Flat calm. Our prayers are answered.

The intrepid crew exploring the Bahia del Aguila at the start of the real adventure.

Puerto Niemann, a home for the dreaded *Rachas*. Site of our near nemesis.

Beagle Channel, Brazo Noroeste. Cordillera Darwin.

Brazo Noroeste, Glacier Alley.

The magnificent Garibaldi glacier. Close as we can go because of brash ice.

View from Olla up the Beagle Channel. Just as Darwin saw it.

The Horn and I meet at last! Two grim old men.

Stanley on its best behaviour.
Mount Tumbledown
battleground behind.

Warmer climes.
Jeremy gives
Mr Franklin a rest.

It took a long time but Fraser finally comes good. Fish for supper.

The waiting game.
Our ever-lovings watch
us come home.

Back on her buoy in
Plymouth, but the old
lady's makeup has slipped.

Having extricated himself from the grip of the Horn, the Commodore, with the remnants of his fleet, had reached the island of Juan Fernandez, the old pirate haunt off the coast of Chile. After badly needed repairs to the ships and the health of their crews, Anson had set about executing his instructions by attacking Spanish shipping. Although a state of war existed Spain looked on Anson as a common corsair, whereas he considered his taking of Spanish ships and relieving them of their precious cargoes as legitimate action against an enemy. Doubtless he would have also held the popular view that these selfsame treasures had been acquired illegitimately by the Spanish in the first place, so justice was being done, except that there was no intention actually to return the plunder to its original owners.

One ship taken was a small cargo vessel in which were three women passengers who were terrified of their English captors. All that the women knew about such men was based on the reputation of the earlier English buccaneers who were considered 'the most terrible and brutal of all mankind'. Considering himself, as a Royal Navy officer, to have come from a different mould, Anson went out of his way to treat the captives well, and in particular the women, who were allowed to keep their cabins, with an armed guard to ensure their freedom from molestation. With their eventual release the story got back to the governor in Santiago. Being a Spanish gentleman it can be assumed he would not want to be worsted in the gallantry and chivalry stakes, hence the magnanimity extended to the fortunate Byron.

The boat journey by the *Wager* mutineers, a story largely unknown today, deserves special mention as it was one of the greatest open-boat achievements of all time.

Following the wreck of *Wager* on what is shown on maps and charts today as Isla Wager, discipline broke down and a group headed by a petty officer, John Bulkeley the master gunner, defied their captain and embarked on a plan to sail the ship's long boat south to the Straits of Magellan, through these and then north up the east coast of Patagonia to Brazil. The ships's carpenter, John Cummins, sawed the boat in half and inserted a new midship section to increase the length to 50 feet, at the same time partially decking her over. Re-rigged as a schooner, hopefully named *Speedwell* and equally hopelessly overcrowded with seventy souls jammed into her, she set off in October 1741.

By the time she got to Cabo Deseado, in atrocious weather, at the entrance to Magellan's *paso*, death and subsequently unexplained personnel disappearances had reduced the boat's complement to a slightly more sustainable sixty men. It took them over a month to

negotiate the hazards of the Straits before commencing the long haul
north. Most of the time this was offshore but there were two brief stops
where some of the company were left behind, voluntarily or otherwise,
on shore. Those remaining on board were in desperate shape, their
numbers being steadily depleted by starvation. The survivors were kept
going by the driving force and ruthless leadership of Bulkeley. Unusually
for one of his class he kept a log and in which he recorded the death of
the purser, Thomas Harvey, 'dying a skeleton for want of food', adding
with gallows humour 'probably the first purser in the navy who had ever
died of hunger'.

Clearing Spanish waters, *Speedwell* reached Rio Grande, in the safety
of Portuguese territory, at the end of January 1742 after three and a half
months of extreme hardship and over 2,500 miles sailed. On board were
thirty starving apparitions. Even the redoubtable Bulkeley had to be
helped just to stand. He eventually got back to England to appear before
a court martial but in the end was pardoned and continued to serve in the
navy.

Their voyage takes its rightful place in the trinity of the greatest open-
boat epics in the history of the sea and, it should be said, all by British
seamen. The second was by Captain Bligh in 1789. After the mutiny in
Bounty off Tofua in the Friendly Islands in the South Pacific, he and
eight others sailed the ship's launch, 3,600 miles to reach Timor near
Java.

The third and perhaps the greatest of them all was Shackleton's
journey in one of *Endurance's* lifeboats, the 23-foot *James Caird*, in
1916 from Elephant Island on the Antarctic Peninsular to South Georgia
with a crew of five. The distance was 800 miles in winter in the harshest
of all the world's waters, the Southern Ocean.

Coming up on our starboard bow in *Marelle* was the entrance to Puerto
Deseado or Port Desire. Discovered in 1586 by Thomas Cavendish, it
became one of the recognised stopover places for recuperation of ships
and men by the early navigators. Cavendish, a Suffolk man, born ten
years after Drake but of higher estate, was a gentleman who enjoyed the
good life and spent his money accordingly. With his finances getting into
some disarray, and being impressed by the financial results of Drake's
circumnavigation, he thought it could help his own situation if he were to
follow in the little Devonian's wake. Some ten years later in his ship
Desire he successfully completed his own round-the-world voyage,
arriving home with a vast fortune in his hold provided somewhat
unwillingly by Spanish ships off Chile and Peru. Cavendish had become

the third European to circle the globe, becoming in the process a very wealthy man indeed. Although it was now open before us we were not tempted to put into Puerto Deseado, today a small working port. There would be nothing to see now of its earlier more exotic past. Moreover the *Pilot* does not give it a particularly good reference. 'In the entrance the tidal stream runs at 6 knots at springs ... winds from west prevail. Severe squalls, which generally arrive without warning, are common.' We were carrying a light but favourable breeze as we passed. On the old maxim that no sailor should ever throw away a fair wind we sailed on. Ten miles further on lay Isla Pinguino.

The island invoked the name because it was the home to thousands of penguins, the species being known today as the Magellanic. Where the word *penguin* originated is open to debate but one popular belief has it that a Welsh sailor, possibly with Cavendish, on his first sighting of this 'aquatic flightless bird' with the distinctive white band over the crown of its head exclaimed in his native tongue 'pen gwyn', white head. A more prosaic and less romantic derivation is from the Latin *pinguis*. Whatever the explanation, the island had more than its share of what is everyone's favourite bird. The island and its sole inhabitants were to feature prominently in the history of Elizabethan seafaring, centring on the second foray south by Cavendish. All too soon after his return home from his highly successful world cruise his fortune had gone, disappearing into other pockets. The obvious solution to his now acute money problems was to repeat his previous success. Besides, the life of a corsair appealed to his nature as an adventurer at heart, daring and flamboyant. An engraving shows a handsome, confident figure with big, bold eyes.

He put together a second expedition of five ships, included in which was his old ship *Desire,* albeit now worn out, command being given to Captain John Davis. This was a wise choice. Davis was one of the greatest seamen and navigators of the period. Under his belt he had three Arctic voyages in pursuit of the north-west passage and later commanded a ship against the Spanish Armada. Added to this he was reputed, unlike many of his contemporaries, to be humane. He was subsequently to make his mark with the development of the backstaff, which was to be the principal tool of trade of the navigator for the next hundred and fifty years or so. Not content with that achievement, he was to become a bestselling author with his enduring bible for early navigators, *The Seaman's Secrets*. He dedicated his book to 'all honest-minded seamen and pilots of reputation', begging of them 'that I receive favourable courtesy' because of 'my friendly good-will towards them' and 'my love'. These words give an indication of the nature of the man.

Cavendish, now Sir Thomas, having been knighted by Elizabeth quite possibly because of an involuntary contribution to her coffers, sailed as before from Plymouth on 6 August 1591, never to return. It all went wrong. This time the Magellan Straits gave him a hard time. After a series of terrible experiences in the *paso* he was driven back out into the South Atlantic. Accompanied by Davis, the remnants of the battered fleet they sailed north with the intention of sorting themselves out in Port Desire. Everything continued to go wrong, occasioned largely through the increasingly bizarre behaviour of Cavendish, who failed to keep to the plan, sailing off into the blue. He ended up off the recently discovered Ascension Island. There, broken by failure, overcome by his misfortunes and possibly suffering from the effects of a brain tumour, he died of a broken heart. Magellan's strait had effectively destroyed him.

Davis, a man for whom only superlatives are befitting, and loyal to the end to his leader, sailed again for the Straits to try to find Cavendish. Ahead of him lay another hammering. Driven offshore by foul weather he stumbled into a group of islands which subsequently became the Falkland Islands, whose existence had not even been suspected. If justice had been done they should be the Davis Islands. Struggling back to windward he re-entered the Straits and again doubled Cape Froward which marks the turning point at the bottom of the boomerang shape of the *paso*. It is the southernmost tip of the American continent. Fighting against the late winter fierce winds he finally emerged into the Pacific only to be driven back into the Straits by a furious unmanageable gale. In a ship badly in need of repair, a crew in equally bad shape, and with no hope now of finding Cavendish in the region, Davis had no option but to give the Straits best and work his way north and back yet again to Puerto Deseado. Here with the aid of scurvy grass he got his crew back into shape. He now had to victual for the return to England. What better place than the nearby Penguin Island, where there was an abundance of fresh meat. Anchored off, they killed and dried 14,000 birds and sailed for home. The number was based on a daily ration of five penguins per four men for an estimated passage of six months. Davis was comfortable with this part of his victualling. On the way they tried to get water and provisions in the bay of Rio de Janeiro, but were driven off by the local natives backed up by the possessive resident Portuguese, only to be faced with a hard time weathering the inhospitable Cabo Frio, which had been *Marelle*'s *bête noire*. Then *Desire* had a torrid time getting through the Doldrums. The rest of the story is nothing but one long tale of unimaginable suffering. The penguins, inadequately dried, became riddled with maggots and the ship filled with putrefaction. The crew became diseased, 'growing raging mad and some died in loathsome and furious pain'.

With only Davis, a boy and the ship's Master still on their feet to work the ship, the stinking, festering wreck that was *Desire* sailed drunkenly into Berehaven in southern Ireland. After sorting out the ship and what was left of her crew, Davis, that consummate seaman with the unquenchable spirit, went home to Devon to an empty house. His wife had left him.

As a sort of postscript, Bruce Chatwin raises the intriguing thought that the story, having been well publicised, was the inspiration for Coleridge's *The Rime of the Ancient Mariner*. The resonant lines in their swinging, powerful stanzas have a particular aptness:

> *The many men so beautiful!*
> *And they all dead did lie:*
> *And a thousand, thousand slimy things*
> *Lived on and so did I.*

Although within the realm of pure speculation, there is an intellectual stimulus in deriving a connection between the fate that befell one of England's greatest mariners and the source of the story that unfolds around the central character in one of England's greatest poems.

The essence of *The Rime* is the concept that love is supreme. It was this in the end which saved the mariner. In Davis's case it played a central role in that it was his humanity which exacerbated his problems because of his support for Cavendish. It continued to show through in his compassion for his crew right to the end of his ordeal, ultimately for him to be saved, as was the Mariner.

It was the act of killing God's creatures that led to the demise of the crews of both ships. In *Desire* it was the birds they had slaughtered which in turn killed the ship's complement. The Mariner's companions died as retribution for their connivance in the shooting of the albatross:

> *'Twas right, said they, such birds to slay*
> *That bring the fog and mist.*

The parallels within the two stories continue. Both benighted ships had come up from the cold and bleak, ice-ridden south with 'fog and mist' and both went though a desperate time in the tropics which

worsened their torment. The famous lines could have been written for
both predicaments:

> *Day after day, day after day,*
> *We stuck, nor breath nor motion;*
> *As idle as a painted ship*
> *Upon a painted ocean.*
>
> *I looked upon the rotting sea,*
> *And drew my eyes away;*
> *I looked upon the rotting deck,*
> *And there the dead men lay.*

The ghastly stories wend their way through to the denouement where
the survivors at last find a haven. The Mariner is helped in by 'the Pilot
and the Pilot's boy', Davis by his boy and the Master, his Pilot.

So was John Davis the Mariner? Who knows?

In *Marelle* we went in close to Penguin Island but as at Puerto Deseado
we were wary of becoming too intimate. It is bare and uninviting, it being
difficult to pick out the spot where Davis had anchored. The *Pilot*
describes two possibilities close on our beam but only in south-
westerlies. For us they were lee shores. We sailed on, marvelling again at
those intrepid souls venturing inshore with their hearts in their mouths
wondering what dangers lurked unseen just below the surface lying in
wait ready to tear open their hulls. Going for those navigators was only
hope and a sublime belief in the Almighty. Ahead of us lay Puerto San
Julian, the setting for performances by another two great sixteenth-
century actors on the maritime stage. Drake and Magellan.

In beautiful sailing conditions we worked south. With the sun's
declination of south 26° 26′.3 the longest day swept over us, marked late
that evening by an encounter with an Argentinian ship, *Transmoola*,
heading north. We took what we thought would be an opportunity to get
a message back to Falmouth. The ship's response was positive. The
officer of the watch called the radio operator out of her bunk. She came
on the air to inform us that for some unexplained reason she was unable
to call the MRCC Falmouth direct but instead would relay our messages
to the Argentinian coastguard, our old friends the Prefectura. They came
back very promptly and directly to us. Reception was poor so our
friendly ship intervened as a radio relay. The Prefectura, true to form,
kept coming back with ever more questions concerning us personally and

about *Marelle*. It was a verbal form-filling exercise, a repeat of Mardel. Overhearing all this was the captain of our ship now out of sight astern. Cognisant of the language problem he took charge of the communication link, in excellent English. Suspecting the Prefectura was primarily interested in fulfilling its function of vessel traffic control, we were not too surprised to learn later that our greetings had not got back to the folks at home. This was to be our only failure using the ship-to-ship route for message transmission, but it certainly was not the ship's fault.

Christmas Eve. At sea. A fresh south-westerly during the night forced us offshore, which reinforced the desirability of keeping close into the land for protection in the event of stern westerly stuff. At the change of the watch I was greeted with Jeremy voicing concern. 'How far off are we? I heard cows mooing!' I was a little surprised. 'You must have better hearing than I thought. We are ten miles off!' A mystery and one not to be solved until later, further down the coast in daylight when we found ourselves in the midst of a large herd of cows. At least that is what it sounded like. The answer lay around us in the shape of Magellanic penguins. Jeremy was not the only one to have been caught this way. In his diary Darwin records, when *Beagle* was off the River Plate, 'We were surrounded by numerous seals and penguins which made such strange noises that the officer on watch reported he could hear the cattle bellowing on shore.'

By late afternoon we were back hugging the shoreline. Totally undistinguished, being almost featureless with no sign of any life, human or otherwise. I noted 'Barograph low but steady. Very comforting to see the land nearby. Very low and flat but an interesting part of the world. It has its own unique fascination. I do like this vast country or what I have seen of it so far; it is so huge.'

Very close on our starboard bow was the entrance to Puerto San Julian. It was a welcome sight to us as a milestone on our progression south but how much more welcome it would have been to Magellan and Drake as a rest area for repairs and water. Primarily however it would enable them to tackle the impending threat of mutiny. There was a remarkable similarity in the circumstances faced by these two voyagers as well as in their personal characteristics. Primarily they were both interested in wealth, Magellan to find access to it on behalf of his king as well as for his own benefit, Drake to acquire it on behalf of his queen, not to mention himself. Both were of humble birth and accordingly suffered from the class system. Although of differing faiths both were highly religious but neither let Christian charity stand in the way of ruthless treatment of those threatening the success of their ventures. In these ventures they were both completely successful but it was a twist of fate that on the way to achieving his success Drake was to find a route to the Pacific Ocean purely by accident whereas for Magellan it had been solely by intent.

When Magellan stumbled onto Puerto San Julian he was in trouble and a desperate man indeed. Following the difficulties at Cabo Frio morale took a further knock when the River Plate, after initially looking promising, turned out to be a dead end. Plugging ever southwards the never-ending sameness of the unbroken and singularly unfriendly shoreline supported the growing sense amongst many in the fleet that the quest for the passage through to the silver sea was doomed to failure. Opinion opposed to their leader was hardening. It was at this time that the fleet was smitten by storm-force winds which inflicted great damage to the ships, threatening the ability of many of them even to stay afloat. Shelter had to be found as a matter of life and death. Magellan in his flagship *Trinidada* closed the land, praying for an opening. One presented itself. A miracle. As we ourselves knew only too well, navigable inlets, or any inlet for that matter, are rare indeed in those waters. Fortune continued to smile on the Captain General as he led his other four ships in through the shoal waters at the entrance to the hourglass-shaped little harbour. It is not an easy entrance even in modern times with up-to-date charts. The *South America Pilot* is also not all that reassuring. 'Two channels lead across a bar at the harbour entrance. Least depth 2.1m with drying banks which keep moving.' With breakers smashing over the bar Magellan had to pick out a channel and career through with little margin for error and no idea how much water he would have under his keel. After him came his retinue, bringing up to anchor in still water and a wind that had died. Understandably Mass was said in each ship. They were safe from the elements but not from themselves. No European had seen the place before. Magellan gave it the name Puerto San Julian as shown on the charts today.

Winter was coming on and the hands were turned to in order to get the fleet ready in time for another attempt on their elusive passage in early spring. But like a subterranean eruption welling up to the surface, mutiny was coming to a head. Its objective was to override the Captain General's authority and sail back home to Spain. Its ringleaders were men of the establishment, higher born than Magellan, enjoying at home power and privilege. From the outset they had resented the imposition on them of authority invested in a person whom they considered an inferior. A Portuguese upstart. They had had enough.

In the forefront was Juan de Cartagena, second in command of the expedition and captain of *San Antonio*. Conspiring with him were Gaspar Quesada of *Conception* and Luis de Mendoza commanding *Vittoria*. Palm Sunday, which occurred soon after they had found their haven, was the day the action started, with a show of defiance and studied insults directed at the Captain General from the three ships. Only the fourth, *Santiago* under Juan de Serrano, remained loyal.

Fully aware this was a prelude to a full-blown assault on his authority and far from confident of how much support he could depend on in the other two ships, a lesser man might have been tempted to negotiate with the conspirators. But Magellan was no lesser man. He took swift counter-action, sending a party with concealed weapons over to *Vittoria* with a note for Mendoza. Whilst reading it he was knifed in the throat above his armour and fell dead. The boarding party took over the ship. The Captain General now had three ships against two. He moved his loyal ships out to the harbour entrance and sealed it off.

Cartagena and Queseda decided to make a run for it but were too late and fortune was not to favour them. *San Antonio* whilst getting her anchor was caught by a sudden blast of wind and dragged onto the flagship. The errant ship was boarded and she surrendered. Cartagena was back in irons. Quesada in *Concepcion* saw all was lost and gave up. He joined his fellow mutineer in chains. The Captain General was back in undisputed command. The mutinous monster had finally been slain, but justice had to be seen to be done.

A court martial was convened in the Captain General's state room. To set the tone the body of Mendoza was drawn, quartered and hung out on a gibbet set up on shore for visual display purposes. The court handed down its verdict. Guilty all round with no appeal. They didn't mess around in those days. Quesada was beheaded, quartered and his parts impaled on the gibbet next to Mendoza. Cartagena was temporarily reprieved; his sentence was marooning at the Captain General's discretion.

The Armada wintered in that grim, bleak and tragic scene. On shore the ghastly display remained as an object lesson to all. The crews were fully occupied with their minds concentrated on getting their ships ready for the next attempt to find Magellan's strait, his *paso* and his obsession.

It was during this time that the local natives began making their presence felt and increasingly threatening. They were a big race, over six feet, dwarfing the Spaniards and in particular Magellan who was quite small. He is popularly credited with giving them the name Patagones, the generally accepted, albeit corrupt, translation being *big feet* in recognition of the outstandingly large fur boots they wore. From this was derived Patagonia, the territory we know today.

The big men and their equally big women were Tehuelche Indians, hunters roaming over large tracts of Patagonia. Darwin over 300 years later was to meet them on the shores of the Magellan Straits. By that time they had become familiar with white people, but it was at San Julian where they first saw these strange little people with such pale faces. The Tehuelche were copper-skinned, adorning their faces with red and black paint, the eyes being ringed round with yellow.

King Charles had ordered Magellan to bring back specimens of natives he encountered in remote parts. Accordingly he tricked two men into allowing shackles to be put on their ankles and after a tremendous struggle one was brought on board *Trinidada*. The other managed to escape. The captive eventually settled down and was actually baptised with the name Paulo. He and his captor were to meet their ultimate fate in the Pacific. Paulo dying of scurvy and Magellan by the sword, a victim himself of trickery. His nemesis perhaps.

Spring arrived. On 24 August 1520, after seeking Divine blessing and with spirits uplifted, the Captain General and his fleet once more stood south.

It was to be nearly sixty years before white mens' voices were heard again in that sombre harbour. English this time with a West Country accent. It was midwinter 1578. What was about to happen bore an uncanny similarity to what had gone on before. A virtual rerun. Over the selfsame bar came another Captain General, Francis Drake in his flagship *Pelican* of 120 burthen. After him in line ahead came his Armada with the same number of ships as Magellan's, five; *Elizabeth* under Captain John Wynter, *Marigold*, *Swan* and the little pinnace *Christopher*. As an add-on bringing up the rear was the Portuguese prize taken off the Cape Verdes, the merchant ship *Mary*. It had been a hard passage down the coasts of Brazil and Patagonia. Drake, his men and the ships were all very much in need of rest and repair. Puerto San Julian, despite its dour unfriendliness, provided that badly required haven just as it had for Magellan. Because the account of his voyage had been published and widely distributed Drake was aware of San Julian and what had happened there. Although the coincidence in their situations was extraordinary there was nevertheless one big personal difference. Magellan was a devout Catholic. All his fortunes, good and bad, were unequivocally laid at the door of the Almighty. Drake was a Protestant with an equal intensity of faith but, and it was a big but, witchcraft and sorcery were real in his mind as they were amongst many of his contemporaries. He was shortly to put this fear of the supernatural to good effect at a time of crisis when his authority was under threat. If nothing else Drake was a pragmatist, which tempered his attitude to religion. Although a firm adherent to the Faith, he had no qualms about using his religion as a useful tool to justify the pursuit of his personal objectives.

Having in the end been successful in the long struggle against Islam, Spain was now the religious superpower in the West with her chosen form of Christianity, Catholicism, being rammed down the throats of her European neighbours, including England. The resultant outraged feelings of anger, hatred and fear fuelled the Protestant movement. It was in this highly charged emotional climate that Drake saw his opportunity. He set about promoting his public image, like an Elizabethan spin doctor, with the objective of becoming a perceived champion of English Protestantism, challenging the Titan that was Spanish Catholicism. This ensured him the backing of a large slice of the Establishment, including that of the Queen herself, for his treasure-seeking forays against the Spanish empire. At the same time it provided him with the righteous justification for his behaviour as a pirate, in all but name, with the wealth that ensued from that activity being no less than his just reward.

Drake also, like his Portuguese counterpart, had a coterie of gentlemen adventurers and court favourites on board causing problems. Drake's Cartagena was Thomas Doughty, who similarly considered himself the social superior of his appointed leader. He was a man of some standing having the ear of both Queen Elizabeth and her Lord High Treasurer, Lord Burleigh, the second most powerful person in England as the Queen's long-serving adviser. Trying to serve these two at the same time was shortly to cost Doughty his head.

Drake, brooding in his cabin and dwelling on the large number of things that had gone wrong in more recent days, developed the belief that Doughty was the root cause. He was practising witchcraft. Not only was this bedevilling the expedition but he was exerting a malignant influence over the crews. The seeds of mutiny were being sown. Doughty had to go.

Here again was the extraordinary parallel with Magellan in the way each dealt with his difficulties. Soon after the fleet had anchored in San Julian Drake convened a court martial and arraigned Doughty before a jury for trial. It was a masterly public relations exercise. Drake had already decided what was to be the verdict. It is quite possible he was consciously taking Magellan as his guide on how to deal with a self-same situation. All on board Drake's ships knew about the earlier mutinies and the subsequent executions. The grisly reminder was plain to see. Still standing was the gibbet complete with bones lying at the base.

The evidence against Doughty was unconvincing and rather thin, but playing into Drake's hands, he sealed his fate by admitting he had informed the Lord High Treasurer that Drake had been commissioned by the Queen with the express purpose of robbing the Spanish. Knowing that Burleigh would be strongly opposed to this as his policy was to improve relations with Spain, she had misled him about what the expedition was all about. Drake could now say that in addition to being a sorcerer Doughty was a plant by Burleigh to wreck the whole venture. As a further blot on Doughty's character there was made known a bizarre incident when in the course of some horseplay Doughty was alleged to have placed his hand on the buttocks of one of Drake's staff. Such an action, and the connotations of what was associated with it, were frowned upon in those days. It was a very serious offence. How times have changed! The accused was found guilty and sentenced to be beheaded. He met his death, it is recorded, with great courage and dignity as befitting a true officer and gentleman. He had in fact been offered the choice of how he would like to be despatched. The options were either beheading or for Drake personally to shoot him. The latter option was totally unacceptable to Doughty. There was no debate in his mind. Drake was not a gentleman.

Having come to grips with his predicament and knowing he was a doomed man, Doughty accepted his fate with equanimity and quiet courage. The drama was then played out to the full. The night before the final curtain-fall, Drake and Doughty dined together. The next day they received Communion kneeling together and, at the execution spot in the shadow of Magellan's gibbet, they embraced. The condemned man wished his Captain and all the company success in the forthcoming venture and then died. Doughty at the end had the supreme satisfaction of knowing he had deported himself in the manner he believed was expected of one of his rank. Drake for his part in all probability did not enjoy the same serenity of soul.

There is a noteworthy similarity between the end that Doughty met and that which befell Sir Walter Raleigh forty years on. Both had been manoeuvred into an impossible position, from which there was no escape, by totally ruthless men each executing his own agenda. James I was to Raleigh what Drake was to Doughty. Both victims saw themselves as gentlemen to the manner born and beholden at the end, when facing death, to the code of conduct appropriate for Elizabethans of that social order. Doughty died with his dignity intact and so did Raleigh, who went even further in the way he publicly presented himself, by joking with the executioner as to which direction Raleigh should face when he placed his head on the block.

Drake, who had not come out of the episode in a particularly good light, then demonstrated his superlative leadership qualities. Holding up Doughty's head before a full muster of the ships' companies, he made the point there was no future in mutiny, in case any others harboured similar ideas. A month later all hands were called to a church service at which Drake himself delivered the sermon. He was then to make a remarkably effective speech about the necessity for all to pull together if they were to succeed. This speech was to go down in history as one of the greatest ever made by a commanding officer to his men. Its central core was 'For I must have the gentlemen to haul and draw with the mariner and the mariner with the gentlemen. What! let us show ourselves all to be of one company.'

Having put his affairs in order he sailed in August from that sinister place, still in the grip of a harsh winter. He was a believer in the old adage that 'Harbour rots ships and men'. He gave the appearance of being a new man, lighter in demeanour and demonstrably clearer in purpose. It can only be surmised that perhaps deep down he was apprehensive about his reception when he returned home, now that the cat was out of the bag about court intrigues. That reception would no doubt be influenced by how successful he was as a pirate. About this he was quite relaxed. All he would be doing was relieving the Spanish of wealth they had plundered from the brutalised inhabitants of their South American conquests; riches to which, in English eyes, the Spaniards had no right of possession.

At drinks time in *Marelle* on our Christmas Eve we were close by the shoals at the entrance to San Julian, looking up the estuary and giving thought perhaps to our own bit of R & R in its embrace. But, as for our illustrious predecessors, the Virgins were now enticingly within reach. Besides, another read of the *Pilot* confirmed that even today there is not too much on offer. 'Fuel not available, fresh water by drum in emergency; provisions, subject to adequate notice.' Not enhancing its appeal is the very considerable tidal range reaching forty-five feet. It could also be assumed that Magellan's gibbet, with or without bones, had not been preserved as a national monument. There would also be no local 'giants' to meet, earlier Argentinians and European immigrants having largely exterminated them. Before a gentle northerly we sailed on, continuing to hug the brown and bare shoreline.

'Christmas Day. Woke to a perfect morning. Clear deep blue sky, bright sun and smooth sea with land close aboard.' Before the others awoke I hung up Daddy Xmas in the centre of the saloon. A family gift, he had been away with me on several Christmas morns over the years; a permanent travelling companion.

We were motionless in the mouth of the Rio Santa Cruz and with us in spirit were two of our fellow travellers. FitzRoy and Darwin. Open before us was the same vista seen by *Beagle* as she lay at anchor before moving into the river to beach herself for careening. She had glanced off a rock when entering Puerto Deseado, carrying away part of her false keel at the bow. FitzRoy decided that she should be put right before carrying on into the Pacific. Whilst the work was in hand, accompanied by the ever-eager Darwin, he set off up the Santa Cruz river with three boats and twenty-three volunteers (?) with three weeks' rations. The objective was to explore the upper reaches where no civilised man had been before. It was harder work than they had imagined hauling those heavy boats upstream and being away longer than planned they went onto half rations. Darwin writes about a light stomach being a 'good thing to talk about, but very unpleasant in practice'. On returning to the ship they found her 'afloat, freshly painted and gay as a frigate'. FitzRoy like all before him then laid off a direct course for the Virgins. We were soon to follow him.

Not much more than a mile offshore we opened our presents and thought of home, enjoying the serenity and waiting for wind. But it has not always been a scene of tranquillity. Where we were had been the backdrop to the final curtain of the tragedy that had been enacted at San Julian.

Here at Santa Cruz Magellan came to exercise the authority vested in him by the court martial. He had anchored his fleet in the estuary to fill their water butts and restock their larders from the plentiful game and fish. The Armada was ready to sail but there was also unfinished business. From the flagship *Trinidada* a boat was lowered, bearing to the shore Juan de Cartagena and a dissident priest, de la Reina, who had aided and abetted him. These unwilling souls were put ashore on the beach. Marooned. The boat went back to its parent and was hoisted smartly on board. The fleet got their anchors and with *Trinidada* in the van stood out to sea, southwards. There is no record of what fate overtook the desperately lonely figures standing forlornly on the foreshore. The poison in the boil which had been lanced in San Julian had finally drained away. Magellan, in the end the winner, was three days away from immortality.

For us the afternoon sea breeze came in and we were off. Only 132 miles to go. Would this remarkably good weather last? To see us on our way a southern right whale, close by off our beam and heading in the opposite direction, laid on a marvellous, acrobatic display of breaching, bursting most of its huge, dark bulk clear out of the water to Fraser's great delight as he stood on watch. He had never seen anything like it before and for all of us it was our first sighting close up of a right whale. It is a very big creature indeed, the species measuring up to 60 feet long and weighing in at 80 tons. Being way above *Marelle*'s size, a chance encounter would have been devastating. Apparently during our passage south there had been a TV documentary shown at home featuring these mammals breeding off the Patagonian coast, leaving our folk concerned that we might actually run into one of them as they lie around just under the surface and get out of no one's way. In fact they can be inclined to do the opposite, as described by zoologist Mark Carwardine: 'Playful and inquisitive: will poke, bump and push objects in the water.' A practice not to be encouraged in our case.

Whales can certainly be a problem for small craft, and I can recall some years ago in the Pacific having a near miss with one. Sailing slowly in calm conditions we saw coming up from astern a large specimen heading directly for us. When frighteningly close it suddenly sheered off and sounded. We were at the time towing a Walker's mechanical log to record the distance run, comprising a long line with a rotator at the end. It could have been that the whale's sensitive skin brushed the line, precipitating the avoiding action.

We were still not quite finished with the ghosts of those parts. One of my Christmas presents had been a pair of singing socks complete with tiny batteries. With movement of the ankle my inspired gift played a traditional air. They were however to cause unrest on the lower deck. Fraser started complaining that when he was just on the point of sleep he would be woken by Auld Lang Syne. As I was duty-bound to continue to wear my socks it appeared the only answer to the insurrection was to follow the lead set by my predecessor and maroon Fraser at Santa Cruz. The impending mutiny died along with the batteries.

Our track, lying close into the coastline of the southern stretch of Patagonia, had been the one followed closely by FitzRoy's famous and infamous predecessors. The list is the *Who's Who* of the early European navigators sailing in Magellan's wake along his trailblazing passage. Amongst the Spanish are names now buried in history. Garcia de Loaysa who took seven ships through the Magellan Straits. All were lost. Close after him came Alonzo de Camargo with three ships of which only one managed to get back to Spain. This ship had been the first to sight Le Maire Strait by being blown through it, continuing on to winter in the eastern approaches to the Beagle Channel, the first European to enter these parts. In Spain no one took any notice of this remarkable voyage. No gold or silver had been brought back and that was all that mattered. The folks back home were in fact so uninterested that the name of the ship and her captain were not even recorded. The Dutch then came onto the scene. With five ships Simon des Cordes was the first from his country to transit the Strait. All his fleet were lost. Success finally came with Admiral Joris Spilbergen who made it through the *paso* in command of six ships. He arrived back in Holland via the Dutch Indies after three years, to a hero's welcome but not in the same ship. In the Moluccas he had been compelled to transfer to another and larger Dutch ship that conveniently happened to be lying there. All the ships in his original fleet had been so knocked about that they were no longer seaworthy. His circumnavigation was noteworthy in that it opened up the trade routes to the east and in doing so underpinned the Dutch East India Company, helping it on the road to becoming an immensely powerful monopoly. In the English section of that *Who's Who* are listed Drake, Cavendish, Davis, Anson, Byron twice and Weddell more latterly prior to FitzRoy, both of whom, unlike most of the self-seeking adventurers in the past, had none but the best of intentions. After them of course was James Cook. In his first voyage, just on thirty years after Anson, he sailed those waters in 1768 in the bluff-bowed, robustly built ex-collier *Endeavour*. Following a stop at Rio for provisions, Cook went down the Patagonian coast to arrive off the entrance to the Le Maire Strait, only to be 'driven out again with great violence' and a contrary tide. When the weather relented the great cartographer, charting as he went, entered the Pacific.

What was so outstanding about the early pioneering seamen probing into realms of high uncertainty was their totally obsessive commitment, coupled with a remarkable proclivity to risk all, not only the venture capital but their own lives. What was equally extraordinary was that they were able to achieve their ends in such ill-equipped ships which were, in modern eyes, so unsuited to contend with those waters. Not only were they consummate seamen but they were very brave men indeed.

The hazards encountered by those men in their struggles to get round South America from the Atlantic Ocean into the Pacific, are starkly apparent when the cost is counted. From Magellan's time to Anson's voyage as many as seventy-nine ships sailed from Spanish, Dutch and English ports. Thirteen returned. The long gruelling ocean passages, the violence of the Magellan Straits and the onslaught of atrocious weather off the Horn had destroyed the rest.

It was at the southern end of this historic track that Drake, once again in parallel circumstances with Magellan, was beset by adverse weather barring entry into the Magellan Straits. It is probable that here, whilst at anchor a little up the coast waiting for the wind to favour him, he changed the rather prosaic name of his flagship, *Pelican*, to *Golden Hind* as a favour-soliciting gesture to his patron Sir Christopher Hatton, a man of great influence as a confidant of the Queen, enjoying the prestigious title of Captain of the Guard. On the Hatton family crest was a hind. In those days patrons were all-powerful, as are today their modern equivalent, the sponsors. *Golden Hind*, much more eye-catchingly descriptive than *Pelican*, was to become, along with Nelson's *Victory*, the most famous of all ship's names.

As we started on our last leg south the weather was getting colder and we were now sleeping with plenty of clothes on in our sleeping bags. But the weather remained benign with fitful breezes during the day and frustrating nights with little wind and equally little progress. We were having to use the engine on occasions. It had been behaving itself for some time. I put this down to doses of biocide conditioner. I had always been sceptical about this as something of a quick-fix potion. To ensure there was no interface in the fuel tank between diesel and any water present causing bacteria to develop I have always maintained a firm regime of regularly draining off any residual water via the drain at the bottom of the tank. However, as no reason had so far been unearthed as to why the engine had misbehaved, I had as a long shot tipped in the recommended dosage of biocide. There had been no further trouble. Seemed too good to be true but the results were there.

Still keeping close inshore we landed in the shoals at the entrance to Puerto Gallegos, totally devoid of wind. We wondered what had gone wrong with the weather and why, apart from a lack of wind, it was being so kind to us. Suspiciously too kind. We would not have too long to wait for it to show its true colours. Rio Gallegos, a commercial harbour, had little for the likes of us but rather out of context we could see on the side of the river a big four-masted barque. We wondered about that. Perhaps in this prosaic setting for a working port, very much a product of today, the romance of yesterday still has its place. The town does feature in Bruce Chatwin's writings wherein he relates a tale of the Wild Bunch, comprising Butch Cassidy and the Sundance Kid complete with beautiful girlfriend Etta Place, riding in to help the local bank with a problem it was having in deciding what best to with its surplus cash deposits. They talked about a loan with the bank manager, who invited them to lunch. They tied him up with the staff and relieved him of his cash problem. Etta entertained an appreciative group of admirers outside, taking their minds off going into the bank, whilst her men got clear away. Then with a chorus of good wishes ringing in her ears she galloped after Butch and the Kid. They vanished in the general direction of the Andes.

Stretching out ahead of us on our starboard beam was a long low cliff coming to a sudden abrupt end. The Virgins! The lighthouse perched on the end marked the final end of our long haul south. They owe their name to Magellan. As he passed the headland, a stretch of clear water suddenly appeared reaching to the west as far as the eye could see. To the south the land could be seen vanishing into the murky distance. There were no doubts in his mind. He had found the opening which would take him to the South Sea. Steeped in the traditions of his faith he was fully cognisant of the significance of the date. As 21 October was Saint Ursula's Day, he gave the headland the full flowing title of Cape of the Eleven Thousand Virgins. This was the number of young ladies who had accompanied Ursula on a pilgrimage to Rome which unfortunately led to her martyrdom and subsequent canonisation as patroness of brides. Ursula's is a sad story. A triumph of piety over evil but at great cost. In consenting to an arranged marriage orchestrated by her father, a Christian king in Brittany, in collusion with a pagan king in Cornwall on behalf of the latter's son Conon, she made various stipulations. One was that the bridegroom had to accompany her on a combined pilgrimage honeymoon to Rome and another that she must also have in attendance ten virgin companions. Each of them in turn had to be provided with one thousand attendant virgins. The party travelled up the Rhine, with the boat loaded to the gunwales with maidens, to Cologne and then proceeded onto Rome where Conon was baptised and Ursula received the sacraments. On returning via Cologne disaster struck. The Huns besieged the city, killing Conon, and attempted a mass ravishment of the virgins but, meeting with no reward, they put the still chaste maidens to the sword. The Huns' chief, reserving the prize for himself, also met with no success. His manly pride was further dented when Ursula conveyed her feelings in public with a gesture which he deemed rather offensive. One of his followers then despatched her with an arrow. On the assumption Ursula was herself a virgin, the correct name for the cape should possibly have been Eleven Thousand and Eleven Virgins. In modern times the name has shrunk to simple Cabo Virgenes, a reflection perhaps on the difficulties there could be in assembling such numbers today.

Magellan's dream of a short cut to the fabulous wealth of the spice islands in the East Indies had become a reality. It was ironic the success of his venture, which had been sponsored by the King of Spain, was not to benefit the Spanish but rather the hated English.

CHAPTER SIX

TIERRA DEL FUEGO

In these regions, in a general way, it is safe to say that the weather is almost always bad and the country is completely uninhabitable. To the west of the watershed, on the Chilean side, it blows a full gale most days, a full storm the rest and a hurricane for three days in every three months.
M. Mason, in an appendix to Sir Alec Rose's *My Lively Lady*

Enter Straits of Magellan – Punta Dungeness – north-easterly gale – anxious night – we attempt Primera Angostura – Armada requests pleasure of our company – stressful night passage to Puerto Sara – see in new millennium – transit Segunda Angostura – miracle weather – Punta Arenas – mishap – Armada to rescue – we start the big adventure – Bahia del Aguila – rest day in Puerto Hope – King – Mount Sarmiento – Niemann – *Rachas* – hard time – Caleta Atracadero – Puerto Engaño – Caleta Cushion – Seno Garibaldi impresses – glacier alley – beautiful Caleta Olla – Ferrari, first sign of habitation – passing view of Ushuaia – arrive Puerto Williams

We rounded Cape Virgins in late afternoon and none too soon. Building up astern to the north-east was a bank of very dark clouds and looking more unpleasant by the minute. The sooner we got into the Straits the better. It was almost as if the weather god was telling us we had had it too good for too long.

The cape is in Argentinian waters and in accordance with the rules we tried to call up the naval radio station. Nothing. No matter, as very shortly we would be in Chile. After rounding the Virgins there are a further five miles to run south-west to Punta Dungeness, marking the border. The Chilean Navy, the Armada, maintains a presence here and wide awake they are too. On calling them up we were subjected to detailed grilling. They wanted to know all about us and our passage plans. We had been clocked in. Over the next few weeks we were to have a lot of contact with the Armada. They were very much in charge.

The name Dungeness, slightly incongruous perhaps for these waters, was given to the point by Samuel Wallis, captain of HMS *Dolphin*, when passing through the Magellan Straits in 1767 in the course of a world circumnavigation. It reminded him of home, seeing a marked resemblance to Dungeness on the Kentish coast. It was a landmark he would have known well when beating down Channel. The voyage by Wallis was noteworthy in that he discovered many Pacific islands including Tahiti. Moreover it was remarkable in that none of the crew suffered from scurvy, the scourge of the times.

Twenty years after Wallis a Spaniard, *El Capitán* don Antonio de Cordova, attempted to change the name to one more acceptable to Spanish ears, but with no success. The title bestowed on it by Wallis has endured.

In drizzle and bone-chilling cold, darkness descended upon us as we entered the eastern end of Ferdinand Magellan's great discovery. My journal notes 'We now have a full gale. What a welcome!' Slocum had the same lament: 'On February 11 the *Spray* rounded Cape Virgins and entered the Strait of Magellan. The scene was again real and gloomy; the wind, northeast and blowing a gale, sent feather white spume along the coast; such a sea ran as would swamp an ill-appointed ship.' The *South America Pilot* is not particularly welcoming either: 'In the E part of the strait winds from WSW or SW blow with great strength, commonly exceeding 50 knots', adding for good measure, 'Violent and unpredictable squalls ... are frequent throughout the strait.' For the present, for us, the weather was contenting itself with a sedate gale Force 8.

The *Pilot* would seem to have its reservations about the attractions of the Straits. Paragraph 7.15 reads 'ANCHORAGES Suitable for vessels are few. Some have only been cursorily examined, and they are mostly from old surveys so care is required when entering them.'

Further into the bay, in calmer waters, and now getting a lee from the southern shore of Patagonia, we hove to for the night under storm jib and trysail. This was the locality where Magellan lay with his fleet whilst he sent his two smaller ships further into the straits just to make sure they weren't in another dead end – which had so disappointed him in the River Plata. It was coincidental he had also been subjected to a north-easterly gale soon after he arrived.

Our immediate objective was Punta Arenas, further up the Straits, which was to be the jumping-off place for the cruise through Tierra del Fuego. But to get there we had to negotiate two difficult channels, Primera Angostura and Segunda Angostura, first and second narrows. They are eight and twelve miles long respectively and two to four miles across. They point towards the south-west, which is directly into the prevailing wind and through them the tidal stream runs at up to eight knots. They are a difficult passage even for big ships but for us they were a formidable obstacle. A strong wind against tide would render them impassable for *Marelle*.

We lay hove-to for the night and in the early hours planned to get under way to tackle the first of the narrows. It was during this period that the value of GPS became very apparent. *Marelle* was fore reaching at between one and two knots, lying comfortably. Fraser was on watch, cold and damp. Jeremy and I were relaxing below, warm and dry, with drinks all round. The only known hazard was an oil rig but this was well down to leeward. I had done a quick vector and after making a very generous allowance for leeway, which I knew would be considerable, we should clear that oil rig with plenty to spare. Fraser gave tongue, 'I don't like the look of that oil rig.' 'Nonsense,' I said, 'we will miss it by a mile.' He wouldn't take no for an answer. What was wrong with the fellow? To shut him up and to confirm what I was saying I glanced at the course made good on the GPS. I couldn't believe my eyes and thought the thing had gone haywire. The leeway we were making was vastly in excess of what I had allowed. Converting the GPS track to magnetic and sighting across the pedestal-mounted steering compass explained Fraser's nervousness. We were going to hit that oil rig! As it was unlikely to move we had to take action and promptly at that. We let the storm jib draw and hardened in the trysail, giving her as well a rag of genoa. With a brief touch of engine for good measure she forged ahead to clear Fraser's rig. He relaxed and the watch below reconnected with the Happy Hour, sparing a thought for the poor chap huddled in the cockpit, wrapped in the night in the wind and rain. Up till then I had used the GPS for not much more than to give a position, but now I was suddenly aware of its hidden talents. An old dog was learning a new trick.

Come the morning the wind had eased and we were getting in position to catch the first of the flood tide for the transit of the Primera Angostura. By early afternoon we were in the entrance to the narrows but the wind was now picking up from dead ahead and a chop caused by wind over tide starting to worsen. It was going to be a hard passage. It was at this point that a Chilean Navy pilot cutter *Toucan* overhauled us and ordered us to follow her into the anchorage off the tiny township at Punta Delgada. She had a mooring there to which she secured, inviting us alongside. I declined, it looked too bouncy, and instead anchored abreast of them. Whereupon we were subjected to another prolonged question and answer session. It wasn't clear why we had been dragged out of the narrows and it may have been because of the deteriorating weather or perhaps because of a ship coming through. Subsequently we were to learn from Noel, owner of the French yacht *Enez* in company with us at Mar del Plata, that probably what they wanted was just to enjoy our company. Noel, unbeknownst to us, was a couple of days behind us and he on entering the narrows received the same treatment. He actually went alongside *Toucan* and at their insistence had all his meals with them over several days. That would figure, as we were to discover how friendly were the Chileans.

A day's rest, which we badly needed, and then we launched ourselves on another attempt at the Angostura. As we were about to do so we heard *Toucan* calling up a yacht entering the narrows. It turned out to be the Swiss yacht *Atmos II*, also from Mardel days. Big and very much a hot-and-cold running-water boat, she was having a problem in communicating with *Toucan*. Neither was able to understand the other's version of English and the Swiss had no knowledge of Spanish. *Toucan* called on us for help and I found myself interpreting Swiss English into Spanish English. Exhausted by this verbal marathon, we followed the Swiss into the Angostura with the warm farewells of *Toucan* and their thanks speeding us on our way. We were in for a tough passage. The wind settled into the south-west, right in our teeth, and progressively built to gale force as we emerged from the narrows. We had something over twenty miles to go across the bay to the entrance to the Segunda Angostura, dead to windward in fifty knots of wind and night coming on. On deck it was bitingly cold in drizzle and spray driving in sheets over the boat. *Marelle* on her ear was going beautifully. On the wheel I was watching her and so proud of her performance. Solid water was swirling down the lee deck, throwing up plumes of foam as it hit the guardrail stanchions. She was in the slot and only required an occasional spoke or two of wheel to keep her steady on the path ahead. I could feel her soul and innate strength. As sailors in the past would have put it, 'everything bar taut and singing' under the strain. The wind was still rising and I kept saying to myself something had got to give but it didn't. I had never experienced sailing like that before. Later on I wrote in my journal 'What a way to spend our occasion!' It was our wedding anniversary.

As the night progressed the wind, true to form, eased and the rain cleared. We were closing the entrance to the second narrows but we were too late. The ebb was starting and we were very tired. It was getting light and ahead of us we could see *Atmos II* looking as though she was having sail trouble. It had to be our friends as the likelihood of there being any other yacht in the immediate vicinity was slim. The eastern half of the Magellan Straits is somewhat lacking in general appeal as a cruising ground with the passage being deemed too dangerous. Boats on their way down the South Atlantic heading for Tierra del Fuego tend to give the entrance a miss and make for the eastern end of the Beagle Channel, further south. For us it had not been easy working our way up the strait and one can only be in awe of how the great Magellan himself, with his consorts in their impossibly unhandy ships, was able to negotiate these turbulent waters, beset by fast running tidal streams and excessively strong winds. We were surprised to see *Atmos II*. A big boat with a big Volvo engine, we thought she would have been out of the narrows and well on her way. These were now shut off to us and with the wind, again true to form, coming back strongly we anchored in Bahia Gregorio off the small oil terminal of Puerto Sara. We had met this lady again. 'It is midday as I write this with Fraser and Jeremy in their bags catching up on sleep whilst the wind howls and we roll in the chop even though we are close in under the protection of the land. We will have to wait until conditions ease before we can tackle the Angostura. It would be impossible right now. Apart from that the last few days have been too wearing with no let-up on boat and crew. My learning curve on small boat handling is almost vertical. I thought I knew something about sailing. I don't. I am only just beginning to learn.'

Puerto Sara, lying in behind Cabo Gregorio at the eastern entrance to Segunda Angostura, has little going for it. A few houses, some oil tanks complemented by a small pier and that's it. The place takes its name from Doña Sara, *la Primera Dama*, wife of *el Presidente*. She lent hopefully some glamour to an otherwise unglamorous occasion, the opening in 1907 of a refrigeration plant to serve the needs of Patagonian sheep barons. One such was José Menendez, a Spanish entrepreneur in a big way, whose 90,000-hectare holding, Estancia San Gregorio, was just to the east of Sara on the north shore of the bay. Following the expropriation of this and the other enormous land settlements by the socialists in the 1960s and the Marxist Allende in the early 1970s, it was turned into a cooperative. As a consequence it became akin to a museum town, a mere shadow of its great past when it had been a major centre of employment with its own school and community services.

The port's most distinguished feature is the wind which continuously sweeps over it from the west with great vigour. But it has its place in history. Once again Thomas Cavendish comes onto the scene to play a rather unheroic role. Embarked on his first visit to these parts in the course of his world circumnavigation he had negotiated the first narrows with little difficulty and still carrying a fair breeze was approaching Cabo Gregorio for the run at the second hurdle. Up till then he had seen no sign of the fires on shore which had been so much in evidence when Magellan had passed that way and on which Drake had commented. Suddenly there was a small flickering of flames to be seen on the beach near where Puerto Sara is today. Cavendish anchored to wait for daylight. On sending in a boat to investigate, three Spanish soldiers were found standing at the water's edge. They were a little put out to discover that their potential rescuers were not their longed-for countrymen but English. As such of course they had to be pirates from whom little in the way of hospitality could be expected. They were right. Their spokesman, Tomé Hernandez, managed to convey to the curious Cavendish sitting in the boat how it was that they were there, in rags, obviously greatly distressed and starving. They were witness to the failure of a disastrous Spanish attempt to colonise the Straits. This venture was part of a plan to fortify them to keep out unwelcome intruders, particularly the English.

Drake's earlier arrival on the coasts of Chile and Peru had thrown the Spanish viceroy into a state of complete panic. How many more Drake lookalikes were on their way in an unbroken procession through Magellan's *paso*, about to plunder Spain's South American shores and her ships on a grand scale? Immediate action was demanded. In Callao, capital and port for Lima in Peru, there was by happy chance a leading Spanish navigator and one of that country's most experienced sailors, Pedro Sarmiento de Gamboa. He was forthwith despatched south with a second ship as consort to explore the straits and determine how best they could be defended. As it happened his heart was in his work as he had himself been a victim of Drake, who had taken Sarmiento's own ship off Callao with the treasure she contained.

The Viceroy had compiled a comprehensive set of Sailing Orders which he read out word by chilling word to the assembled, unenthusiastic crews, comprised largely of impressed men, standing in the waist of the flagship, *Nuestra Señora de Esperanza*, before they sailed south. These Orders included instructions on what to do about 'The Scourge of God', one Francis Drake.

'If you should encounter or receive news of the ship in which Francesco Draquez, the English Pirate, sails, who has entered into this sea and coast of the South and as you know well, has committed robberies and injuries, you will do your best to take, kill or cripple him by fight, at any risk whatever, since it is of the greatest importance to the service of God,' and if this was not enough 'and of the Virgin Mary, our Mother, His Majesty our King and realms.'

The hopeful Viceroy was too late. The astute archfiend Drake, the archetypal weapon of mass destruction, sensing he might have outstayed his welcome, was long gone, way to the north, trying his luck in other lucrative Spanish waters.

Travelling east along the *paso*, alone in *Esperanza*, his consort having given up, Sarmiento experienced freak weather conditions. It was fine, warm and sunny when he spied a likely spot for a settlement. It was just

round the corner from Cabo Froward as you go north to the present-day
site of Punta Arenas. He gave the bay the name of San Juan and the
projecting point of land, on which he could see just the place for the fort,
he named Santa Ana. These names are still shown unchanged on some
charts. Here a colony could be established with an excellent chance of
success. A fort would be built with its cannon effectively sealing off the
strait and any access through to the Mar del Sur. Perfect. Events were to
show how the *paso* had completely deluded him with its false promises.
What was to follow was total disaster. A complete victory of the forces of
nature over those of man. Sarmiento was to exacerbate the impending
catastrophe by kidnapping a couple of the local Indians. He was to regret
his action. The news quickly spread that this new influx of strange, bearded
swarthy men, dressed equally oddly in clothes, were undesirables. The
hostility of the local tribes was significant in the ultimate denouement.

He carried on to Spain with the good news. The favourable report on
the feasibility of colonising and fortifying the straits triggered off frenetic
activity. An expedition with Sarmiento as pilot, and to his chagrin made
second in command, was hurriedly put together and despatched to the
south. It comprised twenty three vessels in varying states of
seaworthiness with a mixed bag of three thousand sailors, soldiers,
priests and would be colonists, men, women and children.

Despite Sarmiento's input it was a masterpiece of muddled planning
and faulty preparation. By the time the armada entered the Straits it was
down to five ships and five hundred souls by now under the charge of
Sarmiento. The original leader had gone home.

The first step to establish Spain's authority over the Straits was to
build a township in the eastern entrance a mile or two west of Punta
Dungeness on the southern shores of Patagonia on the *pampas*. A more
unsuitable site to establish a start-from-scratch settlement would be hard
to find. Brown, bare slopes, lacking water and protection from the almost
perpetual gale-force winds. But build a settlement they did, naming it
Nombre de Jesus. No sign of it remains. Conditions are the same today,
as we were to bear witness. Initially the building programme and the
tilling of the land went well, so much so that Sarmiento felt confident
enough to go west to set up what would be the principal town and fort at
the mouth of the Rio San Julian round from Punta Santa Ana. It was
called Ciudad Don Felipe. Paying respect to the monarch in public was
always considered a good thing to do. With skill and remarkable
motivation the new township like its twin to the east sprang into
existence in just a matter of weeks. Sarmiento was well pleased. All was
well but unfortunately the euphoria was ephemeral. There were those

who did not share their leader's confidence in the future. They wanted to go home. Another mutiny was about to happen. In what was becoming standard procedure in such situations Sarmiento took quick action. The ringleader was beheaded and impaled on a stake for public viewing. End of mutiny. Then at the height of his success Sarmiento deserted his followers, taking off to the east in their one remaining ship. It was an action out of keeping with his character and has never been properly explained. After a brief stopover at Nombre de Jesus he sailed away, never to be seen again by the doomed settlers. The final act was about to be played out.

The true nature of the region reasserted itself as the harsh winter descended on both sites. The crops failed and starvation took over. One by one the emaciated inhabitants, in whom all hope had long gone, perished. The rotting corpses piled up in the streets. No one was left alive also in Nombre de Jesus. At Don Felipe with numbers down to fifteen men and three women the officer commanding, Andres de Viedma, embarked on a last gamble of desperation. They set out to march along the shore to the eastern settlement in the vain hope of finding better conditions there. It was in the course of stumbling along with most of them near death that they fell in with Cavendish close to where we were now anchored off Puerto Sara. Having heard the long dismal story he took Hernandez into the boat, telling his two companions to report back to Viedma that the remainder of his party should come down to the beach to be given passage in the English ships. Back on board *Desire* Cavendish gave further thought to the situation. Apart from the catering difficulties with the sudden influx of a sizeable number of passengers there was the matter of the women. They always caused problems. He sailed on.

Passing through the Straits with no great difficulty, still carrying with him his lucky fair wind, he set about making his fortune up the Pacific coast. He was to do exactly what the whole disastrous Sarmiento operation had been aimed at preventing.

Whereas Cavendish had enjoyed an unusual spell of easterly winds we were in the grip of the westerlies and very strong they were too, effectively shutting us out of the narrows. We had anchored close up to the land in eight metres of water veering over sixty metres of chain. We were on a ledge; a short distance out the depth dropped precipitously to thirty metres and more. If we dragged we were out into space in Bahia Gregorio with next stop the rocky shores around the exit from the Primera Angostura. Our first evening was not relaxing. 'The wind is at fifty knots or more but she is holding position facing the small town of dreary aspect. Spray drives over us in sheets past the cabin windows as she rolls and pitches. Although the shore is close, the wind has built up a chop into which *Marelle* plunges her head, sending solid water sluicing down the decks as though we were under way at sea. However warm and snug down below. Slept in my clothes as there is the possibility of dragging when we would have to start all over again in rain and the blackest of nights to keep being drawn back into the Primera Angostura. No one says anything but concern is in the air. It is very stressful.'

Next night was New Year's Eve. We should have been making our approach to the Horn and not stuck here. There was no change in the conditions except the wind was building more. Subsequently when we next met Noel in Punta Arenas he produced graphs of wind speeds recorded when he had been in the area at the same time. The reading was over seventy knots. It felt like it. We marvelled at the holding power of the single CQR anchor. We could perhaps have used our 'Chum' anchor weight for added security but I have had difficulty before with this cumbersome piece of gear. Being so heavy and with any movement of the bows it is not easy to deploy or recover, even dangerous in severe conditions. And so we saw in the new millennium.

Jeremy had set his alarm for us to catch the start of the flood at 0400 on Saturday 1 January 2000. The great hope was that our southwester would have eased by that time. It normally does at night according to the book and hopefully long enough to let us get through the narrows before 'this blasted, searing wind' started again.

We were to be blessed. On time, with the full weight of the tide under us, we entered the Angostura under power in a flat calm. Like a miracle it stayed like that for us to clear the exit and close Isla Isabel, halfway down to Punta Arenas. Given the name Elizabeth Island by Drake, it has always been home to penguin colonies. Today they are protected as a valuable visitor attraction but life for them in earlier times was otherwise. Magellan on his escape from the Narrows sailed up to the island, noting 'there were many sea wolves and large birds'. He ordered his fleet to lie to and called his captains and pilots to a conference. He wanted a vote of confidence in support of his intention to keep on going down the *paso*. One voice, that of Esteban Gomez, pilot of *San Antonio*, thought they should call it a day and go home whilst they were still ahead of the game. He was shouted down particularly after Magellan made his time-honoured comment that he would go on even 'if we have to eat the leather on the yards'. Something they subsequently had to do. It was surprising that Magellan with his experience of treachery did not heed the alarm bells and take his usual positive action, because very shortly *San Antonio* was to desert him and sail back to Spain. More or less in agreement, the fleet left the island and headed south down the *paso*. No sign of life could be seen apart from pillars of smoke on the land on their port hand. These numerous columns seemed to be moving and keeping up with them. It was the sight of these that inspired Magellan to give Tierra del Fuego its name, the land of fire. Lucas Bridges throws some more light on these fires:

There is another interesting point about the fires of the Fuegian Indians. In the numberless sheltered nooks around the shores, at points where canoes could be safely beached, were Yaghan families living in their wigwams. If a distant sail appeared, or anything else occurred to startle those who remained at home, they would send out a warning to those away fishing by piling green branches or shrubs on the wigwam fire. At the sight of the black smoke signal the fishers would hurry back home. The early explorers of that archipelago would see these countless columns of smoke rising at short intervals for miles along the coast. This is doubtless the reason why they named these regions Tierra del Fuego. It is possible, however, that some tract of grassland on the northern part of the island may have been seen burning.

He further elaborates:

Living, as they did, practically naked in this raw climate, the greatest comfort these people had was fire. Their favourite tinder was 'dunda', the filmy web from the puff-ball, a ground fungus. If this was lacking, they used fine bird's down or insects' nests. The tinder was kept dry in the bladder of a seal or guanaco. To ignite it they employed iron pyrites fire-stone – far more effective than flint for producing sparks.

Drake was to echo Magellan's observations on Isabel's wildlife, remarking on the strange birds that could not fly but yet were not able to run fast enough to get away. His men killed three thousand of them for salting down. The consensus was that they were 'a very good and wholesome victual'. Just when the penguins thought life was settling down again, along came Cavendish who salted down more of them.

   With just the gentlest of breezes we coasted past Isla Isabel to arrive at Punta Arenas at 1300. There was *Atmos II* outside some fishing boats on the one and only wharf, the Muelle Arturo Prat. We went alongside her to a warm welcome. It was a great moment. At last we felt we had got somewhere. The Virgins had been a major milestone on the long haul southward but now at Punta Arenas we were on the launch pad for the Tierra del Fuego channels. The real adventure was about to happen. Up till now it had been just an exercise in getting to this point.

We had received mixed signals about the place as a yacht spot and mostly unfavourable. It was certainly was not all that interested in whether we were there or not, presumably because it is a commercial working port. I had spoken to the port authority on the radio about a berth on the wharf to be told we could go wherever there was space but preferably up in its root at the top end. The inference was anywhere would be okay, but try not to get in the way. The *muelle* is used by everyone. Cruise liners, Antarctic survey vessels, warships, cargo vessels, fishing boats and the likes of us. As evidence of the port authority not being fussed about us, we had no demands for harbour dues or any other charges. The major problem with the harbour is it is so exposed. The Straits are wide at this point with a fetch of seventeen miles across to the east to Isla Grande, the main island, stretching over to the Atlantic. The strait here runs north and south, being swept almost continuously by very strong winds. These present a problem to vessels of our size because of the surge alongside the wharf. With any easting in the wind an alongside berth becomes untenable. The *Pilot* warns that winds from the east 'are dangerous for vessels at anchor or alongside'. Like the River Plate the area has its nasty. 'The *panteonero*, a local wind which occurs in spring or autumn, blows between WSW and WNW at strengths of force 8 to 12.' We were to be spared the top end of this range but had our share of the predominant winds from the north-west quarter which as the *Pilot* aptly puts it 'blow very strongly at times'. Although we agreed wholeheartedly with that comment, who were we to complain? We had chosen to be in those parts. We had planned to be there for a week but in the event we were to become better acquainted with the town than anticipated.

Over its 150 years in existence the character of Punta Arenas has changed markedly as its purpose in life has changed. Its first life was short-lived. It was founded in 1848 by the Chilean government on assuming sovereignty of the newly created region of Magallanes, as a depository for criminals and those with awkward political opinions, but it did not last long. The climate and their way of life not being popular with the inhabitants, they rose up, murdered their guards, destroyed the fledgling settlement and departed for the *pampas* of Patagonia. Not to be deterred, the government built a bigger and better penal settlement which was to survive for twenty-five years before there was a repeat of the earlier occasion. This time the guards were as one with the prisoners.

They all hated the place. Once again the conglomeration of buildings was levelled and everyone, guards and detainees alike, took off for the hills.

Yet again the settlement was reconstructed, but big changes had occurred in Magallanes province. Sheep had been imported from the Falklands and sheep farming on a large scale started on the main island. Fortunes were made with the establishment of enormous haciendas. The region began to develop, with Punta Arenas becoming a significant port to serve the rising economy, based on wool and meat. Parallel with all this was its increasing importance as a coaling station. Into the town flowed a hotchpotch of nationalities, including a strong British influence. The First World War and the opening of the Panama Canal saw a decline in the town's fortunes but signs of its earlier more opulent times are evident today in grand buildings around the central square. In more recent times it has re-established itself with a big development in the energy industry and a build-up of the military presence. Something like 100,000 people make their home there now but frequently the impression given is that like the original inhabitants many, if given the option, would rather be elsewhere. Apart from anything else all are agreed the climate leaves something to be desired.

We were destined to be there twice as long as expected, and although our stay was by necessity and not by choice I began to like the place, even entertaining thoughts of coming back to explore more of its patchwork past. I am not sure however if that view was widely shared.

The team in *Atmos II* seemed pleased to have us with them again and were full of thanks for our help in the communication link with *Toucan* way back at Punta Delgada. They were in the process of tackling the Chilean bureaucracy in the form of the Armada to get their *zarpe*. This is the permit to traverse the waters of Tierra del Fuego. Without this document one can go nowhere. We had heard there could be administrative difficulties in obtaining one's *zarpe* and our friends next door rather confirmed they were experiencing a delay. Consequently I hot-footed it ashore in the hope of getting the ball rolling and at the same time paying my respects to the Port Captain. At the reception desk in the Armada's office I was confronted by a very young and very smart naval rating who knew no English and could make nothing of my Spanish. There didn't seem to be anyone else around but after all it was Saturday afternoon and a public holiday as well, New Year's Day! I was perhaps being a little hopeful. It could all wait until Monday.

Indicative perhaps of the lack of yachting activity was that on Sunday morning a journalist, complete with photographer, arrived on board to do a piece for the local newspaper on the first yacht to arrive in the new year. Sure enough on the front page on Monday there was quite a significant write-up with a photograph of '*Marelle de Gran Bretaña*', with an account of what she had been up to and our future aspirations for Cabo de Hornos. Some of our reflected glory even washed off onto *Atmos,* whose nether regions appeared in the photograph, earning her a mention in the story.

High on the priority list was establishing contact with the folks at home to let them know we were still in the land of the living. As luck would have it on the opposite side of the wharf was a cruise liner and, to provide a communications service to the passengers, beside the ship was a mobile telephone van. We made our calls. It had been over three weeks since we had last spoken. A note in my diary reflected the mood: 'Feel so relaxed. It has been a long, long haul since we left home and it is difficult to hoist in that we have made this landmark point. At times I have felt the odds were against us but dear old *Marelle* has got us here.' Unfortunately the feeling of wellbeing was to be shortlived.

Monday 3 January was Disaster Day! At 0400 the raft of fishing boats on the wall moved out. Outside them was *Atmos* and outside her again were ourselves. As we were to learn later the fishermen had cast *Atmos* off, letting go her shore lines and ours, leaving her adrift with us still tethered alongside. She got under way, heading out to sea under power, banging on our coachroof to get us moving. Understandably she was wanting to lose her appendage. Reluctantly we dragged ourselves out of our warm pits and struggled into our gear. Fraser poked his head out on deck, returning to the cabin to appraise us of the situation which was that we were heading out into the Straits, and it was cold, pitch black and raining. The banging on the roof continued. Bearing in mind Fraser's report, we were a little naughty, grabbing a few extra minutes to get into our oilskins and sea boots before venturing on deck. Casting ourselves off from our unwilling hosts, who surprisingly enough were still friendly, we took stock of the position. What to do next? The south-easterly wind was increasing so there would be no future in going back onto the wall with the surge building up. Shown on the chart to the south-west of the end of the wharf was an area marked for small craft. With *Atmos* showing the way we headed for this. She called us to say that they had found a substantial mooring buoy with a long pick-up line and indicated there was another one near them. We stumbled onto this in the dark, tethering ourselves for the night with a considerable sense of relief. Anchoring conditions were not good, and the thought of beating up and down in such an unpleasant scene was not appealing.

As we were tidying up on deck there was a loud crack above our heads and an apparition descended quite gracefully past our ears into the sea beside us. It was the white genoa rolled up on its furling gear with a ghost-like appearance. I went into slight shock whilst we collected ourselves to lift the casualty out of the water, lashing it down the length of the boat on the guardrail. It was still secured to its stemhead fitting and had done remarkably little damage in coming down. Peering over the stern we could see dangling from the top end of the gear a piece of the heavy stainless-steel bar which takes the upper toggle, the bar being part of the tang assembly at the masthead. It had evidently broken in two.

How incredibly lucky we had been! If it had happened a few minutes earlier whilst we were still banging about in the Straits we could only guess at the damage that would have been done to *Marelle* and itself. We retired for what was left of the night.

Come morning with the weather having taken on a more benign look we went back onto the wharf again. There were our good friends *Atmos* back alongside. They took our lines still with cheery smiles and gave us a copy of the newspaper with our grinning faces on the front. I was promptly back in the Armada offices, this time alive with activity, being directed to the control room for the Straits. I now had two objectives to pursue. Added to the *zarpe* paper trail was to seek help in sorting out our gear problem. Things did not get off to a good start. The non-commissioned officers manning the office spoke no English and I was making only minimal progress in Spanish.

It was at this moment that there was a sudden change for the better. Through the door came a tall young lieutenant who announced 'My name is Yerko. Can I help?' He certainly could. I explained why I was there. There was no problem he said. Apologising quite unnecessarily for his imperfect English he would sort it all out and that was exactly what he did. First was the *zarpe*. He completed the application form with instructions to the petty officer. The system was now working. He explained it all had to go to Valparaiso for approval and that would take twenty-four hours. He would keep an eye on its progress.

Now what about the gear failure? Again no problem. There was a contractor to the Armada who would take care of that. His name was Victor and he would contact me. Having set the wheels in motion Yerko started chatting, informing me he had just returned from a visit to Auckland in New Zealand, spending time with the navy there. He had enjoyed himself thoroughly and spoke well of the people. The opportunity this presented was not to be ignored. On telling him not only was I from New Zealand but also ex-navy, his response was 'What else do you need?' The answer to which was that we required water, diesel and our propane gas bottles refilling. Again no problem. I was beginning to like the sound of that expression.

That afternoon down at the wharf a man appeared dragging a hose over the boats inside us and filled our fresh-water tanks. Shortly after him a team arrived bearing drums of diesel fuel. In turn they were followed by Yerko himself bringing with him Victor for discussion about the repair work. Victor said he would also take care of the gas bottles, which he did, returning later with them fully recharged. It was becoming apparent that when the Armada in that part of the world said jump, everybody did just that. Suddenly the whole picture had changed. We were now full of water, fuel and gas: ready for sea except the furling gear was down rather than up, but that was about to be rectified. In the meantime I had tackled the Chilean bureaucracy to legalise our presence in the country. This was simplicity itself, involving the briefest of interviews with the International Police, linked to Interpol, to cover immigration, and a Customs officer who was wanting to go home to lunch.

No one was worried about our state of health. The longest part of the whole procedure was the time taken to walk between the different offices. I would have loved to have brought our Prefectura friends along to show them how things can be done, hassle-free.

That evening *Atmos II* sailed, having got their *zarpe*. They were off to cruise through Tierra del Fuego, double the Horn then back into the Straits and out into the Pacific. The final leg of their odyssey was to sail to an island which had recently been acquired by the owner. He would take up permanent residency and his crew go home. It sounded rather exotic. We moved off to let them out and they were away with much farewell waving. We were sorry to see them go. It would be a little lonely without them. But as luck would have it we were to see them again.

The wind was rising and with it the now familiar surge alongside the *muelle*. This spelled out an uncomfortable night for us and damage for *Marelle*. We moved out to our buoy for the night. This was to become standard procedure. It was much safer out on the buoy and no one appeared to claim it. We could only guess at the state of its ground tackle but it was more soothing on the nerves than on the wall.

I was still in slight shock over what had befallen us and for which I had a sense of guilt, it being very much my responsibility for gear failure. Jeremy and Fraser came to my aid. They had accepted the situation without any recriminations and were quite relaxed. They made me feel that much better.

It was evident that some of the impetus was slowing on the repair operation. I had been up the mast to inspect the failure. It looked as though crevice corrosion had occurred within the weld zone at the point where the bar had been bent to line up with the angle of the headstay. Fatigue had no doubt exacerbated the weakness to the point that the bar had failed. My feeling of disquiet arose from knowing the bar had been subjected to an alternating load over some years and also, being aware of the unreliability of stainless steel, I had not had the bar crack detected when the mast was off during the refit before we sailed. What was required now was to remove the fitting round the mast, to weld on a new bar and to replace the whole assembly. The furling gear had then to be lifted up. The problem was that the wind, strong most of the time, made working up the mast extremely difficult, worsened by the masthead swaying around due to the surge alongside. The task was going to be very difficult indeed. Victor and his engineer appeared but, as was quite apparent, had their reservations about the operation. So back to the Armada offices for a reappraisal with Yerko. It was beginning to look like a dockyard job. Two miles up the coast on the outskirts of the town there was a repair yard Astillero y Maestranzas de La Armada (ASMAR) for work on naval vessels as well as major repairs on commercial ships. Yerko said he would speak to ASMAR and come back to me. The other option was to do nothing. I thought it was time to review the situation with the team on board. Apart from the repair problem there was the question of the overall reliability of the rest of the stainless-steel components in the roller gear. The alternative was to get rid of it altogether and fall back on using hanked headsails, of which we had a comprehensive wardrobe, onto the moveable forestays. The vote was to stay with the roller gear if possible because of its great convenience. Leaving me with my thoughts the team then went off to progress the restoring programme. It was then I heard voices up top.

Standing on the deck of the next-door fishing boat were three men. Presumably they were something to do with it and if so it would be useful to know if there were any plans to leave. If there were it would involve action on our part to let them out. I launched into a discourse in Spanish aimed at ascertaining something of their movements. In silence they heard me out and then one responded with 'Would it help if we spoke in English?' They were from ASMAR and had come to inspect the repair job. The party was a senior one consisting of Juan Severa, the marketing director, and two technical managers. They were disinclined to go up the mast but inspected the broken piece through the binoculars and departed to think about it, but promised they would certainly fix it. I was to get to know Juan very well over the next few days whilst we explored various solutions, including dangling someone from a crane or to lifting the mast onto the wharf. Juan even suggested hauling *Marelle* up an ASMAR slipway. Fiddling around at the top of a yacht's mast was not really their scene but they were quite firm they would get the job done one way or another. In the end Juan came on board with two young men in tow. They were both mechanics and moreover professional climbers. Apparently in the season they took Japanese parties climbing in the Andes. Perched on top of a mast in a gale of wind would be nothing to them. They would remove the masthead fitting, have a new bar welded on and tested at the university, resecure the assembly in place and lift up into position the roller gear. All this for $380. We agreed warmly with the proposal. The original budget price from the dockyard had been $1,400. Working in the early morning and late in the evening when the wind was at its lightest they completed the work in a couple of days. Once again we were operational. I rounded off their bill and they went off all smiles. So were we. Now that we were once more seaworthy our *zarpe* materialised. It had even been extended to include Cape Horn which meant we would not have to go through the application performance at Puerto Williams. We prepared for sea with hearts uplifted.

Whilst all this had been going on the vacuum left by the departure of *Atmos* was filled by *Enez*. Noel had arrived to wait for his sons to join him for the next leg out into the Pacific. Where in the Pacific he was not sure. He was just going for a sail. Before coming into Punta Arenas he had made a sortie into the channels sampling some of the anchorages. This useful information he was happy to pass on to us over a drink or two. Noel was a very relaxed person. He had divorced his wife, sold his business and set off to cruise the world.

Included in our preparations for sea was to have a shower. Fraser had found one hidden away at the head of the wharf, reporting back on board in triumph. The grim reality was it was cold water only, but no matter. It was our first bodily immersion since leaving Mar del Plata. Any change in the environmental conditions inside the cabin was not remarked upon.

Whilst Jeremy with Fraser completed the store ship programme I went off to supplement our chart library with Chilean charts from *el Instituto Hydrográfico de la Armada de Chile*. These charts, comprehensively covering the region, are works of art in themselves and relatively cheap. Then it was a trip out to ASMAR to thank Juan for all he had done. Later in the afternoon Yerko came on board to say farewell and, with a bottle of Chilean wine opened specially for the occasion, to give us his thoughts on our route. He had a particular request that we should make every endeavour to keep the Armada up to date on our movements in the *canales* by reporting to the couple of control stations in the Beagle Channel, supplemented by relaying our position through any convenient ship we met en route, albeit an unlikely event. I had seen during my last visit to the Armada offices *Marelle*'s name on their operational plot, indicating they would be keeping an eye on us. I gave Yerko my Royal Naval Sailing Association burgee, against all the rules no doubt, as a memento with a little note of thanks. He had done so much to make it all happen. He left and it was early to bed.

Saturday 15 January. The start of the adventure proper. The culmination of all those miles so far. My journal records 'Blew very hard during the night from the west and wondered about our sailing. However the weather was kind to us. The wind moderated and we got away to an easy start at 0735 bidding farewell to Noel in *Enez* lying inside of us, who had popped his head out to wave us off.' We were not to see him again. Another ship passing in the night.

From Punta Arenas the Straits continue south for about forty-five miles before trending round to Cabo Froward where they turn sharply north-west to emerge into the Pacific at the top end of the well-named Isla Desolación. Our first night's anchorage, at Noel's suggestion, was to be Bahia del Aguila thirty-eight miles down the reach to Cabo Froward. We noticed how the terrain had changed since we had left the narrows. In Bahia Gregorio the land, the southern shore of Patagonia, was low, bare, brown and barren. Now as we passed down the coast the land was appreciably higher with forests appearing and dryness replaced by low cloud and mist dampness. Darwin was to remark in similar vein 'It is truly surprising to find in a space of twenty miles such a change in the landscape. If we take a rather greater distance, as between Port Famine and Gregory Bay – that is about sixty miles – the difference is still more wonderful. At the former place we have rounded mountains concealed by impervious forests, which are drenched with the rain brought by an endless succession of gales; while at Cape Gregory there is a clear and bright blue sky over the dry and sterile plains.' Port Famine is near Bahia del Aguila, our choice of anchorage.

By mid-afternoon we were half a mile off Punta Santa Ana, in behind which is Puerto de Hambre. Hambre is Spanish for hunger. This was where Sarmiento built his doomed settlement of Don Felipe from which Viedma lead his wretched band of starving survivors round the shores of the Straits, ending up with the ill-fated meeting with Cavendish near Puerto Sara in Bahia Gregorio.

As he continued west and down the Straits Cavendish was told all about Don Felipe by Hernandez, the one refugee picked off the beach in Gregorio. Rounding Punta Santa Ana Cavendish anchored his ships in the little bay. There laid before them was Don Felipe, deserted except for the corpses of the erstwhile inhabitants who had 'dyed like dogges in their houses, and in their clothes, wherein we found them still at our coming, until that in the ende the towne being wonderfully taynted with the smell and the savour of the dead people'. Cavendish renamed it Port Famine, the name as known to Darwin. Since then the name has had further changes. There are two large-scale charts for the area, each showing a different name. Puerto San Juan de la Posesión and Puerto de Hambre. The latter would be the more appropriate.

As we passed Sarmiento's folly we could see a few small fishing boats in the bay. It is the end of a gravel road, the most southerly road on the American continent, which runs up to Punta Arenas. It allows visitors to come down to gaze at a replica fort on Santa Ana. Why anyone would want to do that I am not sure except perhaps to witness proof of the old adage about history repeating itself. In 1843 the Chileans tried to establish a colony here, including building a fort on Santa Ana. It, like Sarmiento's disaster, ended in failure. The poor soil and hostile climate would not sustain agriculture. It was abandoned and the fort, Fuerte Bulnes, named after the then president, fell into ruins. The reconstructed replica would seem to be a monument to a Chilean authority learning nothing from history.

With no desire to visit such a place we sailed on, heading for Bahia del Aguila, Bay of the Eagle, an anchorage recommended by Noel, ten miles further down the coast. Also we wanted to get further on our way. Tierra del Fuego was beckoning.

Anchoring at 1730 we bedded down for the night using for the first time the tandem anchoring system, the recommended arrangement for coping with the dreaded *Rachas*, otherwise known as williwaws, the horrendous squalls which play such a dominant role in the region's weather. These are violent katabatic winds, the very cold air sweeping down the hillsides, rushing at great speed over the water and then dissipating. Frequently they are up to hurricane strength and can blow a vessel out of the anchorage. Slocum treated them with great respect as he worked up the Straits:

A fair wind from Sandy Point brought me on the first day to St. Nicholas Bay, where I was told I might expect to meet savages; but seeing no signs of life, I came to anchor in eight fathoms of water, where I lay all night under a high mountain. Here I had my first experience with the terrific squalls, called williwaws, which extended from this point through the strait to the Pacific. They are compressed gales of wind that Boreas handed down over the hills in chunks. A full-blown williwaw will throw a ship, even without sail on, over on her beam ends: but, like other gales, they cease now and then, if only for a short time.'

Sandy Point is a translation of Punta Arenas, St. Nicholas Bay is five miles south of our Aguila anchorage and Boreas is the god of the north wind. We were to agree wholeheartedly with Joshua's remarks.

Tandem anchors offered more secure holding than two anchors out on separate cables. With the latter and more traditional method, because of the boat's swing one anchor at a time is taking more than its share of the load, increasing the risk of dragging. Very seldom is the load being borne equally by the two anchors. One anchor in line with the other should mean both are working over a wide range of the boat's swing. The arrangement we adopted was the first anchor down onto the bottom was a 45-pound Bruce onto ten metres of chain shackled onto a CQR which in turn was shackled to the main cable. This was about 62 metres long and into it was spliced a further 30 metres of octoplait nylon rode. We first tried the system in Aguila in deference to the *Pilot's* comments '... good holding; violent squalls at times.' In fact there are few anchorages free of such squalls throughout the channels. For Aguila the *Pilot* adds 'Local knowledge is advisable.' This warning crops up frequently for small craft anchorages throughout the archipelgo but where the authors of the *Pilot* think one can find someone with local knowledge is uncertain. Most of the region is uninhabited. Deserted completely.

It was with some relief that we entered Aguila. The wind had been building steadily, biting into us and bringing up a nasty choppy sea. During the night we were spared the company of any *Rachas* but it blew very hard, reminiscent of Sara. There we were dependent on just the CQR but now we were in more relaxed mode with our double system. I turned over and went back to sleep.

Faced in the morning with the wind still fresh and steady rain, it was tempting to stay put and delay crossing over the Straits to enter the Canal Magdalena. The canal entrance, high-sided and impressive, was enclosed in mistiness, gloomy and uninviting. This was the same vista confronting Darwin when faced with the same passage we were about to undertake:

There was a degree of mysterious grandeur in mountain behind mountain, with deep intervening valleys, all covered by one thick, dusky mass of forest. The atmosphere likewise, in this climate where gale succeeds gale, with rain, hail, and sleet, seems blacker than anywhere else. In the Strait of Magellan, looking southward from Port Famine, the distant channels between the mountains appeared from their gloominess to lead beyond the confines of this world.

In the Magdalena our next anchorage was Puerto Hope, another Noel recommendation, and our first stop in Tierra del Fuego. It was only twenty-one miles but they were to be the longest twenty-one miles I could recall for many a day. With temptation overcome and backbones stiffened we pushed out into the Straits and turned south.

Aguila had been a place of particular interest, marking a complete change from the Straits we had known up till then. From the Virgins down as far as Fuerte Bulnes there was civilisation and development of the land bordering the Straits. Aguila was a complete break from all of that environment. No one lived in Aguila and there was no sign anyone ever had, apart from the ruins of a small building, deserted and being taken over by the bush. Our anchorage was surrounded by silence, sombre and damp, a world unto itself. This was the world of Tierra del Fuego. Here nature was in authority. The freedom from the jarring clamour of people was sublime.

Puerto Hope lies just inside the entrance to the Magdalena on its western side. The canal itself opens out from the south side of the Straits just short of Cape Froward. This cape with a distinct similarity to Cape Horn plays a dominant role in the *paso*. One can only wonder from whence the name 'Froward' originated. Dictionaries have it as medieval English for 'stubbornly self-willed' or 'perverse'. In the *Diccionario Geográfico Náutico* by Alberto Mantellero there are equally unflattering expressions *rebelde, odioso* and *hostil*. Froward has never enjoyed a supportive press. Distinctly uncompromising in mien, it had given its namer, Thomas Cavendish, a rough ride. It certainly would have seemed entirely appropriate to Cavendish to apply such a sobriquet to that obdurate obstacle to his progression up the Straits. Froward was to feature in the denouement of his plot to get at Spanish riches in the Pacific, the vexations associated with the struggle to round the headland contributing to his giving up and subsequent decline into physical and emotional wreckage.

Sarmiento, when he rounded the cape the easy way from west to east, seven years before Cavendish, had a comparatively easy ride which disposed him to name it after a saint, Santa Agueda. FitzRoy, it would appear, was an admirer of Sarmiento as a navigator and was inclined on his charts to use the Spaniard's choice of names, but in the end Cavendish's heartfelt title prevailed.

The cape has a special geographical significance, marking as it does the southernmost tip of the American continent. Successive Chilean governments have felt this should be recognised. On Froward's forehead there is an 80-foot tubular steel structure, erected in 1987 after its two predecessors had been blown away. The occasion was to mark the visit to Chile of the Pope, Su Santidad Juan Pablo II. We were not to enjoy a sighting of *la Cruz de los Mares,* the Cross of the Seas, as predictably enough the 'perverse' one had wrapped itself in dark cloud.

The *Pilot* treats it with respect: 'At Cabo Froward exceptionally heavy squalls are experienced. The weather frequently changes to heavy rain or snow, and the shores are often obscured.' It was a hard passage for us, close on the wind which was blowing very strongly up the Straits, raising a most unpleasant head sea. We were motor-sailing under staysail and barely making a knot over the ground. Over on our starboard beam was the brooding mass of Cabo Froward, wreathed in its misty rain. Ahead stretched the ravine of the Magdalena canal, lost in the distance in misty nothingness. Just when we thought we would never get there the wind freed to let us pass into the canal and enter Hope. It was beautiful. A magnificent, fully protected deep inlet surrounded by scenery reminding me of the southern fjords of New Zealand. We were ringed by steep wooded hills leading up to snow slopes and rocky outcrops. It was completely deserted and there was no sound. I recorded the feeling 'One could say all our journeying and travails have been worth it just to be here, our first anchorage in the land of fire.'

We liked it here so much, and feeling we had earned a little rest, it was decreed the next day would be a rest day. Apart from a pair of kelp geese the place was ours until completely unexpectedly we heard voices hailing us. Passing were two very small fishing boats which went right up to the head of the inlet, dropped stern anchors and thrust their bows into the trees. They would be bomb-proof against any *Rachas*. Puerto Hope would seem not always to have been deserted. There is an early print showing some Yahgan Indian families outside their wigwams on the beach being friendly to a sailor in a boat. In the background is a small sailing vessel which could have been a sealer. Alternatively it may be *Hope*, a tender to Captain Parker King's ship *Adventure.* He had discovered the inlet in 1826. It is a sad scene, witness to how defenceless the Yahgans were against their impending destruction.

We had been flying in the face of fortune, according to the *Pilot*, in coming here. 'The inner part of the cove, a basin known as La Paza, can be entered by small craft but it is subject to violent squalls and is not recommended.' The Good Book was right. That night proved to be one of full-blown *Rachas* with ferocious gusts exceeding anything we had experienced so far. I got up at about 0400, made a cup of cocoa and kept an anchor watch, but I must say in some comfort, watching my shore marks through the galley window. *Marelle* was pulling her cable out in the blasts but would always ride back onto the starting transits. Tweedle Dum and Tweedle Dee on the sea bed were doing their duty. By breakfast time the *Rachas* had lost their viciousness. The fishing boats departed and so did we.

The canal had got a grip on Darwin's imagination and fascinated him.

Captain FitzRoy determined to leave the Strait of Magellan by the Magdalen Channel, which had not been long discovered. Our course lay due south, down that gloomy passage which I have before alluded to as appearing to lead to another and worse world. The wind was fair, but the atmosphere was very thick, so that we missed much curious scenery. The dark ragged clouds were rapidly driven over the mountains, from their summits nearly down to their bases … we anchored at Cape Turn, close to Mount Sarmiento, which was then hidden in the clouds … But it would be difficult to imagine a scene where (man) seemed to have fewer claims or less authority. The inanimate works of nature – rock, ice, snow, wind, and water – all warring with each other, yet combined against man, here reigned in absolute sovereignty.

Darwin was not quite right, historically, with his reference to 'the Magdalen Channel, which had not long been discovered.' In fact it had been found and named by Sarmiento de Gamboa way back in 1580.

Outside in the channel the wind had departed completely. There were twenty-five miles to cover to our next overnight stop at Puerto King. This was to be the pattern over the next few weeks. Relatively short day sails, arriving at the next selected anchorage in time to bed the boat down for the night. It is possible to navigate the channels by night but not desirable and certainly not without radar, something we didn't have. There are few navigational marks, with the added problem of the charted positions being well adrift from the GPS coordinates, particularly on latitude. There is also the undesirability of being under way when hit by a *Racha* at night in poor visibility. The *canales* are very much eyeball pilotage, best conducted in daylight.

Under power we rounded Cape Turn, behind which *Beagle* had anchored, marvelling at the seamanship required to work a square-rigged vessel up these intricate waterways. They are bad enough in a handy, close-winded yacht with an iron horse to call upon. The only thing in his favour with winter coming on (they were there in early June) was a slightly greater chance of picking up an easterly. Nevertheless FitzRoy must have been a superb ship handler. At this point the Magdalena turns to run west and we were overhauled by a Chilean-owned luxury yacht, *Gloriana,* an 80-foot Swan design with a British skipper. Her complement was on deck photographing this rather quaint, weather-beaten wooden boat as they forged past under power. In deference to our instructions we asked them if they would report us to the Armada, a request which the skipper acknowledged. We had encountered this craft in Punta Arenas in which she had made a brief stop, Fraser and Jeremy being specifically requested to help with her shore lines when she came alongside the *muelle.* Her skipper had been a little concerned, not unnaturally, about the manoeuvre. Our two lads had been a trifle put out by the rather cavalier way they had been thanked for their efforts.

Puerto King is tiny. Too small to warrant a write-up in the *Pilot* but covered well in the RCC pilot, albeit with some confusion over its precise position. Find it we did but so tight for *Marelle* to squeeze into that a discussion ensued between Jeremy and me on which way round we should position her. As always the pivotal question was '*Rachas* to be or not to be?' Being katabatic winds, in theory if one was anchored off low-lying land the likelihood of a *Racha* was reduced. The thinking is probably right but we were to learn that not all theories are related to fact. In this part of the world squalls are laws unto themselves. An added factor was the complication in persuading *Marelle* to turn in a confined space. I have mentioned this to her before, always to get the same response 'I was built for sailing, not motor-boating.'

In the end Jeremy's opinion prevailed and we bedded down with the bows to the east, that is pointing out of the little cove. The anchors would then hold her against an easterly blow and as the head of King is low there was not a great likelihood of a *Racha* blasting her out of the anchorage. The issue had boiled down to which was of greater moment. To land up on the beach or be blown out into the strait. As this was an argument that was not going to have a tidy ending we called it a day and retired below for a drink. We had a peaceful night.

Puerto King is a good viewing location for Monte Sarmiento, lying only fifteen miles to the east. It is one of the showpieces of Tierra del Fuego. With a charted height of 7,330 feet it is the tallest named peak in the archipelago, earning a special mention in the *Pilot*: 'Monte Sarmiento, the most prominent and beautiful mountain in Tierra del Fuego … is covered with perpetual snow and is nearly always enveloped in cloud, but with E winds, cold weather and a clear sky it presents a magnificent appearance.' Unfortunately for us the comment about cloud cover was only too true. We were only able to glimpse the lower slopes. Not so however for Darwin when at Cape Turn, just four miles from where we were lying in King. 'In the morning we were delighted by seeing the veil of mist gradually rise from Sarmiento and display it to our view.'

After our trouble-free night we cleared King and turned west into Canal Cockburn. We were still very much in FitzRoy territory, so many names around us being attributable to him. King was after Captain Parker King RN. In command of *Adventure*, with *Beagle* as consort under Captain Pringle Stokes RN during her first period of duty in the Horn region, he commenced in 1826 a survey of those southern waterways. What those dedicated men accomplished is so admirably summed up by Felix Riesenberg:

> The year 1826 saw the beginning of the most thorough exploration and charting work ever done in Tierra del Fuego, an enterprise that found Cape Horn and the Strait of Magellan without any co-ordinated surveys. During an interval of ten years from 1826 to 1836, with some time out between two commissions, the British Admiralty laid the network of our geographic knowledge of the great Fuegian Archipelago. But so intricate are these shores, so difficult are the hydrography and the terrain, that today many hundreds of miles of shoreline and large areas of the interior still remain unknown.

But the work took its toll. In the end Captain Stokes had had enough and shot himself. *Beagle*'s new commanding officer was Robert FitzRoy.

We were expecting the Cockburn Channel to be hard work with a beat of twenty-five miles against the prevailing westerly wind to Puerto Niemann at the end of the channel. The start was not too promising, damp and misty with the cold wind in our teeth. It was along here that FitzRoy had worked *Beagle* for his final departure from the scene of all his endeavours. It would seem to have been a happy moment shared by Darwin.

Cockburn was a well-chosen name bestowed by Parker King on one of the region's significant features. Admiral of the Fleet Sir George Cockburn was a Lord of the Admiralty when Parker King was appointed to *Adventure*. Cockburn was a man of influence and very much a fully paid-up member of the Establishment. Parker King no doubt felt it would do his own career no harm if he were to be perceived as being instrumental in the great man's name passing down in perpetuity to future generations of seafarers.

As we progressed up the channel the situation improved with the wind veering enough for us to lay Puerto Niemann on a close reach. We began to think about arriving in time for tea and cake, anchored and at rest. With only a couple of miles to go, however, the scene changed dramatically. A dense black wicked-looking cloud formed ahead of us. The indications were something particularly nasty was heading our way. It was. A driving hail storm and biting wind lashed down onto us. I was on the wheel and having a hard time. The hailstones were exceedingly painful and nearly blinding me as through slits of eyes I tried to see where we were going. A note in my journal captures it. 'Dear old Jeremy appeared from below wearing his skiing goggles with his face wrapped up and took over. He is a kindly old soul.'

The entrance to Niemann is narrow and then opens out into an enclosed bay three-quarters of a mile across. Where best to anchor? The RCC pilot had two recommendations but they looked as though they would involve some intricate mooring work. Admiral Mantellero's pilot showed a spot under the western shore. This looked nice and simple. Although under high ground and hence good for *Racha* breeding, Niemann was not shown in the pilotage literature as being prone to this problem. The *Pilot* comments 'The harbour is protected from all winds, and no swell enters.' It adds an item of interest: 'secure to trees and take water from a waterfall.' It was just that place we chose to anchor.

Niemann is on the north side of Canal Cockburn where it swings south-west and out into the Southern Ocean. Fifteen miles from Niemann down the channel is the Canal Brecknock, heading south-east towards the Beagle Channel, our ultimate objective. Our next immediate target was the western opening into the Brecknock. Those fifteen miles can be dangerous. The Southern Ocean maintains its uninterrupted sweep round the globe until it hits Tierra del Fuego. Part of it tries to force its way up into the Cockburn Channel and can cut up very rough indeed. The *Pilot* gives it due respect: 'Paso Brecknock, especially at its NW end, is exposed to the full force of the prevailing W winds; it frequently suffers stormy weather with sudden reductions in visibility and squalls of great violence.' One wants to choose one's weather if possible for making the crossing.

Yerko who knew those waters only too well made a big point about us staying in Niemann until we were sure about the weather before making the dash in daylight down to the Brecknock.

Puerto Niemann has only received due recognition as a refuge in the last forty-five years, taking its name from Capitán de Corbeta don Otto Niemann of the Armada. He was looking for a secure anchorage to provide shelter whilst waiting for favourable weather before heading south across the exposed *paso*. We were to put his discovery to good purpose, albeit with some problems.

The water in Niemann is deep and to anchor we had to put *Marelle*'s bow close to the beach before there was anchorable depth. Down went the Bruce followed by the trusty CQR as we went astern into deep water. At the same time to welcome us and to show who was boss in those parts down came a *Racha*, an extraordinarily violent one. Anxiously we watched our shore transits but the tandems took it in their stride; so much so that we broke the golden rule and did not run lines ashore. A big mistake. Getting dark, we were more interested in retreating down below. With the Blake paraffin heater aglow and the oil lamps alight it was seductively snug, warm and dry. Another world to that outside. 'This is what I like,' said Fraser, 'it is one of the best parts of the whole cruise.' And so it was.

We decided a day of rest was called for. Poor old Fraser was suffering with a bad bout of diarrhoea, about which he made little comment but was obviously in some distress. So out with The Book, *The Ship Captain's Medical Guide*. This was its first appearance since the wounding of Jeremy off Brazil. It confirmed liquids, very light meals and no alcohol. I applied the treatment with iron authority, though I suspected Fraser thought I might have been a little too enthusiastic. He liked his food. It was my turn as duty cook, preparing chilli con carne on rice for Jeremy and me and certainly inappropriate for Fraser. He could only sit and stare. I think he thought I had done it deliberately. It was a day of wind and rain. We all went to bed at nine that evening at the end of the dreary day, nevertheless noting 'God this is a wild place but strangely enough I like it.'

The morn brought no improvement. 'Blowing like hell', overcast and drizzly damp. We were cognisant of Yerko's words about sitting it out and waiting for the change. The *Rachas* came back with a vengeance and settled in for the afternoon. We started to drag. First action was to let go the fisherman anchor on its rode but before it took any weight we were too near a beach under our lee. It was only after a tremendous struggle that we were able to recover the anchors but even so had to leave the Bruce hanging under the bows as its recovery line had gone. The tandem system incorporates a line from one anchor to the other to facilitate hauling the first anchor with its length of chain round the bow and up to its bow roller. We went round to the 'bullet proof' niche recommended by the RCC pilot but it didn't look promising with the wind blowing directly into the mooring area. We could never have held the boat in position whilst we got the lines ashore, the problem being compounded by the Bruce dragging under us. So back to the original anchorage, this being the only viable option. It was blowing with unbelievable ferocity. We could see the hurricane-force wind hurtling across the bay bringing with it a white wall, a metre or more high, of solid water under a thick veil of swirling spray, lifted off the sea surface. It would hit us like a hammer blow, heeling *Marelle* over till her lee decks were under water. Slocum used the expression 'a shot from a cannon' when writing about his williwaws. With the boat out of control, Fraser and Jeremy struggling with the anchors on the foredeck could only hang on as best they could on the near-vertical deck. The impact of wind and water brought us up dead, even with full throttle. Then the engine would stop. After weeks of faultless performance it started to play up and dangerously this time; but it would restart. We were being subjected to a series of these knockdowns, each time getting closer to the downwind side of the bay. If the engine could not have been restarted all we could have done was to try to work out under a rag of sail through the entrance and back into the Cockburn, but I would not have given much for our chances in those winds. That dangerous, rocky lee shore was too close. What the conditions were like out there didn't bear thinking about. The engine did continue to restart and we slowly clawed our way back to the original anchorage but further over to gain more protection from the stunted trees. This time we got in even closer, with the bows up to the sandy foreshore before the Bruce dangling beneath us touched the bottom.

There was no question of any dinghy use in that wind to get lines ashore but we held as those terrible gusts continued. We were keeping anchor watches but I could not sleep and was wide awake at three in the morning when I heard Fraser from the cockpit 'Ben, we are dragging and dragging fast out into the bay!' All hands turned to in a rush to recover the anchors but as we turned to clear the anchorage we came very close to a spur of land jutting out from a little sandy cove under our stern. I was in the driving seat and knew we would clear, if only just, but it seemed to the team on the foredeck that all was lost. Jeremy said afterwards he was working out how best to set up a camp on the beach. He had in mind a similar fate that had overtaken Hal Roth, when he and his wife with one crew were blown ashore by a *Racha* onto a beach just north of the Horn. They lived in a makeshift camp until rescued by the Chilean Navy.

It had been a Herculean task for Fraser and Jeremy with the anchors in the wind, rain and darkness. Having sorted out the ground tackle yet again we re-anchored, still worryingly beset with repeated engine failures. Making Fraser and Jeremy turn in, they were exhausted with what they had been through, I kept an anchor watch until breakfast time. Those appallingly violent squalls kept coming and I have a desperate little note, 'God Almighty will this cursed wind ever give up?'

It did. As the morning progressed our world took on a less hostile appearance and belatedly we ran out two shore lines. We started seeing a murky sun with an occasional glimpse of blue sky. We were over the worst and Fraser and I even had a little walk on the foreshore, stumbling through the wind-blown straggly growth and tangled vegetation.

We had survived the fury of the infamous *Rachas*, albeit with all too little to spare. They are a phenomen which has to be experienced first-hand to appreciate to the full their viciousness and menace. We could now have a complete understanding of the typically unembellished reference in the *Pilot* to those wind effects in the region. 'Violent and often unpredictable squalls with, on occasion, gusts in excess of 100 knots occur most often along the S and W coasts of the continent and also around the Falkland Islands. These squalls may, at times, be only of short duration but nevertheless can reduce the visibility to less than 5 cables in precipitation. Some respite from these squalls occurs when high pressure becomes established over the area but this seldom lasts for more than a few days.' In other words get going when the going is good.

Although throughout the archipelago we were subject to the onslaught of *Rachas* or williwaws, in our experience they were possibly more frequent in the western isles and also perhaps more violent. Certainly they featured prominently in the log kept by the tragically fated Captain Stokes of *Beagle* during her first commission in those waters. His observations are transcribed so graphically by Riesenberg in his absorbing book *Cape Horn*:

The south-west gales, blowing from the southern ocean with extreme force, are scooped up by the mountains impeding them. They roar over the lee cliffs of steep bare precipices, tearing off as it were, and descending perpendicularly. The surface of the water, when struck by these mighty downward blasts, boils with foam, picked up by the winds. Clouds of heavy scud drive screaming across the Strait. A ship may lie at anchor close under a high shore, seemingly safe, when *williwaws* suddenly throw her over. The next moment she rides upright; again a squall strikes her – as like as not, on the opposite beam – and back she heels. Up she rides on her cable, is caught again on her nose, surges back with a tremendous shock, her riding bitts straining. All hands are at stations ready to veer [cable], but there is no room. To stand out, casting into the storm, especially at night, would have been madness.

Old Slocum would have joined us in *Marelle* in appreciating to the full what the captain was on about.

With the passing through of the lows we planned an 0430 start next morning to tackle the run down the Cockburn Channel and to gain the shelter of the Brecknock before the next front arrived.

I was awake at 0400 and it felt calm outside. With the feeling we should get away and not waste this gift from God I was thinking about calling the others when the alarm went off. As is his wont, Jeremy had set it early. A good move as it turned out. Emerging on deck there was a moment of panic. During the night the wind had gone right round and we were now on a lee shore. All that was holding us off the beach was the great bight of chain lying on the bottom. We held her clear with the engine whilst the lines were let go and anchors recovered. This was where Fraser was so good. In record time we were under way through the entry passage and out into the Cockburn. There was almost no wind with a long, high swell lazing in. Ahead there was no sign of any broken water. The Southern Ocean was sleeping. We congratulated ourselves on the success of our tactics in sitting it out in Niemann and at the same time doing our best to put on one side the price we had paid whilst in there.

Seven or eight miles ahead to the south were the East and West Furies, isolated rocky patches, between which *Beagle* had sailed before turning northwards into the Pacific. I wondered whether they had been just as docile when Darwin and FitzRoy had viewed these same Furies, so named because of the hundred-knot squalls to which they are prone. Perhaps not. Rather as a postscript Darwin adds 'a little further northward there are so many breakers that the sea is called the Milky Way. One sight of such a coast is enough to make a landsman dream for a week about shipwrecks, peril, and death,' concluding, 'with this sight we bade farewell forever to Tierra del Fuego.'

With the breeze picking up we cut the corner into Paso Brecknock by passing down Canal Ocasión to enter the Brecknock proper at 0930. We relaxed with a feeling of being home and dry. From now onwards we would be heading east, having reached our most westerly point, closing the longitude gap with home even though that seemed a long, long way ahead. Niemann had been an experience we would never forget and one to echo Darwin's final sentiments as *Beagle* cleared the Furies.

From now onwards, we fondly thought, we should have predominantly fair winds. Reality was not to be quite like that but at least we got off to a good start. No matter it was raining and very cold. 'We were with instead of against,' as Fraser put it. A grand sail with eased sheets down the Brecknock brought us to the chosen anchorage for the night at a hole in the wall, Caleta Atracadero. The name means quay, but of one there was no sign. This time we were going to it properly in accordance with the book. All anchors down and the full outfit of shore lines. But what a performance it was to be with the wind deciding to go into the east which meant blowing straight into the anchorage. We had to drop the tandems well out, turn M*arelle* and try to persuade her to ease herself stern first into the niche. Not being very good at this, she needed help. Again in situations such as these Fraser's contribution was so valuable. He had become our shore-line party, an exclusive role. He was rapidly perfecting the art of running four lines ashore and finding suitable trees or boulders as anchorages. He was getting it all together now with smooth efficiency. On this occasion he had to add to his repertoire by first having to pull *Marelle*'s stern around. As a grand finale the poor chap had then to take, in the dinghy, the fisherman with its chain and warp to lay it all out well ahead. I felt I might have been playing the age game a bit but Fraser stoutly maintained he enjoyed all this dinghy work. I believe he meant it. With three anchors down and four lines ashore we felt reasonably relaxed. The mooring arrangements were not put to the test. It was a *Racha*-free night.

In my bunk that night I did an audit of where we stood now that we were halfway through the Tierra del Fuego cruise. The balance sheet was looking healthy, it seemed to me. For *Marelle* the only significant problem remained the engine, suspected as being a victim of contaminated fuel. I had run out of biocide, but hopefully would be replenishing stocks in the Falklands. I had asked Susan to bring some with her when she flew down to Stanley. On the human side, although I could only speak for myself, I was happy about that and felt I could congratulate myself on my crew. 'Old Jeremy is a stabilising influence and Fraser a pillar of strength and reliability.' I was pleased to see how well they got on together. Both were extraordinarily well informed about the sailing scene in the West Country and in particular on boats and personalities around the Falmouth waterfront. The harmonious dialogue was beneficial and I was happy for them to chatter on. Two factors I thought which contributed significantly to the good degree of compatibility prevailing in the boat. Firstly, we were busy. Working the boat in frequently demanding circumstances took up much of our time and in a sharing way. There was no time for boredom leading to dangerous idle thoughts. Secondly, each individual was able to enjoy a measure of privacy despite living on top of ourselves. After dinner, our time was our own, assuming the elements outside were obliging. Reading and listening to music through headphones, or writing, we were each in our own world, to be followed by an early turn-in for a long night's sleep through to the 0730 morning cup of tea. At sea there was no problem. The days were taken up with the sea routine.

With the bows pointing down the channel leaving Atracadero was fairly painless. With the fisherman holding the bow and one stern line we could get the tandems in and the other lines recovered in a relaxed manner. We were off down the Canal Balleneros, the next channel taking over from the Brecknock. There may have been a Welshman here at some time as Brecknock or Brecon is a town in south Wales. However the *Diccionario* states that the Brecknock was surveyed and named by Robert FitzRoy in 1830 '*en honor al Conde de Brecknock*'. Whoever that gentleman was, he certainly has an impressive memorial.

Ahead lay Puerto Engaño in which is tucked Caleton Silva, our next haven, on Isla Londonderry thirty-five miles further on. To get there we had to cross over Bahia Desolada. This was to be our last direct exposure to the Southern Ocean until later when heading south to the Horn. It deserves its name. The general appearance is one of barrenness and desolation. What growth there is struggles for a foothold in whatever shelter it can find from the salt-laden wind, relentlessly sweeping over the bay, more often than not with gale-force strength.

It was an area that caused FitzRoy considerable stress and aggravation. Whilst anchored under the doubtful protection of the equally well named Cabo Desolación at the south-western approach to Bahia Desolada, *Beagle* lost one of her whaleboats. It had been stolen by some Canoe Indians, known as the Alacaluf, whilst a party from the ship was ashore surveying. To get back to *Beagle* they constructed something resembling a coracle from reeds, caulked with clay. They referred to it as their 'bloody basket'. The scene of their embarrassing misfortune is on the chart as Isla Basket, the top of which we passed close to when entering Atracadero.

No trace of the whaleboat was found except an oar and on another island the boat's leadline. Desolada Bay is studded with exotic names like Isla Burnt and its neighbour Smoke, as well as a Cabo Longchase, dating back to the whaleboat incident.

Ahead of us as we crossed the bay we could see a sail which on getting nearer was none other than *Atmos II*. She was on her way to the western channels and then up to Puerto Montt before entering the Pacific. They reported a rough doubling of the Horn and spoke well of the anchorage at Caleton Silva which they had just left. They enquired if we had any news about other fellow-cruisers, in particular of Roger, last seen in Mardel. We both, it would seem, were worried about that intrepid little chap all on his own. Motor-sailing they disappeared westward towards Canal Brecknock. We were not to see them again.

It was extraordinarily peaceful and relaxed at anchor in Silva. We could only guess it had been named after Nuñez da Silva, Drake's pilot when in these waters. In bright sunlight and no wind we enjoyed our evening drink. Our world of our own ceased to be just that as out of the gap between the islands lying to the east of us emerged a cruise ship. She had come through the Canal O'Brien down which we would transit, come the morning. We wondered vaguely about the ship's destination but one thing was sure, as she made her exit from the Brecknock, in this weather sundowner drinks were not likely to be spilled. We could only hope so.

It had been a restful night, wet with heavy rain but no vice. In a grey, cold morning we headed out into Whaleboat Sound, yet another reminder of FitzRoy's trials and tribulations, with Isla O'Brien looming large and mist-enveloped before us. Along its southern flank is the Canal O'Brien, narrow with strong currents overlooked by steep, frowning hillsides, covered with stunted beech forests, plunging into the sea. The island itself is high, over 2,000 feet, and front-of-stage to the Cordillera Darwin which extends in the background to the north for eighty miles from Canal Magdalena down to where the Beagle Channel proper starts. At the western end of the mountain range, the Cordillera, is Monte Sarmiento and at the south-eastern end rises Monte Darwin, reaching 6,965 feet. Spread out along the length of the Cordillera are peaks of comparable height, permanently snow-enshrouded. Interspersed are extended fields of snow through which protrude outcrops of black jagged rocks riven with deep clefts of ice. 'Strong outlines, marked on a lurid sky' as seen by Darwin. It was so beautiful.

This southernmost thrust of the mighty Andes remains an outpost, isolated and completely remote from human existence. It was not until 1962 that Eric Shipton was the first to put a footstep onto its largely inaccessible heights but even today it occupies the world of the unknown.

Emerging from this completely silent and still passage we entered the Paso Timbales. Somewhere here was an Armada reporting point, and

Yerko had made much of us contacting this station to report on our progress. He had told us they had been forewarned of our impending arrival in their space. On calling them up there was an immediate response but no visible sign of the station whereabouts. We were questioned at great length on our wanderings, where we were going and our personal details. With their imperfect English and my equally imperfect Spanish the dialogue was protracted. We finally got there and in the typical Chilean friendly and courteous way they wished us well, finishing off by thanking me for our help! Some time after this exchange we emerged from the *paso* to be called up again. The station wanted to confirm that what they were looking at was in fact *Marelle*. I was pleased we had done the right thing. A little further on we sighted what we assumed was the Timbales station. It had to be, as nowhere else in the area was there any sign of human existence. Just a couple of small buildings clinging to a steep slope running down to the sea. Totally isolated. The voice had explained there was only himself and his family and it sounded happy.

A mile or two on we bedded down for the night in Caleta Cushion at the eastern end of Isla Chair. This was typical FitzRoy. In the course of his survey the names would have offered themselves as self-evident when drawn out on the chart. What a special little place it was too. A gem. A little tricky to get into with once again the wind blowing in rather than out but this time we were better organised. Fraser was launched in the dinghy to go in ahead of us, taking with him the first of the lines and securing them ashore. A return to collect the other lines and then a trip out to sea with the fisherman, complete with its buoy. With this secured from the stern we were nicely in position.

A feature of all these anchorages and indeed throughout the archipelago is kelp. It was something we had to watch constantly. The *Pilot* makes special mention of it: 'Kelp grows on most dangers having a rocky or stony bottom, especially in channels and inlets.' Growing kelp should invariably be regarded as a sign of danger; ... vessels should never pass through growing kelp if it can be avoided.'

Darwin was fascinated by it, or brown seaweed as he referred to it. 'I believe, during the voyages of the *Adventure* and *Beagle*, not one rock near the surface was discovered which was not buoyed by this floating weed. The good service it thus affords to vessels navigating near this stormy land is evident; and it certainly has saved many a one from being shipwrecked.' As a naturalist it provided him with an interest transcending the navigational. 'The number of living creatures of all orders, whose existence intimately depends on the kelp, is wonderful. A great volume might be written describing the inhabitants of one of these beds of seaweed. I can only compare these great aquatic forests of the southern hemisphere with the terrestrial ones in the intertropical regions.'

A mere four miles from Cushion is the entrance to Seno Garibaldi. Eight miles up it at the head is a clutch of glaciers, dominated by Ventisquero Garibaldi itself which according to Mantellero is 'the most beautiful glacier of the Darwin cordillera'. We were not to have any cause to doubt him. The glacier takes its rather out-of-context name from a small sailing vessel of that name, an affectionately regarded veteran of the *canales*, commanded by an old *lobo de mar*, old sea wolf or rather dog, with the imagination-stirring name of Fortunato Bevan. About Garibaldi we had some discussion. There was a marked difference of attitudes. I had seen glaciers before in the Antarctic and the south island of my native New Zealand but Fraser had not. He was all for an excursion up to the Garibaldi. Jeremy agreed with him. He quite rightly pointed out that 'we should be seeing these major sights in this once-in-a-lifetime trip.' I weakly stated my preference was to force on and cover another thirty miles and moreover conserve fuel. I was worrying about the fuel situation. Jeremy demolished this argument with 'You are always saying we are short of fuel when invariably there is more in the tank than you admit.' We left Cushion and turned into Seno Garibaldi. I was very glad we did.

The wind blowing in the narrow sound was all over the place so it was a case of engine all the way to get as close to the face as possible. Garibaldi comes right down to the sea with brash ice spilling out from the base, keeping us a little way from the actual face. The glacier is a wonderful spectacle. Blue and white, filling the wide ravine between steep cliffs, its wide sweep escalating upwards to vanish into the mists of the cordillera. Down the centre was a narrow clearly defined discoloured streak. This apparently is known in geological circles as medial moraine and is the result of two glaciers coming together higher up in the mountains with the scrapings from the sides of the ravine joining forces in the middle of the new combined flow. Our visit had been a tremendous experience.

Passing back down the seno we met a small cruise ship, *Terra Australis,* which had been in and out of Punta Arenas during our stay. With a cheery salutation from her bridge staff she carried on with her band of tourists, although none was evident on deck. Maybe it was tiffin time, which would be more important perhaps than looking at what was around them. Sightseeing for the confirmed tourist can be so boring.

Emerging from Garibaldi we crossed over the canal into Babia Tres Brazos in which lay Caleta Julia. Small and pretty. Jeremy put us neatly in between two outcrops of rocks whilst Fraser had the lines ashore and the fisherman out off the bow with naval precision. This was definitely not a *Racha* breeding locality so we could dispense with the heavy weights, the tandems. The rough and tough conditions in the west of the region were moving into the realm of nightmare memories. The improvement was largely because of the changed terrain with its gentler slopes rather than the climate looking more kindly on us. Here in the east it was still cold, damp and gloomy but the wind was inclined to be less aggressive. The eastern coves tended to be more gentle with tree-lined shores and wild fuchsias growing. The colour seemed a little out of place in the stern surroundings.

I had a special motive in coming in to Julia, having a little friend of that name, a fan of *Marelle*'s who with her parents has sailed with me. I knew she, also being small and pretty, would like this Julia. It was certainly lovely, completely still and as nature had formed it. A peace descended on our souls. 'I still find it hard to take in that here we are in this wild, magnificent and hostile outpost of civilisation. So far away from all that is familiar to us in our "natural" world at home.' Caleta Julia was not hostile at the moment but the threat in the air was present.

Seventy-eight miles to Puerto Williams with Caleta Olla next stop twenty-five miles down the channel, which by now had become the Brazo Noroeste, that is the north-west arm of the Beagle Channel. Puerto Williams, the jumping-off point for the Horn, would also mark the end of the Tierra del Fuego cruise. I wanted to get there but at the same time I did not want this to finish. We had to resist the urge to linger on in attractive Julia.

With a good following breeze down the Brazo we entered Glacier Alley. Over the next six-and-a-half miles marched a row of six big glaciers side by side like a parade of soldiers on an inspection. They are all different and each in its own way spectacular. Some flow down to the sea, others stop further back, hanging over bold rock precipices. Down the cliff faces pour waterfalls. The glaciers have been given exotic names with a national flavour. Ventisqueros España, Romanche, Alemania, Francia, Italia and Holanda. It was probably at the foot of Romanche where FitzRoy and Darwin working up the Brazo in two of *Beagle*'s boats took a lunchtime break. This was to bring them to the brink of disaster. Let Darwin recall what happened:

The boats being hauled on shore ... we were admiring from the distance of half a mile a perpendicular cliff of ice and were wishing that some fragments would fall. At last, down came a mass with a roaring noise, and immediately we saw the smooth outline of a wave travelling towards us. The men ran down as quickly as they could to the boats: for the chance of their being dashed to pieces was evident. One of the seamen just caught hold of the bows, as the curling breaker reached it: he was knocked over and over, but not hurt; and the boats, though thrice lifted on high and let fall again, received no damage. This was most fortunate for us, for we were a hundred miles distance from the ship and we should have been left without provisions or fire-arms.

Darwin was most impressed by these glaciers and describes the scene so well. 'It is scarcely possible to imagine anything more beautiful than the beryl-like blue of these glaciers, and especially as contrasted with the dead white of the upper expanse of snow.' Fittingly they all have one thing in common. Their birthplace is high up in the Cordillera Darwin.

Fraser, who up to a few days before had not seen a glacier, was now getting his fill. All too soon we were at the eastern end of the Brazo and with a stiffening wind sailed into the most beautiful of *caletas*, Olla, which lies at the junction of the Brazo and its parent Beagle Channel. It is here that Ventisquero Holanda, the last of the line-up of the ice cascades, ends its majestic descent.

Olla was one of the scenic gems of our cruise. A good well-protected anchorage, even though Mantellero warns of williwaws down the high slope on the north side. Ringed around by a beach with tall trees and a landscape rising through wooded slopes to faces of bare rock and on to snow fields. It is a most pleasing sight. From a knoll above the cove there is a grand sweeping view up the length of the Brazo Noroeste vanishing in the far distance into a backdrop of snow-covered peaks. Deserted, no one lives there or has lived in the cove since the Indian tribes were made extinct. But not completely deserted. Fraser on the beach checking his shore lines disturbed a fox gnawing at them. Darwin refers to two kinds of foxes he found, on one of which he bestowed the name *Canis magellanicus*.

On the south shore of the Beagle Channel, a little further down from Olla, is Caleta Awaiakirrh, mentioned in Mantellero's *Navigator Guide* as a useful anchorage but also with star billing. 'This cove is very special ... if you are fond of the history of this Beagle Channel tribe (Yamanas).' Situated on the north coast of the large island of Isla Hoste, it is connected to its southern shore by a low, narrow isthmus over which the Yahgans (or Yamanas as they called themselves, meaning 'people') transported their canoes. This gave them easy access to the fishing grounds to the south.

Wooden ways over which the canoes were slid can still be seen today. As such these remains would be almost unique in that they bear enduring witness to the existence of the Canoe Indians. They have left virtually no sign in the wilds of the region that they have ever lived there. Today the cove, like the area around it, is dark and deserted.

Hoste was the rather unusual name of a Royal Navy captain after whom FitzRoy had named the island. Sir William Hoste had been a protégé of Nelson's and had fought under him at the Battle of the Nile, subsequently distinguishing himself against combined French and Venetian forces in the Adriatic.

As well as the rare distinction of having his name recorded in perpetuity on charts of the southern extremity of the world, he had the further distinction of a statue to him being placed next to Nelson's in St Paul's Cathedral.

But our world, centred on *Marelle* and our immediate surroundings, was changing as we approached an inhabited environment. On the beach there were the remains of camp fires and the litter of alien visitors, charter boats and fishermen. We were moving back amongst people and very reluctantly had to accept this unpalatable fact. Ushuaia was only thirty miles ahead and Puerto Williams not much further on.

To emphasise the point we met three yachts heading west as we left Olla and headed out into the channel. One, a small American, came over to welcome us. They had come down the Atlantic to pass through Le Maire Strait and spoke well of Puerto Williams. They sailed on carrying with them an easterly wind which was great for them but it put us hard on the wind. Beating down the Beagle in a choppy sea, cold and damp did not appeal. My inclination was to run back to Olla and take it easy whilst waiting for the westerly wind to come back as surely it would. However once again I was faced with a counter view, namely we should press on. I was beginning to think I had with me a latter-day Cartagena or Doughty. Carry on we did for a while but in the end succumbed and ran into Bahia Yendegaia at the head of which is Caleta Ferrari, mentioned by both Mantellero and the RCC pilot as being interesting spots. The area certainly is so. Virtually on the Argentina and Chile border there was a Carabineros post on the eastern slopes of the bay. This Argentinian police station just inside the border was substantial and we had to wonder at its purpose. An outpost against a possible Chilean invasion, perhaps?

These two countries have strong feelings about each other and have harboured them for some time. There has long been a problem on where to put the border in this no-man's-land, neither country wanting to be seen to give ground literally to the other. They are both very proud peoples. With the line originally settled along the ridge of the Andes there nevertheless arose disputes about the boundary south of there. The British got themselves involved, with Queen Victoria doing her best to mediate at the end of the nineteenth century. Subsequently a British arbitration commission tried manfully to quieten down the hotheads, but bickering remained rampant until a measure of agreement was reached in 1966. Dividing Tierra del Fuego there is an unreal border. Ruler-straight lines have been drawn which take no account of the terrain, with mountains, rivers, ravines and other obstacles of nature being ignored as though they are not there. Perhaps the task of policing such a border was so daunting that the Carabinero had given up. No one was in evidence as we passed.

In the late evening and the wind gone we came in under power to anchor off a little settlement of a couple of houses and some farm buildings above a rather doubtful-looking jetty. Apparently one could hire horses at the hacienda and stay there for hiking tours. Access would be perhaps a problem. Maybe by boat from Ushuaia or alternatively there was a tortuous track which runs all the way down from Isla Grande. To tackle this one would need to be determined. As the anchors went down so did the engine. It would seem to have been in need of another dose of its tonic, biocide. Ferrari is accused in the pilots of suffering from more or less permanent strong winds off the beach but we were spared these. The authority on high had apparently decided enough was enough. We had endured our share of the hard stuff whilst we were in the west of the region.

At 0600 next morning the hands were called with the mandatory mug of tea and we were away on the last leg. As evidence that changes in the weather are mercurial in these parts, the morning was near-perfect, bright sun out of a clear blue sky. Passing the anchorage at Dos de Mayo below the police station, once again there was no sign of life. Outside the entrance to the bay, the breeze filling in from the north-north-west, our course took us south of Ushuaia. This brought back strong memories of when Susan and I had been there two years before. That had been the start of the long journey back to where we were now, tramping past the town under sail in my old *Marelle*. The sense of achievement was heightened on looking back up the deep, misty cleft that is the Beagle Channel. The equally beautiful and now all too familiar waterway stretched a long way astern for many miles, symbolising the distance we had sailed on this whole adventure.

The Beagle Channel was so named in 1830 by the sailing master of HMS *Beagle*, Lieutenant Matthew Murray, who in one of the ship's boats had sailed up the narrow channel, known today as Canal Murray, on the west side of Isla Navarino, the island south of Ushuaia. On reaching the top of the channel, there, stretching as far as Murray could see, running east and west, was a magnificent waterway. It was to strike a deep chord in Darwin who rapturously entered in his diary that 'it is a most remarkable feature in the geography of this, or indeed that of any other country.' Then continuing in the same vein, 'it … is throughout the greater part so perfectly straight that the view, bounded on each side by a line of mountains, gradually becomes indistinct in the long distance.'

Canal Murray provides a short cut to the Horn when sailing down the Beagle Channel from the west, but for their own good reasons this has been declared a prohibited area by the Armada. Woe betide the unwary who attempt to traverse it without special permission.

The name Navarino is evocative of the days when Great Britain was in fact great. The greatest of the maritime powers. The island was so named by FitzRoy in 1828 to commemorate the Battle of Navarino which had been fought only the year before. It had featured prominently in the Greek War of Independence which resulted in Greece freeing itself from Turkish rule.

A combined fleet of British, French and Russian line-of-battleships under the overall command of Admiral Sir George Codrington had been assembled to support the Greeks. It confronted a Turkish–Egyptian fleet under Ibrahim Pasha anchored in Navarino Bay, off Peloponnese, the allied fleet having anchored immediately to seaward to prevent Pasha leaving. It was intended to be a sabre-rattling exercise, it not being the British government's intention to become involved in actual fisticuffs. Codrington had other ideas. A boat was sent in, with its crew armed, to order a Turkish ship to move inshore but the Turks, believing they were about to be boarded, fired on the boat with their muskets. This was enough for Codrington and battle was joined, resulting in the destruction of Pasha's fleet. Whitehall was not amused, taking the view Codrington had deliberately provoked the Turks into attacking, thereby disobeying his orders not to engage in battle. He was recalled to face a court martial but so robust was his defence that the court, with some misgivings, acquitted him. It can be assumed the grateful Greeks took a different view of his actions.

The battle has a special niche in the history of the sea, being a milestone in the evolution of maritime warfare. It was the last major action to be fought under sail alone. The 'wooden walls' of the Nelson era had reached their sell-by date, much to the delight of the environmentalists of the day, it now being a case of 'woodman spare thine axe' on the oak trees of old England.

In the late afternoon we closed Puerto Williams, wondering whether we would make it in time before an ominous build-up of black cloud unleashed its fury on us. We didn't make it. As we entered the little inner harbour a vicious, biting squall swept over us. It made us feel quite at home.

CHAPTER SEVEN

THE HORN AND BEYOND

*Where ... the Atlanticke Ocean and the South Sea, meete in a most large
and free scope.*
Captain General Francis Drake, 1578

Alongside the yacht club – limitations of dining out in Puerto Williams –
friendly Armada – *Micalvi* warmth – pisco sours and crab salads – worth
coming all this way – re-stock – wait for break in weather off the Horn –
sail – difficult night passage – calm rounding of the 'brooding malignant
rock' – easterlies – trying time in Le Maire Strait – difficult passage up
the Falklands coast – enter Stanley

Puerto Williams is unique. A purely naval town with no commercial
shipping apart from deep-sea fishing vessels and bunkering tankers, it
nevertheless provides a service for the benefit of the sailing fraternity.
There is no other facility for the yachtsman anywhere near. Ushuaia is,
like Punta Arenas, a harbour where small craft have to make do the best
they can. Otherwise to the north there is nothing for them until one gets
to Mar del Plata on one side of South America or way up the Chilean
coast on the other. To the east is Cape Town and to the west New
Zealand.

What Puerto Williams has to offer is a secure little berthing area and a
delightful yacht club. This is disguised in the form of an ex wartime
munitions carrier, *Micalvi*, now moored securely with her bottom firmly
on the sea bed. Boats secure alongside or to a pontoon projecting out
from her stern.

With our squall persisting we positioned ourselves parallel to a large
American yacht berthed on *Micalvi*. We let the wind do the rest. As
though under some giant's hand we were pushed smoothly alongside.
Better than any fancy bow thruster.

Whilst we were minding our own business and securing the boat an
Italian woman arrived from a yacht on the pontoon to supervise
proceedings. Why she had been compelled to assume this role was not
clear. Fraser ignored her and she departed 'like a woman scorned'. It had
looked nasty for a moment or two, with the makings of an international
incident, but it did not develop. We were to meet the lady later in the bar
and it emerged that she and her husband were going to winter in
Williams in their boat, but in the meantime they had been commissioned
to take a visitor down to the Horn and back. Knowing the ropes about the

rock, the husband extended an invitation to have a chat about the passage down there. Some time later I accepted this offer and went round to their boat. The husband, pleasantly inoffensive, was up the mast. No sooner had we started to chat than the female dragon thrust her head out of the hatch and addressed her man. 'You have too much work to do to waste time talking!' That was that. I never did benefit from what they knew about Cape Horn.

Having secured ourselves comfortably alongside the American the unanimous vote amongst all hands was for a meal ashore. It being Sunday there was no point in going round to the Armada to hammer on the door to commence the formalities. Equally as we were to discover Sunday evening is not the busiest time of the week in Puerto Williams. We could find nothing open and, looking lost, we were taken in hand by a vaguely drunken local who appeared from nowhere and was kindness itself. He insisted on taking us to every likely and unlikely place, but to no avail. Back on board to a DIY supper, but at least we had found the telephone bureau in the post office open and got through to home.

Puerto Williams is not big, having a population under 2,000, most of whom like those in Punta Arenas quite possibly don't want to be there. Small it may be but the place has considerable strategic significance, in Chilean eyes at least, it being the capital of the Chilean Antarctic Territory. Chile, like several other countries, considers it owns a part of Antarctica. Chart No. 12 has Territorio Chileno Antarctico starting at Polo Sur, the South Pole, sweeping north in a wedge to take in Tierra del Fuego, and carries on to embrace Chile itself as we know it. The geographical centre of the whole territory, which they call Chile, is located in Puerto del Hambre close to Fuerte Bulnes.

We pondered how this place, so remote and so far from home, had for a name one so common in England, or Wales for that matter. All was revealed in the Mantellero *Diccionario*. The port was given its name in 1953 for *Commandante* don Juan Williams of the Armada who led the team to assert the Chilean government's authority over its part of Patagonia and Tierra del Fuego. Previously to that one learns it was called Puerto Luisa, after the daughter of the missionary Martin Lawrence, whose flock presumably were the very few remaining Yahgans. There still remains unanswered the small question as to how don Juan managed to be called Williams.

Puerto Williams is very much the Armada, the tentacles of which are all-embracing. The hospital, supermarket, Club de Yates *Micalvi* and supply of such items as diesel fuel and propane are all the Armada. About all that is not controlled by the Navy is fishing for *centolla* or spider crabs, the local delicacy. On our *zarpe*, however, written in English in Yerko's handwriting, was the warning 'Don't eat sea food. It's prohibited.' It was actually more dire than that. It could be lethal. We assumed the *centolla* to be acceptable. It certainly was most palatable.

Also not directed by the Armada was the scenery. Behind the township, which from the sea has the appearance of a frontier town, the land sweeps back through wooded slopes up to the snow fields, jagged peaks and broken skyline at the centre of Navarino Island. It is typical of the untamed scenery of the region.

Next morning, Monday 31 January, it was around to the Armada to check ourselves in and once again to be received courteously with a friendly willingness to be helpful. This included the form-filling procedure. Having secured the full *zarpe* in Punta Arenas which included Cabo de Hornos there was the minimum of formalities. The young chief petty officer, Marco, who appeared to be secretary to the Commandant, had workable English and went out of his way to assist. There was a temporary hitch when he explained that if we wanted to land on the Horn to sign the visitors' book we would have to return to Puerto Williams for a new clearance to exit Chile for the Falklands. If we did not want to do that we would have to take an immigration official with us to the Horn. This seemed to me to be an operation fraught with potential problems. What would happen if the weather precluded us from landing? We would be stuck with a guest on board for who knew how long. Where would we land him in that event? It all seemed extraordinarily complicated, or perhaps there was a hidden agenda. They could have seen a convenient opportunity to get one of their people down to the Horn. In the event Marco said he would speak to 'someone' and we were to hear no more. The issue appeared to have been quietly shelved.

Concurrently with my discussions with the Armada, Jeremy and Fraser were seeking out sources of fresh provisions and chasing up mail. This had been directed to the yacht club but appeared to have been re-directed back to the post office. I followed them into the town and to put another call through to home. The bureau also sold newspapers which I endeavoured to read whilst waiting for my call. They were giving full coverage to the court actions in Britain to decide on General Pinochet's fate. The literal translation of one headline was the general had 'one foot in the air'. I was having difficulty with this until it became clear the reference was to Jack Straw being expected to give clearance for Pinochet to be allowed to fly home. Overall the reporting was favourable to the general. I had been a little concerned that he being supported by the armed forces, there might have been a problem in our dealings with the Armada, but there was no sign of any antagonism.

Whilst the others were still roaming the streets I went back to use the showering facilities in *Micalvi*. Like on the *muelle* in Punta Arenas the water was stone cold, but it got the thick grime off, albeit the immersion time was not protracted.

Alongside us was a Swiss charter boat *Philos* which had come in shortly after we had berthed. In the course of conversation with her skipper it transpired he was also a regular user of biocide and he very kindly donated a jam jar of it to keep us going until we reached the Falklands. He suggested he and I went over that evening for a drink aboard *Micalvi*. This was my first introduction to a very Chilean drink, *pisco sour*, and the delights of the yacht club bar. Situated in what would have been the officers' wardroom mess below the bridge, the bar was a welcoming home from home with a roaring open fire, the ambience being enhanced by a charming young woman serving the drinks. Eric insisted on the first round with the unequivocal statement 'There is only one drink round here! *Pisco sour*. It's the best.' He was right. Mantellero in the back of his pilot gives it special attention including full details on its preparation. The ingredients are essentially pisco spirit with icing sugar, lemon juice and white of egg, the whole being put in a blender and served with crushed ice. We were to find it a taste very easily acquired, with the pleasure enhanced by watching a pretty girl doing the mixing.

An interesting character, Eric. Speaking fluent Spanish, he had been operating his charter boat business out of Puerto Williams for some years, living on board with his wife and small son. She seemed an interesting person as well, away at the time on a camping tour with the boy further north in the unfrequented channels of Chile.

Eric's current charter party was a group of German climbers whom he was taking down to the Antarctic peninsula. They were no doubt used to the rigours involved in climbing peaks but he was wondering how they would handle Drake Passage, the turbulent stretch of water between the Horn and the Peninsula, if the weather didn't behave itself. Its reputation is not the best. It was useful chatting with him as he was only too happy to pass on pointers about the route from Williams down to the Horn, a passage with which he was very familiar.

In the midst of enjoying our sours a local walked through the door and espying Eric, whom he knew, addressed him in Spanish. I understood he was some sort of shipping agent. 'I have had a fax from a cruise ship containing a message for a Jeremy Burnett in a British yacht *Marelle* expected in Puerto Williams. Do you know the boat?'

'Well as a matter of fact, yes I do,' replied Eric. 'I am sitting with her skipper right here.'

It all sounded exciting. Adrie had been on a cruise down to the Peninsula and on the return passage the ship was calling in at Stanley. The impression conveyed by the agent was that she would be waiting there to meet Jeremy when we arrived in the Falklands. I thought this was great news and told it all to him when shortly afterwards he and Fraser appeared in the bar. Knowing Adrie's itinerary, Jeremy was sceptical, feeling that the message had suffered a translation mishap. Unfortunately this was to prove correct. It was a great pity but he swallowed his disappointment in his inimitable way.

The *Micalvi* was more than a yachtsman's facility. It was also a social centre for visitors of one sort or another to Puerto Williams from back-packers to tourists released from the occasional cruise ship. Our old friend *Terra Australis* at the end of her sight-seeing trip through Tierra del Fuego came in to anchor off the naval base and disgorge some of her passengers. Exhausting what the town had to offer, almost in a matter of minutes, they descended on the yacht club bar. Suddenly it had become crowded. Rather irrationally perhaps we resented this intrusion as we had come to regard the bar as something special and personal. Akin to the situation in which one can find oneself at a cocktail party I was cornered by a middle-aged American female of solid proportions and obviously on her own. I was informed her life consisted of non-stop world cruises. When one was completed she would embark in another vessel and set off for yet more exotic destinations. She had become supersaturated with the globe's scenic spectacles. Money would not appear to have been a problem but loneliness was. In due course it became apparent that a contribution to the conversation was called for from me.

'Did you enjoy the Garibaldi? We passed your ship *Terra Australis* when you were heading up the *seno* to the glacier.'

'I don't recall that. Perhaps I was below decks some place. Was it good?'

I was beginning to feel trapped with a sense that a permanency in the relationship was developing. With the ruthlessness one develops at cocktail parties I escaped. Where is that Flying Dutchman tourist now, I have wondered since. Sad.

We had not been planning an extended stay in Williams, the purpose being to obtain fresh provisions and to meet the mandatory requirement to secure our exit clearance from Chile. There is not a great deal in the place to see but there was one item of particular historical interest to us. The bow section of the Chilean tug that went south and succeeded in collecting Shackleton's men from Elephant Island in the South Shetlands is mounted as a public monument. We liked to think it was a recognition of the long-standing link with England in maritime history. This goes back to 1817 when Admiral Lord Cochrane was invited to take over command of the Chilean Navy and to further its development. His exploits played a major role in Chile, securing its independence from Spain.

The town lies on the north side of Isla Navarino, home to the Yahgan Indians who featured in FitzRoy's great social experiment, when members of this tribe were taken to England in *Beagle*, supposedly to benefit from exposure to a higher form of life. A well-meaning act that was to do more harm than good in that it strengthened the Fuegians' distrust and fear of the white man's intrusion into their lives. The missionaries who followed soon after FitzRoy's incursion into the area were to feel the full and fatal impact of that hostility.

FitzRoy was not alone in adopting the practice of taking locals, found en route, back to the home country of the world traveller. But he was different in that his motivation was laudably to impart the advantages of Christianity to the heathen. Before him had been Magellan with his kidnapped Patagonians, removed from Puerto San Julian to satisfy the curiosity of his patron in Spain. Later had come the French frigate captain, Bougainville, a contemporary of Cook's, who had taken a South Sea islander named Ohutoro back to France. He was to prove a great success in Parisian society, lending on-the-spot credence to the popular conception of the 'noble savage'.

Cook himself was likewise to become involved in 1773 in the course of his second voyage. Captain Furneaux in command of *Adventure*, sailing as consort to Cook's *Resolution*, brought on board in the Society Islands a young Polynesian, Mae. Taken back to England, he was presented to the King by the First Lord of the Admiralty, the Earl of Sandwich, at whose home he stayed. Mae was considered to be 'well conducted, appearing to possess a good understanding and honest principles'. The fact that he had difficulty in getting his tongue round the King's name of George, and addressed him as King Tosh, was of little moment.

Mae, known popularly as Omai, was well received by London society, even having his portrait painted by fashionable artists of the like of Sir Joshua Reynolds. It is worthy of note that in recent times the Tate accorded Reynolds' work, *Portrait of Omai*, the status of a 'national icon' with a market value of £12 million.

Cook on his third and fateful voyage brought Omai back with him. In New Zealand, Omai, having seen how things were done in the better circles in London, acquired two young Maori lads as his personal servants. A symbol of his new importance to impress the folks back home.

In due course on arrival back at his own island of Tahiti, Omai, complete with entourage, was put ashore after Cook had arranged for the ship's carpenters to construct for him a suitable furnished residence. Omai returned the kindness he had received, by entertaining Cook and his officers to elaborate dinners which he prepared himself of 'fish, fowls, pork and puddings'.

As *Resolution* prepared for sea, Omai went out to her for an emotional farewell with the ship's company and broke down in front of Cook.

During the next couple of days there was movement in our little haven. The American boat inside us left, to be followed by *Philos* with her German adventurers. Something went awry with her sailing. Having just slipped from us she came to a halt with the loud sounds of heavy hammer blows coming from her inner depths. We never did learn what was the problem but eventually she got under way and disappeared down the channel, hopefully with her passengers' confidence still intact.

Next to leave was *Wanderer III*, the Hiscocks' old boat, now being lovingly looked after by a young Dane, Thies Matzen, and his Austrian wife Kiki. They were on board for drinks, giving us the opportunity to hear about a completely different lifestyle, essentially one of permanently sailing the oceans of the world. They supported themselves with casual work, the finding of which was not a problem particularly for Thies who was a skilled boatbuilder. They had recently arrived from South Georgia where their relationship had been formalised by a romantic marriage ceremony held in the small chapel in the old whaling station. The chapel had been restored by Cornishman Tim Carr who, with his wife Pauline, had been living down there more or less permanently in their boat *Curlew*. Tim Carr had given the bride away. On the return passage Thies and Kiki had stopped off in the Falklands before working south through Le Maire Strait and up the eastern end of the Beagle Channel to Puerto Williams. They were able to give us news of our little Mardel friend Roger. They had been in company through the strait in extremely difficult conditions. Apparently Roger against foul wind and tide, having just emerged from its southern end, had been driven right back through it again. Having eventually won clear, both boats experienced atrocious weather on the beat up the Beagle. They had last seen Roger fighting his way on to Ushuaia. They had maintained regular radio contact and what had impressed them was how Roger had continued to be so cheerful throughout the ordeal. Thies happened to mention that he wished he had a copy of Tilman's *Mischief in Patagonia* which gives a good account of sailing in the *canales* up the west coast where they were bound. We had been in Tilman's wake through the Magellan Straits from the Virgins as far as Cabo Froward, where he had carried on up the *paso* and we had turned down into the Canal Magdalena. I carried a copy on board and had found it a most useful pilot. Although it was falling apart it gave me considerable pleasure to donate the book 'To *Wanderer III*, with much love, *Marelle*'. A delightful couple, but we did not envy them their beat up the Beagle and the contiguous *canales* out into the Pacific. *Wanderer* would not be the most weatherly of vessels and had only a tiny and apparently extremely temperamental engine.

Our own sailing day was nigh. This called for a last shower in *Micalvi*. In the shower cubicle I got organised, rereading the instructions on how to conjure hot water out of the system, getting undressed and correctly positioning myself. With shampoo and soap at the ready the button was depressed. Nothing. This time neither hot nor cold. The Horn would have to accept me as I was.

It was into the yacht club bar that night for one of its famed crab salads. It was out of this world. Consumed in front of the log fire with a bottle of wine, the stage having been set with a *pisco sour* or two, we began to wonder why we were leaving. Perhaps overwintering here might be worth thinking about as an alternative to bashing about in the Southern Ocean. The thought passed on and next morning it was into the Armada for check-out. The prospects did not look too promising. Our barograph had plunged and its message was confirmed by the weather fax handed over by Marco. On his initiative he obtained for me each day, ahead of the scheduled time and free of charge, the fax from Valparaiso. The weather chart showed only too clearly things weren't too good off the Horn; in fact they looked decidedly nasty. There was consensus we should stay put. Fronts in that region move through fast and if we let the current low pass on we should have a chance to cover the ninety miles or so to the Horn before the next one hurtled through.

There is a positive side to everything and in this case the delayed departure meant we could indulge ourselves that night with another of those superlative crab salads. Back on board the barograph had risen and steadied so it was to bed with the expectancy of getting away on the morn. An introspective note in the diary observes 'To the Horn tomorrow. WHAT WILL IT BE LIKE? Feel tired and a little apprehensive.'

Sure enough the fax next morning looked healthier. I settled our dues, which included the yacht club charges, all very modest, had my hand shaken by a senior officer and said my farewells to Marco. He said he would arrange for the immigration officer to come down to *Marelle* in the next ten minutes and we were free to leave. I gave him our address in Falmouth with the invitation to stay with us. He accepted gracefully saying it would help his English. I hoped he would take up on it.

No sooner had I arrived back on board when down came the immigration man. He stamped our passports, shook our hands and left. Through my head for some strange reason ran the refrain 'Don't cry for me Argentina'. What a difference!

We slipped, cleared the yacht basin, dipped our ensign to the naval vessel in the harbour and pointed our bows down the Beagle Channel. A day away from the great moment!

With the wind gently up our stern the weather was in its normal state. Grey, overcast and cold with the feel of rain in the air but for the moment with no vice in it.

Suddenly the channel became crowded. Heading towards us was a big schooner hard on the wind who called us up to say they had been asked by the Argentinian Navy station on its side of the Beagle to supply information on our movements. Strange way to go about things, I thought, but the information we relayed seemed to satisfy the Argentinians because we heard no more. There was little point in looking up the *Pilot* to find the radio channel for us to pursue direct communication. On reflection the Argentinians' approach was probably correct. They had no authority to query directly with us on what we were up to, as we had made a point of keeping well within the Chilean half of the Beagle Channel. The boat acting as radio link had told us they were on their way from the Antarctic to Ushuaia, so in all likelihood they had already been in contact with the Argentinian port authorities. The incident could have been read as an indicator of the suspicion that lies between the Argentinians and where we had just left.

The radio had only just gone quiet when it burst into life again with an English voice, the first we had heard for a very long time. Shortly afterwards the vessel herself appeared in the channel to the north of us heading west. She turned out to be English, *M'our Bruin*, en route from Mar del Plata to Ushuaia having recently passed through Le Maire Strait. The encounter was interesting in that this was the first British-flagged vessel of any kind we had met since the Canaries, sadly evidence of the near demise of Britain as a major maritime power. It is not so many years ago, and certainly in my life span, that half the ships at sea had the 'red duster' waving over their taffrails. But even in the yachting scene in modern times the red ensign has continued its vanishing act. The blue ensign, usually defaced with some strange emblem, has taken over more and more. Seemingly today to be seen to be a yachtsman one has to be seen to have a blue ensign. The humble red version would never do.

In the early afternoon we turned south out of the Beagle to pass down the eastern coastline of Isla Navarino and into Paso Picton. Nine miles ahead of us to the east lay Isla Gardiner. This little island has a significance quite out of proportion to its size. It lies across the entrance to Caleta Banner on the north side of Isla Picton, the island which we were now about to pass. Picton had been named by FitzRoy after General Sir Thomas Picton who fell at Waterloo.

Banner was to feature prominently in a tragedy that should never have happened. The Cape Horn region has had more than its share of disasters and human catastrophes, but this one with its starting point in Banner was the greatest. Its central character was Captain Allen Gardiner, ex Royal Navy, who at the height of his career suddenly was compelled to obey the call from God to save the heathen. Gardiner, more or less a contemporary of FitzRoy's, was eleven when the Battle of Trafalgar was fought. This inspired him to enter the Royal Navy, in which service he was well liked and successful. He had all before him. As a child he had received a strict Christian upbringing against which he rebelled. Tall, handsome and charismatic, he enjoyed life to the full. It was then personal tragedy overtook him. Bereft at the sudden loss of his wife and child, he swung hard the other way, retiring from the Navy with an all-consuming dedication to become a full-time missionary out in the field. The publication of Darwin's journal gave him the signal that the Fuegians were calling out for his help in their redemption.

Also, as it happened, ten years before FitzRoy and Darwin, Captain James Weddell was in Tierra del Fuego with his ships *Jane* and *Beaufoy*, the very ones which had been with us in spirit in Santa Elena in Patagonia. Weddell spent three months in islands south-west of Navarino where he is remembered today by Cabo Weddel and Cabo Brisbane, as well as a Monte Beaufoy. Brisbane was the skipper of *Beaufoy*.

During his stay Weddell took an intense interest in the Fuegians, developing a more kindly and charitable view of them than Darwin, as is reflected in his writings. 'The philanthropic principle which these people exhibit towards one another and their unoffensive behaviour to strangers

... they are the most docile and tractable of any savages we are acquainted with.'

But even he couldn't leave them to themselves. They should 'be instructed in those arts which raise man above the brute'. Gardiner had probably read Weddell's published works, and his comments would have been just what Gardiner wanted to hear.

He formed the Patagonian Missionary Society and after a hard fund-raising struggle accumulated enough money to enable him with six companions of a like mind to take passage in the barque *Ocean Queen*. She dropped them at Banner Cove. It was November 1850 and his second attempt, but this time he was completely confident, with God's help, of success. The ship's captain, himself a caring man, having satisfied himself that he could do no more for the new-found mission, sailed on to round the Horn and out into the Pacific. The last sight the captain and his crew had of the seven men was of them singing hymns on the beach. Gardiner and his followers now got on with their new life. First step was to sort out their stores. It was then that they made the cataclysmic discovery that through some inexplicable oversight they had left their ammunition in the ship, now miles away. They had thus no means to defend themselves against any possible attack by unenlightened natives. Gardiner was realistic about this contingency, but faced the added grave misfortune they would be unable to shoot for food. However there was a positive side. Gardiner had brought two 24-foot decked-in launches. It was also fortunate in his party there were three devoted, stalwart fishermen from the tiny fishing harbour of Mousehole in Cornwall who apart from their evangelical efforts would be useful with the boats.

An early objective had been to try to establish contact with the Fuegians who had been to England with FitzRoy and now were back on Navarino, the island just next door. This was not to happen, and instead the mission found itself being threatened by the local natives arriving in substantial numbers by canoe. The missionaries were now having to defend themselves from the intended converts. They had to take to their boats but wherever they tried to land they were attacked. The situation was becoming progressively more desperate, their provisions starting to run out and their physical condition deteriorating. What was not affected was their belief in their mission and their unquenchable faith in the Almighty. But their mortal existence was now in extreme jeopardy and just to stay alive they had to find sanctuary. Gardiner had the belief that the further east they went the greater were their chances of freedom from the continued harassment.

On a rock face at the entrance to Banner Cove they painted in large white letters 'DIG BELOW GO TO SPANIARD HARBOUR MARCH 1851'. At the foot of the rock they buried a bottle containing letters and a plea for help. It was never to come.

In the launches they sailed the forty miles to what is known today as Bahia Aguirre, just to the west of the southern entrance to Le Maire Strait. In the north-west corner of the bay is a good anchorage shown on current charts as Puerto Español. Here for a few days Gardiner thought they had found their sanctuary, but salvation was not to hand. Their pitifully few remaining food stocks which they had stored in a cave for supposed safety were ruined by an abnormally high tide, heightened by a storm, which also destroyed one of the launches. They now knew in their hearts they were doomed.

An exceptionally hard winter set in and scurvy made its appearance. The situation is best summed up by Lucas Bridges, who was intimately involved with the Gardiner legacy. 'The rest of the food must have been finished in spite of the strictest rationing, in July. Then, with the exception of a fox they trapped, they had to live on a few fish or sea birds they found washed ashore, together with some shell-fish and seaweed.' By August only Gardiner and one other, Dr Williams, were still alive but, in Gardiner's journal entry, 'in a wonderful peace'. Williams was next to go. In his last letter, recovered later, he wrote 'Even in our last distress, I would not change my situation with anyone on earth. I am happy beyond words.' Gardiner lasted another two weeks and, again to quote Bridges, 'His last words were written on the 5th September, and show that he was not only resigned to his fate, but was also in a condition of ecstacy.' There is a terrible twist to this story of outstanding bravery, total devotion and utter foolishness. The Bridges, father and son, were the spiritual heirs to Gardiner, bringing his plans to fruition by setting up the mission in Ushuaia. The missionary movement struck at the very core of the Fuegians' existence and played a key part in their disappearance. It is extraordinary that what happened to those people could be so facilely rationalised as is shown in Lucas Bridges' own words:

He [Gardiner] left clear suggestions in writing as to how the work he had attempted could be carried forward. These plans were followed as closely as possible through trials and disasters to a successful conclusion. Though I am well aware that, within less than a century, the Fuegians as a race have become almost extinct, I deliberately use the word 'successful'.

It is estimated at the time there were between one and two thousand Yahgans. It took not much more than fifty years virtually to exterminate them. It could be said that they had atoned in full for Captain Allen Gardiner's death.

There were four Indian tribes inhabiting Tierra del Fuego, the Yahgan, Ona, Aush and Alacaluf. What happened to the Yahgan was representative of the terrible fate to befall the other tribes. Each tribe had its own quite different and distinctive customs and language, but had one thing in common. They needed to be left alone.

The Alacaluf lived to the west of the Brecknock, centring on Desolation Island, at the Pacific end of the Magellan Straits. To the east of them the Yahgan, or as they called themselves Yamana, occupied the central islands stretching from Ushuaia down to Cape Horn and as far east as Spaniard Harbour. The remaining south-eastern part of the region over to Le Maire Strait was home to the Aush, otherwise known as the eastern Ona.

The Ona, greatly feared by the other tribes, occupied Isla Grande, the main island of the archipelago bordering the South Atlantic. They were relatively big men, skilled hunters with bows and arrows, living off the land, whereas the Alacalufs and Yahgans were people of the sea in their canoes, existing mainly on fish and small crustaceans with their principal weapon the spear. They were a small race, the men averaging five feet, but physically stronger than their white counterparts. Their source of clothing was the skins of otters, seals and more rarely the fox. As all of these were in short supply the Yahgans had adapted to their environment by being largely naked, both men and women, relying on fire for creature comfort. They had the distinction of being the most southerly inhabitants of the globe.

The Alacaluf and Yahgan were widely known as Canoe Indians and had inhabited their regions for thousands of years, living as Stone Age people, remaining unchanged and largely unmolested until *Beagle* arrived. Thereafter they were to be subjected to all the abuse that man is so good at inflicting on his fellow man.

In 1870, when the senior Bridges was establishing his mission in Ushuaia, the Indians of Tierra del Fuego across the four tribes were estimated to total between 7,000 and 9,000. Seventy years later there were less than 150 full-blooded Fuegians left. At the time of our stay in Puerto Williams, one surviving Fuegian, a Yahgan of mixed blood, was understood to be living there. Clothed and Christian.

The Canoe Indians became extinct through a combination of disease and the well-intentioned but disastrous ministrations of the Anglican missionary. The Ona were the victims of genocide perpetrated by white men, gold seekers and sheep farmers with repeating rifles, spreading south over the Magellan Straits, plus some tragically misguided attentions from a Silesian Fathers' mission which succeeded in killing the converts' spirit. The unfortunate tribespeople had been incarcerated, supposedly for their own preservation and good, but they did not survive for long. As Lucas Bridges remarked, 'Liberty is dear to the white man; to untamed wanderers of the wilds it is an absolute necessity.'

A fateful anomaly pertains to the relationship between the foreign, uninvited visitors to the Land of Fire and the Yahgan indigenes during the brief period of their coexistence. It concerns the survival of a species.

Over the years there had been countless shipwrecks, most of them unrecorded as well as unwitnessed apart from, one can presume, the occasional sighting by the local Indians. The ships and their crews just went missing. The fate of any survivors thrown up on the rock-bound shores was never known. However, that was to change with the white men taking up permanent residence in the region, consequent on Thomas Bridges setting up his settlement at Ushuaia. He informed the locals they would be rewarded with gifts if they brought in information about shipwrecks, but at the same time issuing a warning to the potential recipients of these gifts, mostly used and often soiled, quite unsuitable clothing from England, that they would be in serious trouble if the unfortunate mariners were not given assistance. This stick and carrot approach was to work.

Lucas Bridges relates the story of the British sailing vessel *San Rafael* which, in January 1876, was in dire distress. Heading west, having just beaten round the Horn, her cargo of coal caught fire and the ship had to be abandoned. One boat with the captain, his wife and eight men got past the outcrop known as False Cape Horn and landed on the south-west shore of Isla Hoste which forms the western side of the Canal Murray.

They were eventually discovered by a canoe party of Indians who, they claimed, offered assistance to the two remaining survivors still alive and then came on to report to Thomas Bridges. He lost no time in setting out in the mission supply vessel, the schooner *Allen Gardiner*. 'After an exceedingly stormy voyage' they located an anchorage, landed and found the bodies of the woman and all nine men. They had succumbed to starvation and exposure even though it was summer. Also found was a note written by the captain to his stepson. 'When you receive this your mother and me will be no more,' and ending 'we hope … you may live long in happiness and peace in Fear of the Lord, and … may God bless you all.'

Their story has a moving, close similarity to what befell Allen Gardiner and his party. Physically, in both cases they could not survive in their surroundings. Spiritually, although their deeply held religious faith had enabled them to face death it had not preserved them from that ultimate fate, whereas the pagan savage with no faith of any kind was able to continue with his normal way of life. This was just so long as he was left to live it without interference. This did not happen. The faithful were to be party to the destruction of the faithless.

If there was a message here for Bridges he ignored it, proceeding remorselessly on the path to convert the heathen, until their demise terminated the programme. Bridges and his successors appeared blissfully unaware of the ghastly irony of what had happened.

A report by Thomas on the *San Rafael* tragedy was subsequently published in London, which resulted in a Notice to Mariners being issued, giving advice to distressed sailors on what to do and how to reach Ushuaia. Appropriate notes were then inscribed on charts for many years as recorded by Riesenberg:

In the event of a crew being wrecked or abandoned westward of Cape Horn, the best course to Ushuaia is eastward of False Cape Horn ... where the natives will be ready to pilot any shipwrecked men to Ushuaia.

He goes on to state that as comparatively recently as 1937 he saw these 'pious platitudes' repeated on a US Hydrographic Office chart. Thomas Bridges would have been a happy man to have been aware of this. It was just unfortunate that for a very long time there had been no would-be rescuers around.

Caleta Banner had been on our list as a possible stopover. It is a secure anchorage for small craft with good holding and protected from all winds. It is understandable why Gardiner, an experienced seaman, chose it for his base but for us the Horn was now in our sights. Moreover we had a fair wind and of course that could not be wasted. That is the rule in that part of the world.

Our next stop for consideration was Puerto Toro on Navarino and a little further down the *paso*. We could see a few dwellings in what is one of the original settlements in the region. It is a leftover from 1881 when the harbour was the centre of the gold rush which enveloped the three neighbouring islands of Picton, Nueva and Lennox. This event would no doubt have helped to fuel the animosity between Chile and Argentina

over the islands' ownership. This reached a peak in 1978 when they came
close to war. Papal intervention helped to quieten down the would-be
combatants, the island group remaining part of Chile. This was an anti-
war success for the Vatican and went largely unnoticed. It is easy to see
why the Argentines would like to hold them. They would then be astride
the entrance to the straits, giving them control of the main channel. But in
fact did it really matter? After all the Beagle Channel is not one of the
world's major seaways.

We decided to sail on. Ahead lay Bahia Nassau which does not have a
good reputation, and we wanted to get it tucked in behind us. To quote
Mantellero, 'You must cross Nassau bay with precautions because the
weather in this area is very changeable.' It is open water of fifteen miles
and can get very rough, wide open as it is to the east and exposed to a
considerable fetch from the west. Albeit night was closing down we
sailed on, wanting to capitalise on a helpful break in the weather. We
could not afford to waste such a rare opportunity.

It was not to be a happy crossing for Fraser. As we entered the bay on
clearing the lee of Navarino he took over from Jeremy just as the rain
came down. It continued to come down in heavy sheets throughout his
watch. The night was intensely black and very cold and the fact the
compass light was playing up did not help to lighten his mood. I got the
impression he was not too unhappy to hand the wheel over to me at
midnight.

The rain obligingly eased off for me and by the time Jeremy took over
we were across Nassau and running down the shores of Wollaston Island.
The wind had gone into the east and it was getting even colder but we
were safely over that notorious bay with no drama. I felt relieved but the
problem now was one of judging distance off shorelines I couldn't see.
The hillsides, black as the night, ran down to an equally black sea with
no indication where one ended and the other started. The GPS being of
little use this close in on a chart of doubtful datum, it was 'by feel'
navigation and somewhat taxing.

It was starting to get light as Jeremy took over the watch to thread
through the passage at the foot of Wollaston and emerge into the channel
on the north side of Isla Herschel, passing as he did so Isleta Adriana,
Adrie's full name. A family reunion as it were. It was here that we turned
west to cross the top of the island, heading towards Isla Hermite, a short
leg of five miles, before turning south down the west side of Isla Hornos
for the ultimate goal, Cabo de Hornos itself. It was 0700. We had a total
of fifteen miles to go to what all these past months had been all about. I
think this point was one of the worst moments for me in the whole cruise.

I was so tired and so cold. Under our lee just then was Caleta Martial, earmarked as a bolt hole in case we met a bad westerly at this stage. I felt an overwhelming desire to turn down into that cove just to get warm and to sleep. Fortunately there was no thought in the minds of the other two about not carrying on and this gave me the spur to collect myself. Once again I thought privately to myself how blessed I was with my team.

Apart from the desire to benefit from the badly needed succour that Martial had to offer, I would have liked to call in to experience it for what it was, unique in the area with interesting connections. The *Pilot* is friendly towards it with the encouraging comment for the likes of us that it 'affords anchorage for small vessels … in 10m, sand and mud' continuing helpfully that it 'may be identified by its yellow beaches.' These, being a rare phenonomen in such waters, would make the cove worth a visit just for that reason alone.

The only other strip of foreshore we had encountered which could with any justification call itself a beach was at beautiful Olla. Elsewhere in most of our other anchorages, in stark contrast to the serenity that goes with a bare, sandy beach, the boundary between land and sea was witness to the chaos of nature in conflict with itself. There, on the ill-defined shore line, it was dank confusion as the matted, stunted growth and dense proliferation of shrubs and bushes fought amongst themselves to survive in the hostile climate where, as Darwin, oppressed by his surroundings, lamented 'gale succeeds gale, with rain, hail and sleet … and the atmosphere seems blacker than anywhere else.' From his writings, studded with comments like 'I never saw a more cheerless prospect', it was evident he really did not want to be in those waters. The impending onset of winter in that environment would no doubt have depressed him even further.

It was terrain virtually impossible to traverse any distance on foot. The roots of twisted beech trees and fallen trunks lay in swamp, holding within itself peaty soil lodged amongst rocks and stones, with kelp swirling amidst the rotting vegetation. A smooth, firm sandy beach, with nature at peace with itself, would have the feel of an earthly paradise.

The cove's attractions as a place of refuge were also apparent to the Armada, as it was the only anchorage officially approved by them for vessels navigating the island groups in the immediate approaches to the Horn. Having, in the past, had to rescue yachts in trouble in those waters and on occasion with little in the way of thanks, the Armada keeps its finger pressed tightly on the pulse.

The *caleta* owes its name to a nineteenth-century reincarnation of the rather glamorous earlier explorer, Comte Louis Antoine de Bougainville, apparent in the form of Capitaine Luis Martial who was checking out the region in 1882 and 1883 on behalf of the French government, who possibly thought that as the British had been active down there it was time for a French involvement. Sailing in the ship-rigged frigate *Romanche*, equipped to make life easier by having *un motor de vapor* (steam engine), achieving a useful speed under power of 10 knots, the captain was to bequeath his ship's name to various bays and anchorages and not least of all, to that majestic *ventisquero*, the Romanche, in Glacier Alley. This was the great river of ice that nearly had Darwin and FitzRoy in serious difficulties.

Clearing the top of Herschel we turned south-east with the island of Hermite on our starboard beam. This large rugged island commemorates the Dutch admiral Jacques L'Hermite, one of the ablest and also the most unfortunate of the early explorers. Supplied with a massive fleet of eleven ships and sixteen hundred men he was despatched in 1623 by the Netherland's legislative body, the States General, to destroy the Spanish monopoly on trade in the Pacific. Rounding Cape Horn in good order he made the first sighting of the island, which was named Hermite as a gesture by the fleet to their admiral. They had then proceeded up the channel down which we were sailing. He carried on up into the bay which we had just traversed and named it Nassau after the Prince of Orange, Maurice de Nassau. The fleet needing water, boats were sent in to land a party, which was by mischance unarmed, to fill the water barrels. The weather suddenly turned hostile and the boats had to return to their ships. Next morning they were shocked to find seventeen of the shore party had been murdered in particularly brutal circumstances by Canoe Indians. On top of this misfortune L'Hermite fell ill from a terminal complaint. From then on the expedition fell apart. However, his name has a permanent record in history as being the first to anchor in behind Cape Horn and make the first landing. That is to say the first verifiable landing. Drake may well have had that honour but this has never been established beyond any reasonable doubt.

In *Marelle* we were now on the last leg. It was typically grey and damp with low cloud cover. The wind had shifted into the north-west and was getting lighter, so much so that we were having to use the engine intermittently to make any reasonable progress. It was all very reminiscent of our first venture into the Southern Ocean when we made the crossing from Niemamn into the *canales* Ocasión and Brecknock. The same long, high, lazy swell in relatively gentle weather. In our path was the small abrupt Isla Hall, and on passing close to this we laid a course to clear the clusters of dangerous-looking rocks off the western slopes of Hornos

Island. They bear a strange mixture of names, Catedral, Robinson and Bascunan, and take the first impact of the Southern Ocean. The swell had broken out of its temporary lethargy and was smashing over the rocks with explosions of spray. Cascades of white broken water poured back down the faces of the rocks into the trough of the wave as the crest passed on to burst against the base of the Horn itself.

Even on this non-violent day there was a pronounced awareness of the force and awesome power of all that heaving mass of water in motion into which the great storm-ravaged rock forced itself.

Rounding the last of the outlying rocks, Ra Bascunan, we turned east. Cabo de Hornos itself was one-and-a-half miles ahead. As we altered course the sun came out, doing its best to soften that formidable headland's grim features – and grim they are too. Rising 1,400 feet straight out of the sea with its bare face riven by vertical, jagged, broken spurs of rock, its whole demeanour is one of uncompromising hardness. The concept Naomi James had of that 'brooding malignant rock' is very apt. It has been at war with an equally malignant stretch of water since time immemorial.

We passed close in to the southernmost point at 1150. There, sheer before us, was the age-old enemy of sailors who had gone before, their Cape Stiff and our ultimate objective which, as we sailed past, became our success. It was 5 February 2000 and apart from the timing we had achieved all we had set out to do. 'Mixed feelings' is the expression usually applied to such occasions but I think for me the predominant emotion was just quiet satisfaction. To have cracked the usual bottle of champagne would have been an intrusion into the mood. Strangely there was no sense of elation at the realisation of a lifetime's ambition but I was reminded of Bernard Moitessier's remark, 'There are two terrible things for a man: not to have fulfilled his dream, and to have fulfilled it.' Rather extreme perhaps but I could understand the sentiment. Although it was within his reach he did not fulfil his dream to be the first person to sail single-handed non-stop round the world. He sailed on into the Pacific after rounding the Horn, happy to continue living his dream and let Knox-Johnston take the prize.

Over the next two miles as one sails east along the length of the island, the land drops down to a point behind which on its north side is Caleta San Leon. From this anchorage, temporary at best, a pathway has been cut leading up to an Armada reporting station and a lighthouse with nearby memorials to sailors lost off the Horn. The site has become something of a tourist attraction. Cruise ships, if the weather permits, land their denizens who march obediently up in line ahead to the station to have their passports stamped, take each others' photographs and have their postcards mailed. This activity was to be a discussion point amongst ourselves. Jeremy was keen to land, advancing the understandable view, reminiscent of the Garibaldi debate, that we should avail ourselves of this favourable opportunity. We would never be here again. My view was we should take advantage of the weather whilst it was being so favourably inclined towards us and sail on. I did not trust it. Moreover the obligatory lighthouse and site visit seemed to me to be somewhat contrived and a little trippery. But perhaps I was not as enterprising as Jeremy.

Fraser I think was also for pressing on. After all we were now homeward bound. The weather as always was the final arbiter. The wind was strengthening and steadily working round through north to the east which meant the landing spot, which is wide open to the north and east, would be insecure. At least that is what I maintained and Jeremy was gracious enough to accept the decision not to attempt the landing. Clearing Deceit Island, lying immediately to the east of Hornos, we went onto the starboard tack to make northing, the wind now firmly in the east. To have it from that direction in these waters was a little disappointing but no matter, for the first time we were closing the difference in latitude as well as the longitude gap with home. It was a good feeling as up till now our progression had been ever southward.

Isla Deceit has been one of the villains in the history of Cape Horn disasters. Mistaken for the Horn itself by vessels beating westward in poor visibility it could have deceived ships' captains, with most unfortunate results, into thinking they had safely weathered that headland.

It was so named by Captain Henry Foster RN in HMS *Chanticleer* undertaking scientific work in 1831 on behalf of the Royal Society. Realising there was deception about the Horn's actual whereabouts, he hauled his wind to claw clear and named the island to the north Wollaston, after William Hyde Wollaston, another Fellow of the Society.

Deceit Island has a partner in crime, lying to the north-west of the Horn, appropriately named Falso Cabo de Hornos. In this case ships headed east under the impression they had got past the Horn with clear safe water now before them, could have been in serious trouble. There is a lot of land still dead ahead.

We had been let off lightly with our Horn rounding, aided by some ability to choose our weather. Earlier navigators of course had to take it as it came, such as experienced by *Beagle* and duly recorded by Darwin:

We closed in with the Barnevelts, and running past Cape Deceit [bottom of Deceit Island] with its stony peaks, about three o'clock doubled the weather-beaten Cape Horn. The evening was calm and bright, and we enjoyed a fine view of the surrounding isles. Cape Horn, however, demanded his tribute, and before night sent us a gale of wind directly in our teeth. We stood out to sea, and on the second day again made the land, when we saw on our weather bow this notorious promontory in its proper form – veiled in a mist, and its dim outline surrounded by a storm of wind and water. Great black clouds were rolling across the heavens, and squalls of rain, with hail, swept by us with such extreme violence that the captain determined to run into Wigwam Cove. This is a snug little harbour not far from Cape Horn, and here, at Christmas Eve, we anchored in smooth water.

Up till now Darwin's exposure to the Fuegians had been confined to the Aush tribe in Buen Suceso and the three Yahgans aboard *Beagle* whom FitzRoy was bringing back home, the bright young Jemmy Button with his delightful little wife Fuegia Basket and the rather difficult York Minster. It came as a tremendous shock to him to meet the Fuegian Yahgans in their natural state, no doubt having gained a completely false impression of these people through his association with the three in *Beagle*. On them sat a paper-thin covering of civilisation masking their natural selves.

The culture shock for Darwin is made so evident in his account of the first encounter with a Yahgan tribe. These writings, so widely publicised, signified in effect the firing of the starting gun for the race to the finish for the Fuegians. Darwin's reaction to the local tribespeople possibly tells as much about Darwin as it does about them. They were an affront to him and one to which he responded with the unseeing arrogance of someone who believed himself to be of a super-race.

While going one day on shore near Wollaston Island, we pulled alongside a canoe with six Fuegians. These were the most abject and miserable creatures I anywhere beheld ... these Fuegians in the canoe were quite naked, and even one quite full-grown woman was absolutely so. It was raining heavily, and the fresh water, together with the spray, trickled down her body. In another harbour not far distant, a woman, who was suckling a recently born child, came one day alongside the vessel, and remained there out of mere curiosity, whilst the sleet fell and thawed on her naked bosom, and on the skin of her naked baby! These poor wretches were stunted in their growth, their hideous faces bedaubed with white paint, their skins filthy and greasy, their hair entangled, their voices discordant, and their gestures violent. Viewing such men, one can hardly make oneself believe that they are fellow-creatures, and inhabitants of the same world. It is a common subject of conjecture what pleasure in life some of the lower animals can enjoy; how much more reasonably the same question may be asked with respect to these barbarians!

Wigwam Cove does not exist under that name on modern charts covering the vicinity of the Horn, but as Darwin remarked 'every bay in the neighbourhood might be so called with equal propriety ... The Fuegian wigwam ... merely consists of a few broken branches stuck in the ground, and very imperfectly thatched on one side with a few tufts of grass and rushes.'

Where *Beagle* anchored was quite probably in Bahia Alsina in the north-eastern corner of Wollaston Island. We had passed within three miles of its entrance after we had cleared the southern end of Bahia Nassau. Alsina was in our passage plan as an anchorage to seek shelter, if needs be, but as I took *Marelle* down that coast it was just a black hole in the absolute darkness of the night.

They were holed up in Wigwam Cove for six days through very bad weather, before sailing to double the Horn for the purpose of landing their Yahgan trio to the west of Navarino Island. They had a terrible time, at one time nearly losing *Beagle* in the violent seas. It took them twenty-four days to get round and FitzRoy, giving up on getting further to the west with his crew exhausted, ran in behind False Cape Horn and 'dropped our anchor in forty seven fathoms, fire flashing from the windlass as the chain rushed round it. How delightful was that still night, after having been so long involved in the din of the warring elements!'

Beagle's travails were reminiscent of those that Commodore George Anson had suffered when he with his small fleet of six ships, almost a century before, had fought his way round the Horn into the Pacific, the much sought-after South Sea. As Riesenberg commented, 'Anson's voyage included one of the greatest of all Cape Horn adventures.'

Unlike *Beagle*, which was well found and manned by a strong, healthy crew, Anson had to contend with ships badly in need of refit and totally unseaworthy. Moreover his crews, including the surviving pensioners, one of whom was eighty-two, were in dreadfully poor physical and mental condition with their ranks decimated by scurvy and dying daily before his eyes.

Having passed down the Patagonian coast Anson's nightmare began with his entry into the Southern Ocean via Le Maire Strait. At first all was well. The morning of the transit was noted for 'its brilliancy and mildness', but the entry in his chaplain's journal went on 'We travers'd these memorable Streights, ignorant of the dreadful calamities that were then impending … and this was the last cheerful day that the greatest part of us would ever enjoy.' It was 7 March 1741 and late in the season with autumn coming on and winter's gales building up.

Ahead of the fleet the sky was darkening, heralding the violent squalls from the south which blew the squadron twenty miles to the east of Staten Island. Thus began a three-month ordeal to double the Horn and get north. Their lot was to be one of almost continuous westerly gales with huge seas besetting them with hardly any respite.

It was not until mid-April that Anson, navigating under the conditions by guess and crude dead reckoning, felt confident that they were safely past Cape Horn and could head north in his flagship *Centurion* plus his two remaining ships. Two others had been beaten into submission by the Horn and in a sorry state had turned back for Brazil. A third, HMS *Wager*, carrying Midshipman Byron, the future 'Foulweather Jack', was partially dismasted and wrecked on the wild coast of Tierra del Fuego.

But on 14 April the leading ship, and the one down to leeward, through the murk and with total disbelief, saw land only two miles away. How could this be when their estimated position was 300 miles to the west? With hindsight we know now they had assuredly grossly underestimated their leeway and made insufficient allowance for the Cape Horn Current, flowing east at up to one-and-a-half knots.

It is believed they were looking at Isla Noir, which lies close to the west of the Furies at the entrance to Canal Cockburn, on the fringes of the dreaded Milky Way, about which Darwin wrote so feelingly. Anson was now in very great peril indeed. The waters he was driving into are considered to be the most dangerous in the world. Knowing personally the area, it is easy to believe the overwhelming fear that would have clasped the hearts of those desperate men with an icy grip.

The only escape was to wear ship and claw their way south. Their situation was now a rerun of what happened to Drake when he had emerged from the western exit of the Straits of Magellan only to be hit by a violent storm and blown south, only just escaping that same unspeakably hostile shoreline.

Anson and the remnants of his fleet were to end up 60° south, that is well below the Horn. The ships had taken a terrific beating. Sails were worn out, continually splitting at the seams, and rigging failures with hull and spar damage combined to impair the ability even to stay afloat, let alone beat to windward. It was to take them another month to regain their lost northing and win clear of 'this terrible coast'. During all this time the agony continued. The appalling weather, malnutrition, injuries sustained in working the ships, cold and above all scurvy had steadily weakened the crews. In *Centurion* alone 43 men died in April, and nearly twice that number in the following month.

Amongst his many problems, the one that had so very nearly been his downfall was that which he shared with every other ocean voyager. The inability to determine longitude accurately. No real method of measuring time at sea had as yet been devised. The solution was not far off but it was to come just too late for Anson.

Four years before the expedition sailed the first chronometer had been built by John Harrison. His prototype, H-1, had so impressed the Admiralty that in 1736 they put it aboard, of all ships, HMS *Centurion*, with the inventor in attendance, for a trial run to Lisbon and back. The clock passed its test with flying colours. Everybody gave Mr Harrison, now recovered from his seasickness, a resounding pat on the back, including the Board of Longitude. This body had been set up by an Act of Parliament to award a prize of £20,000, a very big sum in those days, to the first person to provide a means of measuring time with a consistent error of not more than plus or minus three seconds in twenty-four hours.

The prize lay within Harrison's grasp but he was a perfectionist and his was the only voice of dissent. He told the Board he could do better. So back home the clock went with him for further work. This he said would take a couple of years. It was to be thirty years before he presented himself again before the Board with a timepiece that finally met his own standards. The Admiralty squirralled away the masterpiece and arranged an exact duplicate to be given to Captain Cook to take round the world to prove its worth. It was the dawn of precise ocean navigation.

Thus it was that H-1 was no longer aboard *Centurion* when Anson set off on his circumnavigation. It would have made all the difference in his struggle to double the Horn and would have alleviated so much of the suffering.

In *Marelle* our course made good from Isla Deceit would take us just clear of the Islas Barnevelt, lying ten miles ahead. These islands are another monument to the great days of Dutch maritime expansion in the seventeenth century. John van Barnevelt was one of the founding directors of the Dutch East India Company, which developed into a huge monopoly, immensely wealthy and wielding great political influence.

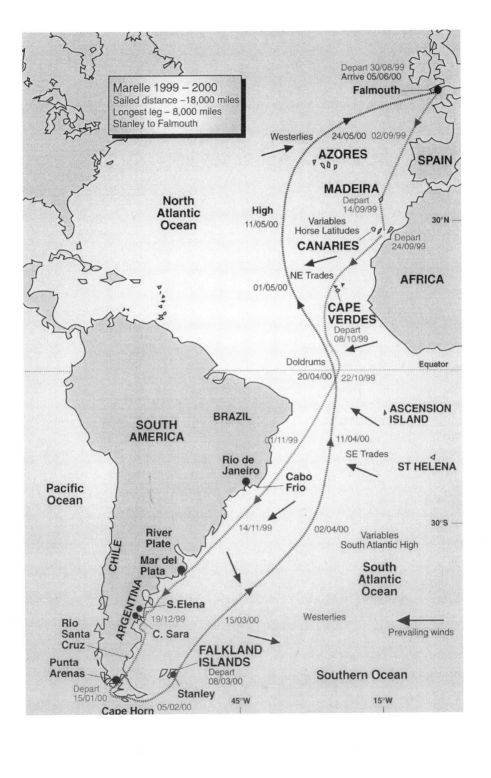

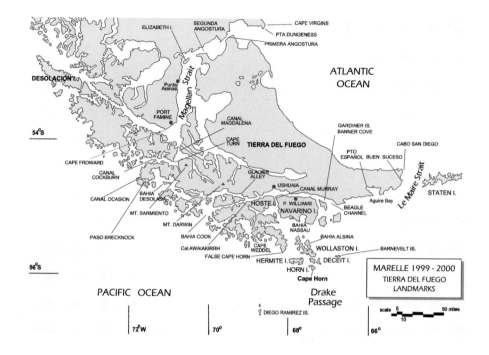

ELIZABETH I.
SEGUNDA ANGOSTURA
CAPE VIRGINS
PTA DUNGENESS
PRIMERA ANGOSTURA

ATLANTIC OCEAN

DESOLACIÓN I.

Punta Arenas

Magellan Strait

PORT FAMINE

54°S

CANAL MAGDALENA

CAPE TURN

TIERRA DEL FUEGO

GARDINER IS.
BANNER COVE

CABO SAN DIEGO

PTO ESPAÑOL BUEN SUCESO

CAPE FROWARD

CANAL COCKBURN

GLACIER ALLEY

USHUAIA

CANAL MURRAY

STATEN I.

Le Maire Strait

BAHIA DESOLADA

CANAL OCASION

HOSTE I.

P. WILLIAMS

NAVARINO I.

Aguire Bay

BEAGLE CHANNEL

MT. SARMIENTO

MT. DARWIN

BAHIA NASSAU

PASO BRECKNOCK

BAHIA COOK

BAHIA ALSINA

Cal.AWAIAKIRRH

CAPE WEDDEL

WOLLASTON I.

BARNEVELT IS.

FALSE CAPE HORN

HERMITE I.

DECEIT I.

56°S

HORN I.

Cape Horn

MARELLE 1999 - 2000
TIERRA DEL FUEGO
LANDMARKS

PACIFIC OCEAN

Drake Passage

DIEGO RAMIREZ IS.

scale 5   50 miles
      10

72°W   70°   68°   66°

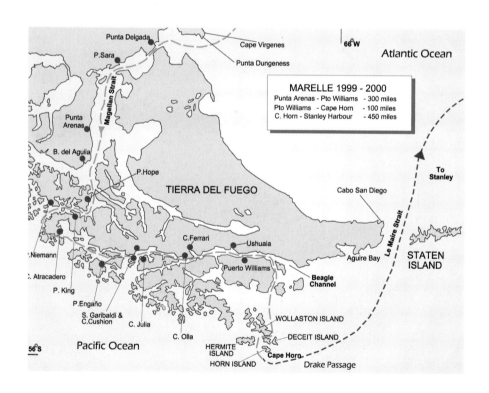

Punta Delgada

P.Sara

Cape Virgenes

66°W

Atlantic Ocean

Punta Dungeness

Magellan Strait

Punta Arenas

MARELLE 1999 - 2000
Punta Arenas - Pto Williams - 300 miles
Pto Williams   - Cape Horn   - 100 miles
C. Horn - Stanley Harbour   - 450 miles

B. del Aguila

P.Hope

TIERRA DEL FUEGO

Cabo San Diego

To
Stanley

C.Ferrari

Ushuaia

.Niemann

Le Maire Strait

STATEN ISLAND

Aguire Bay

Puerto Williams

C. Atracadero

Beagle Channel

P. King

P.Engaño

S. Garibaldi &
C.Cushion

C. Julia

WOLLASTON ISLAND

C. Olla

DECEIT ISLAND

56°S

Pacific Ocean

HERMITE ISLAND

HORN ISLAND

Cape Horn

Drake Passage

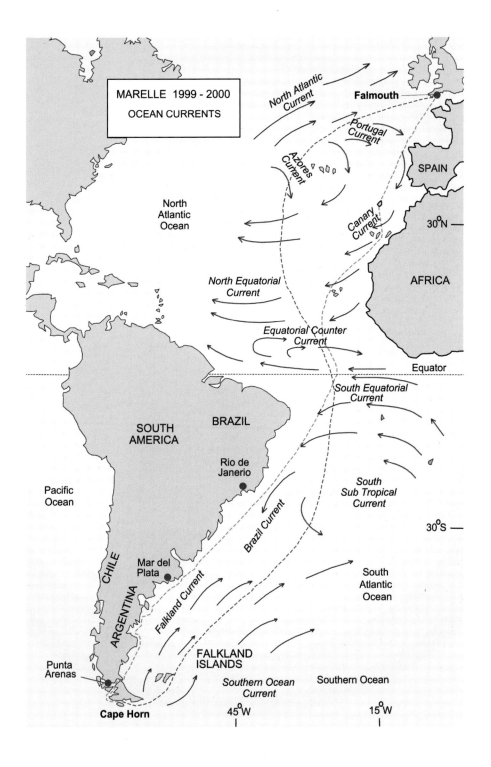

Marelle, in a photograph by Beken of Cowes.

The bestower of his name on these rocks was Captain Willem Cornelisz Schouten, it being ironic that he had done so, because to foil the machinations of Barnevelt and his fellow directors was the reason Schouten was down there at all.

To strengthen its hold on the highly lucrative trade with the East Indies, the Company had been successful in having an edict issued which forbade any vessel other than that owned by the Company to sail round the Cape of Good Hope or pass through the Straits of Magellan. The basic premise was that the land south of those Straits carried on unbroken to Terra Australis, the large continent believed to be at the bottom of the earth. Drake's discovery had not been accepted into the 'public domain'. It was just the English making mischief.

One of the Company's directors, Isaac Le Maire, did however believe there was another route through to the Pacific and having fallen out with the other directors planned to pursue his idea. If he were correct he would be able to bypass the edict and hence free to trade direct with the east and all its riches. To that end he formed the *Compagne Australe* and purchased two ships, *Unity* being placed under the command of Willem Schouten and the smaller *Hoorn* in the care of his younger brother John. Isaac's eldest son, Jacques Le Maire, was appointed supercargo and to keep an eye on the new company's affairs. The Schoutens, experienced mariners both, were from the small port of Hoorn and Willem, being of the same belief as Isaac, put some of his own money into the venture. The objective was thus quite simple. Find open water south of Magellan's *paso*. The expedition was so competently planned and organised that it had to succeed.

The ships sailed in June 1615 for the south, a stop being scheduled at Cavendish's Port Desire. This was becoming something of a regular bus stop on the southern route. Here the expedition suffered a major setback. *Hoorn* was beached on the top of a high tide for a bottom scrub, she having become very foul with marine growth. The method was to light fires to burn off the weed but these, fanned by a strong wind off the *pampas*, got out of hand. The ship's timbers caught alight, leading to her total destruction. Fortunately *Unity* was big enough to absorb her crew and taking everything of value from the stricken ship they sailed on.

Keeping well offshore from the eastern end of the Magellan Straits they sighted in due course further to the south land spreading out to the east and away to the west of them. As they closed with the land a gap opened up leading through to open water. They surmised correctly that the land to the west had to stretch right back to the *paso* of Magellan, but what about that to the east? Mountainous, with its peaks snow-covered, it had to be part of Terra Australis. In honour of Holland's States General, the authority for their enterprise, Schouten named it Staten Land. Today it is still referred to as Staten Island, the geography having been put right. On the chart it is shown under its Spanish translation as Isla de los Estados.

With the wind fair they sailed into the sixteen-mile-wide entrance of what is known today as Estrecho de Le Maire, named after old Isaac. They congratulated themselves on having found a second opening into the South Sea. They now had to get into it and then out into the Pacific to head for the East Indies. Fighting grimly against the weather, which had turned foul for them with gale-force winds from the west laced with snow and sleet, they struggled to make westing. All things come to an end even down there and after the fourth day the wind shifted back into the north-east. Ahead loomed two islands. By midday they were on the beam and duly named Barnevelt. Although they didn't know it these islands were the gateposts to the great discovery that lay just ahead of them.

Later as the day retreated before the advancing darkness they saw on their starboard bow an abrupt sheer cliff with land receding from it as far as their eyes could reach to the north. It appeared at that distance to be unbroken. To the west and south there was only clear open water. The enormity of what they were looking at hit them. They were rounding the uttermost end of the world as they knew it. The Schoutens knew they were now on their way back to their homeport. Spontaneously Willem shouted 'Cape Hoorn! Cape Hoorn!'

The story brought back by Willem Schouten did not thrill either the directors of the East India Company or Philip III of Spain. It could be that their worst fears had been realised and perhaps the rumours of what Drake had found may have had something in them. Now it would appear there was not only a clear sea passage around the bottom of America but it was wide enough to take whole fleets of ships without let or hindrance apart from the weather. The new route did not have the problems associated with Magellan's strait, so navigationally restrictive and dangerous. Moreover it could not be sealed off with forts and cannon.

If his story were true it would be calamitous for Spain's wealth in their Silver Sea as well as for the Company's stranglehold in the Spice Islands. Competition would now be wide open to business rivals in Holland and hordes of marauding English ships. But was it true? Proof was not to be long in coming.

In *Marelle* as we passed the Barnevelts we were on a reciprocal course to that of *Unity,* taking us inshore just to the west of Schouten's strait. Opening up next morning before us was Allen Gardiner's Spaniard Harbour in Aguirre Bay. It is a good anchorage and as the RCC pilot observes 'the last shelter available before entering the Estrecho de Le Maire', twelve miles further to the east. The tidal streams in the strait are strong and it might have been appropriate for us to have taken a breather in the bay near Gardiner's last resting place to wait for the next tide change. But the anchorage is exposed in an easterly so there was no real choice. We sailed on. Making a gentlemanly five knots we made the entrance in time to catch the remainder of the flood tide, which flows north through the strait.

I had been undecided about whether to go through the strait or pass round the eastern end of Staten Island. The distance to Stanley is about the same but as it turned out there was no debate. With the wind now fair in the south-west and with all of four hours to cover only fifteen miles before the south-going stream started, we turned up into Le Maire Strait. With the wind dying we fell back onto the engine to maintain boat speed. It was all very relaxing. Evening was on us and a celebratory drink was called for to mark the doubling of the Horn. Additionally we had passed another highpoint by leaving the Southern Ocean and entering the South Atlantic. That left just one more ocean to go, the one in our home backyard, the North Atlantic. Unfortunately it was soon to become apparent we had gone into the feel-good state a little prematurely.

Halfway up the Strait on the western coast is Bahia Buen Suceso, a good anchorage to such an extent it has been used by ocean voyagers over the centuries. Another bus stop on the route. It had been discovered in 1619 by the Spanish brothers, Bartolomé Garcia de Nodal and the younger Gonzalo. They had so named it because by anchoring in that new-found haven they had successfully avoided being driven back out of the strait by the fierce tidal flow and heavy weather. The Nodals, hailing from the same port in Galicia as Pedro Sarmiento, were highly experienced mariners with a fearful reputation as fighting sailors. They were in those waters to put the King of Spain out of his misery, or not. Agonising over whether or not the Schoutens' story was correct, he had decided there was only one way to be sure. Go down and see. That was the Nodals' commission. In Buen Suceso they were the first Europeans to meet the Aush, the eastern Ona Indians. These were related to the 'giants' of Patagonia, encountered by Magellan and Drake. The Nodals went out of their way to cement good relations with the local tribe, in marked contrast to the normal practice followed by their countrymen.

The brothers cleared their Bay of Good Success and headed west, encountering their share of headwinds and tough conditions. Passing close by the Barnevelts, which they charted, they sighted the Horn and struggled on to make westing in the face of deteriorating weather. A seemingly endless series of gales, laced with driving hail and snow, held them back from getting clear of the Horn. However, they were making ground despite the conditions and with the dawn of 12 February 1619, Shrove Tuesday as they noted, islands were visible between the squalls. They were given the name Diego Ramirez after the cosmographer sailing with the Nodal brothers. Today the main island bears the name Bartolomé and its neighbour Gonzalo. The group lies sixty miles south-west of Cape Horn and has played a significant role as a navigational aid in those waters. In the age of sail the big ships running their easting down from Australia could, on sighting them, check the rate of their chronometers. Now apart from an Armada outpost they remain uninhabited, the birds in their sanctuary undisturbed.

For the Nodals their mission was now complete. They could confirm Schouten's findings and they were free to go home. Steering north they opened up the western end of the Straits of Magellan which they passed down, through the Narrows and out into the Atlantic via the Virgins. Back in Spain they told Philip what he didn't want to hear, but at least now he knew for sure. The brothers were rewarded and honoured as they so richly deserved. In nine months they had confirmed the southern sea route and had been the first to circumnavigate Tierra del Fuego without drama or mishap. Theirs had been a voyage of consummate seamanship, probably the greatest of the early voyages. Three years later both brothers, still sailing together, were lost at sea in a West Indies hurricane. They died as they had lived, audacious adventurers.

One hundred and fifty years later, the Nodals' exercise in good racial relations was to be repeated when Captain James Cook anchored in Bahia Buen Suceso in the course of his first voyage to the south seas. The Aush received Cook and his party in a friendly manner, on their stepping ashore. He made a point of reciprocating accordingly. Three of the natives were taken on board *Endeavour* to be given clothes and provisions for them to take back to their families. Cook, a man of an enquiring mind, initiated a detailed study of the tribe and its way of life. One rather surprising observation of the womens' role in the scheme of things was that 'they were generally employed in domestic labour and drudgery.'

Cook surveyed the Bay of Good Success and other parts of the coast, finding the few charts that were in existence virtually of no value, derived as they were from crude drawings by Schouten and Le Maire as well as L'Hermite. Sailing from the strait, *Endeavour* doubled the Horn and set her course for Tahiti on which Cook was to observe the transit of Venus, the principal purpose of the voyage.

In the course of his second voyage Cook in *Resolution* was back in those waters, arriving in the western approaches to Tierra del Fuego in December 1774. With thoughts of Christmas Day, their third away, being spent at rest rather than banging about off the Horn, Cook entered a bay which was named Cook Bay, finding a sheltered anchorage in Christmas Sound to celebrate that day. They were just thirty miles to the west of Weddell's anchorage. Cook surveyed the surrounding islands leaving the results of this work on the chart today, Isla Sandwich, Cer Catedral de York and Bahia Trefusis amongst a veritable plethora of English-sounding names. The Earl of Sandwich in conjunction with the Royal Society had promoted Cook's three voyages of discovery. Goose Island is on the chart because there it was that fourteen geese were shot for distribution to all hands for Christmas dinner.

Cook sailed on to double Cape Horn for the second time and in weather similar to the conditions we had experienced. Entering Le Maire Straits *Endeavour* hove to off Good Success Bay and fired a two-gun salute which was answered by a smoke signal from a hill overlooking the bay. A boat was sent inshore but there was no sign of their earlier friends. But they left with good memories, charted some of Staten Island and sailed on to Table Bay. They were homeward bound.

Just over sixty years later the great surveyor's successor, Captain FitzRoy, brought *Beagle* to anchor in Buen Suceso. Darwin commented that on their first night 'it blew a gale of wind and heavy squalls from the mountains swept past us. It would have been a bad time out at sea, and we, as well as others, may call this Good Success Bay.'

The same cordial contact was established with local tribespeople, Darwin making an interesting observation. 'These Fuegians are a very different race from the stunted, miserable wretches further westward, and they seem closely allied to the famous Patagonians of the Strait of Magellan.' At this stage in his own personal evolution Darwin appears not to have accepted that the Fuegians as a whole needed understanding not condemnation.

From the cockpit of *Marelle* the bay looked attractive as we passed across the entrance. Tucked up at the head a yacht was at anchor. Perhaps like the Nodals she was working the tides and waiting for the start of the ebb. The *Pilot* in its description of the anchorage intriguingly mentions 'a shelter with room for eight persons stands in the centre of the beach'. Shipwrecked mariners perhaps, or stranded, intrepid backpackers?

Ahead of us lay Cabo San Diego at the north-western exit from the Strait. It is notorious for its attendant overfalls. These are marked clearly on the chart and the fact that this hazard should be taken seriously is brought to the mariner's attention by the *Pilot*. 'OVERFALLS. A heavy and dangerous race extends 5 or 6 miles from Cabo San Diego, as indicated on the chart.' Clear enough. The RCC pilot reinforces the point with 'Care should be taken to stay at least eight miles off Cabo San Diego.' But I knew better. Conditions in the Strait were ideal. The flood stream was slackening, carrying with it the light breeze. Not overfall weather. Fraser was on watch, and at my request kept reporting no sign of any broken water ahead. Our course would take us six miles comfortably clear of the cape. There should be no problem. Suddenly there was and in a big way.

Without warning we were in a world of chaos. Short and extraordinarily high waves were rising and falling with great rapidity, tumbling about, completely irregular and patternless. Broken water, a feature of the normal race and the giveaway of its presence, had been absent. The sea was just jumping up and down virtually on the spot. The motion in the boat was awful and frightening, causing me to be worried seriously about the stresses and strains throughout *Marelle*, let alone in her crew.

Then there was the matter of our supper. It being Sunday I was in the middle of the traditional skipper's fry-up. With the eggs taking off in one direction, beans and bacon in another and myself in motion as though in a tumble dryer the supper prospects were not promising. Doomed in fact, and I gave up for the time being in favour of something requiring less preparation, like biscuits.

With little wind either to propel or steady us it was a case of engine to get us out of the nightmare which seemed never-ending. The area covered by the overfalls was much larger than the chart would have us believe. Noted in my journal was 'Took us an hour to get out of it but the trauma stayed with me.' I felt exhausted physically and drained right out emotionally. It had been a navigational blunder and one that was entirely mine, creating what could well have been a serious situation for boat and crew. But once again I was let off the hook.

It was in fact to take more than a day before we encountered seas that had any system to them. The strong tidal streams, three knots across the top of Staten Island, coupled with the variable winds we continued to feel, were having their effect. The lumpy seas were knocking boat speed back such that it took all of the next day to drop the ice-strewn heights of Staten Island below the horizon to the south. This left me engaging in a little private agonising on whether I had made another navigational error in not having gone round the eastern end of the island. We would then have benefited from the current flowing out of the Southern Ocean, as indicated in a note on the chart. 'The Cape Horn Current predominates, flowing east to north-east with rates sometimes exceeding 3 knots.'

For Fraser the situation was not improved by not feeling well and off his food with a seasick feeling. By coincidence we had chilli con carne again that night, prepared on this occasion by Jeremy. 'Great and plenty of it,' I noted. Poor old Fraser. He would have been thinking of his affliction in Niemann. But by next morning things started to look up. With only two hundred and fifty miles to Stanley the sun came out, the sea levelled off and the breeze picked up, the ingredients for one of our best day's sails for many a day. We all felt better and successfully were able to ignore the fact that the wind was inexorably veering into the north, consequently heading us. The barograph embarked on a steady decline.

We were mindful of listening to Ray, the Canadian single-hander in Mar del Plata, relating the difficult time he had had in rounding the south-eastern corner of East Falkland with contrary winds and difficult tidal streams. It took him days of hard work to get up to Stanley.

We were having something of the same problem. The steadily freshening northerly wind was pushing us further offshore, leaving me with the concern that if we got too far to the east we would have a hard beat back to the land should the expected strong westerlies set in. Under reefed genoa, storm jib on the inner forestay and two reefs in the main, we were tramping along but not towards our target, Cape Pembroke. This marks the entrance to Stanley Harbour. I had done a *volte face* and was now congratulating myself we hadn't gone east about round Staten Island. We would now have been even further offshore because of this wind.

We went about and stood in to close the rock-girt shores of East Falkland. A good move, as late in the evening we benefited from the land breeze. Under full genoa and reefed main it was most pleasant sailing in smooth water now on course for Cape Pembroke, forty miles or so ahead. At midnight I reluctantly dragged myself out of my bag and up into the cockpit to relieve Fraser, to be greeted with 'Go back to your bunk. It's a grand night and I am enjoying myself. I will call you when I have had enough.' He was rather inclined to do that sort of thing from time to time, but I didn't complain. Pushing aside any feelings of guilt, I enjoyed that extra hour.

Our world had changed with the awareness that once again we were entering an environment that had people in it. On shore we could see the loom of the lights from scattered settlements and a bright display from the airport and military base at Mount Pleasant. Offshore were the lights of large fishing vessels passing close to us.

As the night wore on and came the dawn the breeze was deserting us as we rounded the cape. It was gratifying that we could now rely on the engine. Eric's biocide from Puerto Williams had made all the difference.

After rounding Cape Pembroke the course is west up the outer harbour of Port William for five miles and thence a turn to the south through what is known as The Narrows. On passing through these Stanley Harbour opens out, with the town itself spread out along its southern shore. The impression the place gives can best be described as homely. On our way up Port Williams the bareness and rather dreary nature of the land, much of it being covered with very coarse tussock grass, made an immediate impact on us. It presented an unattractive vista, but as we were to discover later there is another side to what these islands have to offer. The initial impression the landscape had on us appeared to have been the same for Darwin. 'An undulating land, with a desolate and wretched aspect, is everywhere covered by a peaty soil and wiry grass, of one monotonous brown colour. Here and there a peak or ridge of grey quartz rock breaks through the smooth surface.'

On emerging from The Narrows I called up Port Control to report our arrival and try to find out from the Harbour Master where we should berth. I didn't get the impression our arrival was the big event in his day, limiting his response to the suggestion we anchor off the public jetty and call up Customs and Immigration, who would board us to give us clearance. He added helpfully they might have a thought about where we could go for a longer-term berth. It was evident Stanley was not a yachtsman's home from home. This view was not one we would have occasion to alter.

On calling up that office, they amended the advice we had just received, saying we should go straight alongside the jetty and their man, Ken, would come down and step on board. Going out by boat to us at anchor did not appeal to him.

Jeremy put us alongside, doing his best to avoid the bits that were falling off and hanging down. On these the breeze, by now having freshened considerably, was trying to impale us. We were to learn later that the outer half of the jetty had been condemned but no one had thought it useful to inform us of this.

It was 1200 on Friday 13 February in this more or less last outpost of the British Empire.

CHAPTER EIGHT

FALKLANDS INTERLUDE

We had a sore storm ...and were ...driven in among certain Isles
never before discovered by any known relation.

John Davis, 14 August 1592

Alongside rotting town quay – where next to go? – no one wants to know – local doctor steps in – no fish and chips – Canache – meet up with Susan – ashore to stationary bed – into Camp – planning for 70 days at sea – friendly cooperation over fuel and water cans – wildlife – ship graves – war sites – Mission to Deep Sea Fishermen – wait for weather break – sail

We were here, now what? Several issues required attention and all at the same time. We had to find a secure berth before nightfall and I had to establish contact with Susan, who would be here by now. But more importantly Jeremy and Fraser wanted fish and chips.

However, before we could launch ourselves into these activities, a figure armed with brief case was espied picking its way with great care over the rotting decking of our jetty. It was Ken of Immigration who with great difficulty got himself onto our deck and then with a deep sigh of relief down into the cabin. He soon made it clear that although we might well be British taxpayers making a major contribution to keeping the Falkland islanders in the way they wished to be kept we were not one of them. He was affable and friendly but had no option other than to follow official policy. We were welcome in the Islands but there was a limit to that welcome. British passports or no British passports we could stay for three weeks and that was that. As our plan was for a ten-day stopover that should not be a problem, or so we thought. He asked us to pay him the standard harbour dues for a yacht, regardless of size, of £44. He was relaxed about its actual collection. 'Drop it in next time you are passing.' Although we might have felt a little miffed that the Islanders did not appear to want to enjoy our company indefinitely the pill was sweetened in that we were not asked to pay Customs Entry and Clearance charges, each of £30, also a standard fee for all ships coming and going within the islands.

Ken departed, walking over the jetty's planks as though treading on eggs, to be followed by Fraser and Jeremy to seek out the world's most southern frier of fish and chips. At the same time they wanted to test the communication system to call home. This left me free to get on with finding a bed for *Marelle* and to locate Susan.

The first step was to break the code made up of the acronyms FIC, FIPASS and FISHOPS, which were to feature prominently in our stay in Stanley. FIC is the Falklands Island Company, which has a dominant role in the Islands' affairs with a controlling finger in many of the local pies. One of these was a jetty next door to us, from which operated a harbour patrol craft, *Speedwell,* whose skipper had been monitoring our radio chats with the Harbour Master and Customs. He was most helpful on the berthing front, suggesting we try the FIC jetty. No berth there, or rather there was one but it would not be available as from tomorrow when something was going to be done to it, so the girl informed me. *Speedwell* then came back on the air and proposed FIPASS as being a good bet. I knew from my earlier homework that yachts had found a berth here. FIPASS stands for Falklands Interim Port and Storage System, which needless to say is managed by the FIC. It is a large facility towards the eastern end of the harbour, comprising seven permanently moored barges alongside which sizeable ships can berth. The barges, on which sit storage sheds and workshops, are connected to the shore by a vehicle and pedestrian ramp. Tucked in behind the barges is a pontoon for workboats with something left over for two or three yachts. If one is lucky. Located in FIPASS is FISHOPS, the Fisheries Department Operations Centre, which was to prove very helpful to us over the days ahead. On calling up FIPASS they confirmed that quite often they were able to accommodate the odd yacht but we were out of luck. They were keeping the only vacant berth for another British yacht expected in within a few days, manned or womanned by an all-female crew. I bit my tongue on complaining about this blatant sexism.

In the middle of these exchanges the skipper of *Speedwell*, who had not given up and seemed to know everything about everything that went on in Stanley, called up to say he had reported our arrival to Carl Freeman, the Ocean Cruising Club's local man, adding for good measure he knew Susan had been in town. He signed off with 'Will see you later.' He didn't.

I was getting a little nearer on the Susan front but nowhere with attending to *Marelle*'s needs. Seemingly the only option remaining was to move out onto a buoy or anchor in the harbour. Apart from the inconvenience of having to use the dinghy the harbour is swept by the prevailing westerlies. These were reputed to be very strong most of the time, frequently reaching gale force. We were to discover this uncomfortable fact to be correct. With a fetch of two miles or so to the head of the harbour, conditions could become decidedly uncertain.

At this point salvation arrived in the form of a little reception party standing gingerly on the jetty. The group consisted of Richard Davies, complete with wife Sarah and young family, accompanied as well by a man who spoke with some authority on the waterfront scene. It transpired he was the erstwhile Harbour Master, now recently retired but nevertheless taking much more interest in our activities than the present incumbent. Richard revealed he was a doctor in the local hospital and by chance had seen us arrive, noting the red ensign. He had come down to say hello. On hearing there was something of a problem over berthing, Richard announced he was a rare breed in the Falklands in that he was a yacht owner. To house his boat he had created a secure alongside berth in a small cove up at the far eastern end of the harbour in an area known as The Canache and marked as such on the chart. The name is believed to have been derived from 'careenage', as it was in this niche that small ships had dried out for bottom cleaning and underwater repairs. We were to discover later that The Canache is a graveyard for abandoned smaller vessels, sealers and the like, just left there with no economic way of otherwise disposing of them, their working lives over. It had also been the site for a floating base for army operations consequent on the Falklands War, the steel piling now rusting away against the rubble on the shore. The whole area is one of decay and desolation but it was to be good to us.

Richard went on to say he was in the process of building a more sophisticated pontoon arrangement against the old army piles, but although the present one was rather rough and ready it would provide a home for us, sharing it with his boat *Cowrie*. Constructed of steel and somewhat larger than *Marelle*, she had been built in Penryn near Falmouth and had been sailed out by Richard with Sarah in the course of a world cruise. However, she becoming pregnant, they had called a temporary halt to this grand plan with a stay in Stanley. He would presumably have been welcomed with open arms by the health authority as one cannot imagine there is a long queue of doctors in UK eager to further their careers in the Falklands. Although he would be careening *Cowrie* in The Canache next day and would be coming and going for day sails, we could use his berthing facility throughout our stay. A most generous gesture. This was the breakthrough we needed and put my mind at rest. In the meantime the shore party had come back with long faces. The fish and chip shop was closed.

Slipping from the jetty we proceeded down harbour to The Canache, passing on the way a small yacht lying inshore on a buoy. I noted in particular the very long buoy rope as an indication of the rough conditions, more often than not likely to be present. It transpired that here lay a sad story. The elderly yachtsman, 'like you' as someone so kindly put it, whilst on his way round the world alone, had stopped off in Stanley for repairs to his engine. On arrival he learned that his wife had died. The following day he had gone, with next stop Cape Town where he had been expecting to meet up with his wife. A long, rough, lonely and unhappy passage lay before him.

Sure enough in The Canache lay *Cowrie*. We went alongside, bringing *Marelle* and ourselves to rest. We drank to the successful achievement of the original objectives, Tierra del Fuego and doubling Cape Horn. This time the celebration was completed in peace, unlike its sudden termination in Le Maire Strait. The Southern Ocean was now really behind us.

My personal requirement now was to catch up with Susan. In light of his comment about seeing me later I had been rather expecting the *Speedwell* skipper to appear, but of him there was no sign as evening descended. Subsequently I was to learn 'later' meant any time in the future, years even or never. I set off, with toothbrush in pocket, to walk into Stanley to locate Carl and his wife Dianne. It is a walk of three miles or so over some rough bits of road, hard going and getting dark. However I had not gone very far when a four-wheel-drive appeared coming towards me. In it were the Freemans on their way to The Canache to bring me up to date on Susan's movements. She was staying overnight, they said, in a lodge on Pebble Island way up on the top of West Falkland but would be back on the plane in the morning. She was soon to know we had arrived, the communication system working with smooth efficiency, from *Speedwell* skipper to the Freemans, to Kay the owner of the guesthouse where Susan had been staying in Stanley, to the Pebble Lodge, to the pilot of the inter-island light aircraft, and finally to Susan as she stepped off the plane. The pilot then enquired 'Would you like to come back with me now to Stanley?' 'No, thank you very much. I want to see Pebble. He can wait one more night.' I was competing with an island, according to the Tourist Board, that features most of the more important wetlands in the group with their wildfowl breeding areas. It is also home to penguin colonies and southern sea lions. 'All of these should not be missed.'

The whole of the Falklands outside of Stanley is known as 'Camp'. To get there one travels by light aircraft, Britten-Norman 'Islander', flown by pilots with great nonchalance in frequently difficult weather and on very basic grass airstrips. Every morning the local radio station broadcasts the complete passenger lists on each flight to each destination. There is no future for the hopeful businessman wanting to take his secretary away for the weekend.

Sure enough, next morning, by courtesy of Freeman transport, I was reunited with Susan at the Stanley Air Terminal, only to be reminded, in the inimitable way wives have, that I was an idiot. She had told me in a letter posted to Puerto Williams the intimate details of her Falklands itinerary.

Our immediate plan was that we would have a week together in shoreside accommodation, leaving Jeremy and Fraser to themselves in *Marelle*, about which they were probably not too unhappy. A break from the old man would not come amiss.

The all-helpful Dianne drove us to the guesthouse where Susan had been staying, run by the truly delightful Kay McCallum, a born-and-bred Falklander and known to everyone. An outward-looking widow, she loved having people in her house. She had a clientele who kept coming back, year after year, like the retired Rear Admiral who came for his fishing.

The Falklands interlude was to be a short R and R break to catch our breath and restock for the Atlantic passage. For Fraser this long ocean leg was a challenge. Something he wanted to do. For Jeremy and certainly for me it was a chore. It was what had to be done. I am not an ocean sailor who looks on ocean sailing as an end in itself and I think Jeremy was of the same inclination. Nevertheless ocean sailing had been instrumental in getting me to the Falklands and I was interested to learn something about this unique archipelago and what it contains. Their very remoteness was in itself an attraction. Despite the Falklands conflict putting them in the spotlight, this group of islands and rocks set deep in isolation way down in the South Atlantic is something of an unknown quantity to most people.

Although John Davis reigns unchallenged as the accredited discoverer of the Islands in 1592 the possibility exists they were sighted by a Spanish ship in 1540. This in itself is a curious story. Don Alonzo de Camargo had been sent with three ships to determine the viability of Magellan's *paso* as a route for Spanish commercial shipping to Peru and Chile. Camargo himself won through but one of his ships was wrecked in the Straits whilst the third under stress of weather was blown south. The captain of the ship, the name of neither is recorded, mentioned in the log sighting islands, with descriptions of their appearance and the wildlife which fit the Falklands. The ship carried on and it would appear sailed down through what must have been Le Maire Strait, turning west into the approaches to the Beagle Channel to winter in an unidentified anchorage. The following year, battered and bruised, she retraced her steps to Spain and was promptly forgotten for a few hundred years. There was little media coverage for any endeavour that did not come back laden with gold or information on how to lay hands on it.

A couple of years after Davis, the Falklands were sighted by Sir Richard Hawkins, sailing in the wake of Drake, but he did not attempt a landing. The best part of a century was to pass before one was probably made. This was in the person of that likeable rogue the privateer William Dampier in the course of a memorable world cruise. However it was in 1690 that Captain John Strong of the Royal Navy made the first confirmed landing, from his ship *Welfare*. He named the stretch of water between the main islands Falkland Sound, after the then First Lord of the Admiralty. The name remained and was subsequently given to the whole archipelago. Hot on his heels came the French, whose explorations were eventually to lead to a colonisation attempt. It was during this period that another redoubtable English seafarer, Captain Woodes Rogers, made a landfall in 1708, the notation in his log referring to Falkland's Land. There is a link between Dampier and Woodes Rogers. Both circumnavigated the globe, Dampier three times, and both wrote entertaining and valuable books about their travels. Dampier's publication *A New Voyage Round the World* remained in print until quite recent times. However they are best remembered because of Alexander Selkirk, the inspiration for Robinson Crusoe.

In the course of Dampier's second voyage, second mate Selkirk was marooned on Juan Fernandez Island off Chile. This was partly at Selkirk's instigation. He had had enough of Dampier's autocratic ways. Four and a half years later the ship in which Dampier was sailing as navigator to Captain Woodes Rogers appeared off the island. A boat was sent inshore and Selkirk brought back to the ship. On clambering over the bulwarks the first person he saw was Dampier. He immediately demanded to be put ashore again. Fortunately he was forcibly restrained and brought back to England. Otherwise Defoe would have been denied the material to write his book.

The French interest in Les Malouines, their name for the Falklands, culminated in 1764 when a young French aristocrat, Captain Antoine de Bougainville, landed a group of artisans and would-be colonists to establish a settlement at the head of Berkeley Sound. As an outpost of

France it was shortlived. The Spanish complained to France about the French incursion into what they considered their space, so Bougainville sold the colony to them. Port Louis then became Puerto Soledad. Bougainville was to complete a successful circumnavigation via the Magellan Straits in which he did some useful survey work over two months. Today he is remembered by a cape and a bay in Tierra del Fuego bearing his name. He was also the first to take soundings around Cape Froward, actually landing on its base to raise the tricolor. The French never seem to give up. The voyage was memorable on several other counts. One is the beautiful South Seas flower the Bougainvillea and another was an unwitting, or supposedly unwitting, involvement with a young French woman. Sailing with Bougainville was a botanist who had a personal assistant, Baré, who was just another member of the ship's company. However, on arrival in a Pacific island the locals, who have a feel for such things, immediately identified Baré as female and were not slow to make their findings known. There was some embarrassment all round when this was established to be a fact but on returning to France it all ended happily. She was of course treated as a national heroine. It was all so romantic. The first woman to sail round the world.

Whilst the French and Spanish had been having their affair in East Falkland the British, unaware of all this, had been attempting to colonise West Falkland with a settlement at Port Egmont on Saunders Island in 1766. Port Egmont had been given its name the year before by the up-and-coming Captain John Byron, 'Foulweather Jack', who had been commissioned by the Admiralty to carry out a survey of the islands. What better name could he have chosen than Egmont, who happened to be the reigning First Lord of the Admiralty? Byron no doubt had his eye on the future, which was in due course promotion to Admiral.

The early history of the archipelago is one of occupation and then abandonment. Port Egmont was vacated in 1774, to be followed by the Spanish who evacuated Port Soledad in 1806. The whalers and sealers moved in for lawlessness to prevail.

Having achieved its hard-won independence from Spain, the new government in Argentina repossessed Port Soledad in 1820 with a new but equally abortive attempt at establishing a colony. In 1832 the governor was murdered by a gang of mutineers, his death signalling the end of Argentinian occupation of the Falklands.

In the tortuous path of claim and counterclaim to the islands the British Ambassador in Buenos Aires, rejoicing in the name of Woodbine Parish, had a little earlier lodged a formal claim on behalf of the British government. When no positive response resulted two Royal Navy vessels were despatched. On 5 January 1833 'Right of Sovereignty' was exercised and the British have been there ever since. Gunboat diplomacy was in its ascendancy and it worked. It was also to mark the end of violence and outright lawlessness but not quite. Captain Matthew Brisbane, old shipmate and valued friend of James Weddell, was appointed British Resident only to be murdered in brutal circumstances five months later by a gang of ex-convicts and gauchos. The Royal Navy restored order. A few months before this tragic event *Beagle* had been anchored off the settlement, with FitzRoy being very favourably impressed by Brisbane. It was at this time that Darwin had gone off on a tour of the area on horseback accompanied by some gauchos of whom he spoke well. One can only wonder about his subsequent reaction on hearing about the murder. The colony continued to develop, a significant step in its progression being the resiting of the seat of administration in 1845 to where Stanley is now.

To make the position clear to friend and foe, the Islands were later to be classified as a Dependent Territory of the United Kingdom, the 'executive authority being vested in Her Majesty the Queen'. The population at the last census was 1,640 resident in Stanley and 590 in Camp. Stanley refers to itself as 'the smallest and most remote capital city in the world'. In recent years the way of life has changed as the economic base has shifted from an almost total dependence on sheep and wool, the main source of revenue now coming from the issue of licenses to specialised squid jigging vessels from the Far East, and a healthy revenue it is too.

In the limited time we had together Susan and I wanted to experience as much as we could of what the Falklands are all about. Within the bounds of this objective, however, *Marelle*'s needs had to be addressed. One of the lessons Jeremy and I had learned on the way south was the need for diesel fuel and lots of it, as a way of helping to keep our sanity in the Doldrums. The purist would stoutly maintain that for complete fulfilment, and to be totally at one with the environment, the true sailor would have nothing to do with an engine. Not being of that school we had a pressing need for extra fuel containers to bolster our fuel stocks for the return crossing of the Line. Similarly we needed to increase our fresh-water storage capacity with more containers. The run up to the Azores would be longer than any of the previous legs and moreover there were going to be three of us. I undertook the task of finding containers, leaving Jeremy to concentrate on the stocking-up programme in the no-frills shopping on offer in Stanley.

In the quest for all these containers it soon became evident there was a dearth of them. Feelers were put out. An army liaison officer, Major Phillip, learning of our quest volunteered to track down as many five-gallon jerry cans as he could find, suitable for water. Looked hopeful. Then following up on a useful suggestion I spoke to the local radio station, who agreed to broadcast throughout the day a feature on our quest. This brought in a mixed collection of diesel cans which were dumped on poor old Kay McCallum's doorstep. Although there was no luck with water cans at least we were making progress on the fuel front. We could now carry the best part of fifty gallons of fuel on board. Where these extra cans were going to be stowed was a problem to be worried about later.

Having got the action under way it was sightseeing time. An excellent government publication *An Introduction to the Falkland Islands* makes, *inter alia*, the point 'Penguins are perhaps the most striking feature of bird life in the Falklands, with five breeding species (Rockhopper, Magellan, Gentoo, King and Macaroni).' Susan and I whilst in Antarctica had seen all these except the King. This and the mighty Emperor were on our 'must see' list. The Emperor we probably would never see, living as it does in the very depths of Antarctica, but we could now see the King. A major colony exists at Volunteer Point, at the north-eastern tip of East Falkland, access to which is by four-wheel-drive from Stanley. Unfortunately the town had been temporarily taken over by a touring American glee club, commandeering many of the local operators such as the man who did the Volunteer Point trip. But all was not lost, as we had learned that in the midst of a Gentoo colony nearer to home there were half a dozen Kings as permanent live-in guests. This commune is also over in the north-east at Kidney Cove but we were lucky through Kay to organise a visit to this rare sight with another local, Neil Rowlands. After collecting Jeremy from *Marelle*, Neil took us at high speed in his powerful rigid inflatable boat out through The Narrows, across Port William and into Sparrow Cove. Here a spanking new pontoon bad been installed by an enterprising land owner with a view to building up a tourist interest. Alongside this Neil kept his Land Rover, into which we climbed for an hour's drive over rough country covered with tussac grass to the colony. There were the Kings. They are magnificent birds and they know it. Standing with their bills, or mandibles as the serious birder would say, pointed to the sky, they maintained an upper-crust aloofness amongst the homely Gentoos. We were delighted to have seen them and been allowed to pay our homage. After lunch in a Portacabin which Neil had recently erected for bird-watchers to stay in overnight, it was back to

Sparrow Cove for a near airborne passage to Stanley. It was in this cove that Brunel's *Great Britain* lay on the beach for many years, as an abandoned hulk, from 1933 until 1970 when she was rescued and brought back to Bristol for restoration. Launched in 1843, she was the first ship built of iron and with screw propulsion to cross the Atlantic. At the time she was the largest ship in the world, a monument to a genius and British shipbuilding skills. It was her first and only return to where she had been built after exactly 127 years.

We admired Neil's efforts to build a business to attract tourists for wildlife spotting and fishing. Our regard for his enterprise was not diminished when some time later he deposited on board *Marelle* a three-pound trout.

Whilst waiting for *Marelle* to turn up Susan had made various trips into Camp and was keen to revisit one of her favourites with me. Port Howard in West Falkland. It was a trip I am so glad we made, providing a glimpse of the life that had been at the backbone of the Islands' economy for a hundred and fifty years.

Boarding, as the only passengers, the Islander light aircraft at the little Stanley Airport, we hopped from one airstrip to another dropping off packages and collecting others until crossing Falkland Sound, we touched down or rather bounced down onto the grass at the Port Howard settlement. Waiting for us was Hattie, owner of the lodge. This was a fine rambling, old-colonial style building and charming as was Hattie. She had not had it easy. Coming out a year or so back as cook and hostess at the lodge, she had ended up marrying the owner. Robin was a member of the family that had run the station for many years and operated the 200,000-acre farm with its forty or so inhabitants, as the Tourist Board informed us. Robin was not there, having been taken ill, and for some time had been in hospital in England, leaving Hattie, with a lot on her hands. Sadly he was not to return home. Hattie, despite having so much on her shoulders, gave unstinting attention to her guests, preparing superb meals and making our overnight stay a delightful experience. The Islanders are a mix of inertia and initiative.

On arrival it was all action. In the ubiquitous Land Rover Hattie drove us around the estate, which included a school room, with a stop to witness the shearing shed in full operation. This was on an impressive scale. It had to be for a station running over 400,000 sheep. Next it was down to the little jetty for a cruise out into Falkland Sound in a retired RNLI lifeboat which Robin had arranged to be shipped out from UK. We were fortunate in being the only passengers, thereby enjoying the undivided attention of the skipper, highly knowledgeable on the wildlife.

Two other lodge guests had been scheduled to come with us but had called off when they saw what was involved in climbing on board. They were too fat. Permanent world travellers, they had enjoyed, it would seem, too much rich fare for too long in too many places.

We were given a good exposure to the wetland wildfowl grounds and enjoyed a close encounter with another of the residents, a big southern sea lion. He stood his ground for a while then, getting bored with the whole thing, slid into the water and swam off back to mum.

Back on shore there was no let-up in the action. We were sent over to a small workshop producing high-quality Falklands knitwear. On entering we found the armed forces in occupation. This was not unexpected as our friend the major had told me he was accompanying the newly appointed officer commanding the British Forces on a tour of his parish. They would be in Port Howard at the same time as our visit. A fortunate coincidence as it was to turn out. Phillip introduced Susan and me to his boss, Brigadier Peter Sheldon, and the other aide, Squadron Leader Fiona. Philip explained how I happened to be in the Falklands, mentioning he was endeavouring to get some jerry cans for us. The Brigadier, himself a yachtsman, was interested and turning to Phillip and Fiona remarked 'I am sure we can do something, can't we?' I knew then our procurement problem had ceased to exist. The military moved on and we returned to the lodge for drinks and a Hattie dinner. It had been a good day.

We had been warned in advance that flying round the Islands can be uncertain. Sure enough next morning Stanley Airport rang through to say it was too foggy for our plane to take off. How fortunate! This gave us the opportunity to see more of the geography of Camp, once again in the Land Rover driven this time by a well-informed member of the farm community. With us also was young Luke, on a work programme from Inverness, who had obviously taken to the life, feeling not out of place in the rigorous climate.

The landscape, completely devoid of trees, is essentially grassland interspersed with heath and stunted shrubs in the peaty soil doing the best they can in the searing wind. It was over this type of country that Darwin rode with his two gauchos, the excursion bringing forth reference to 'these miserable islands'. A prominent feature of this terrain is the widespread occurrence of highly distinctive rock formations described in the promotional literature as 'stone runs' ('rivers' of angular quartzite boulders). These 'rivers' certainly were of considerable interest to Darwin:

In many parts of the island the bottoms of the valleys are covered in an extraordinary manner by myriads of great loose angular fragments of quartz rock, forming 'streams of stones'. These have been mentioned with surprise by every voyager ... The blocks are not waterworn, their angles being only a little blunted: they vary in size from one or two feet in diameter to ten, or even more than twenty times as much. They are not thrown together into irregular piles, but are spread out into level sheets or great streams. It is not possible to ascertain their thickness, but the water of small streamlets can be heard trickling through the stones many feet below the surface. We may imagine that streams of white lava had flowed from many parts of the mountains into the lower country, and then when solidified they had been rent by some enormous convulsion into myriads of fragments. The expression 'streams of stones', which immediately occurred to every one, conveys the same idea.

The geology of the Islands held his attention more than their zoology, much of which seemed to have passed him by, although he does make an illuminating observation on the Magellanic penguin. 'This bird is commonly called the jackass penguin, from its habit, while on shore, of throwing its head backwards, and making a loud strange noise, very like the braying of an ass: but while at sea and undisturbed, its note is very deep and solemn, and is often heard in the night time.' Shades of the experience common to *Beagle* and *Marelle* with cows out at sea off the South American coast.

The gauchos and the way they set about their business had first attracted Darwin in South American Patagonia, this interest being maintained in the Falklands. He makes special mention of their ability to make a fire in the Islands under seemingly impossible conditions with everything being damp. There is a marked similarity with the way the Fuegians were able to light fires in equally wet surroundings.

The best fuel is afforded by a little green bush about the size of common heath, which has the useful property of burning while fresh and green. It was very surprising to see the Gauchos, in the midst of rain and everything soaking wet with nothing more than a tinder-box and piece of rag, immediately make a fire. They sought beneath the tufts of grass and bushes for a few dry twigs, and these they rubbed into fibres; then surrounding them with coarser twigs, something like a bird's nest, they put the rag with its spark of fire in the middle and covered it up. The nest being then held up to the wind, by degrees it smoked more and more, and at last burst out in flames. I do not think any other method would have had a chance of succeeding with such damp materials.

He was further intrigued that the gauchos used bones as fuel, observing 'to my great surprise' the skeleton of a bullock 'made nearly as hot a fire as coals'. Lucas Bridges would have been interested in these fire-lighting techniques and the comparison with those adopted by his Fuegians. The added dimension was that Tierra del Fuego was densely treed whereas the Falklands were virtually treeless but man had successfully adapted to each setting.

With our guides we tramped over the low hills behind Port Howard and walked up a sombre valley. Scattered over a large area lay the shattered remains of crashed Argentinian Mirage aircraft. They had been damaged when attacking British troop concentrations near Goose Green and could not make it back to safety. One could imagine the desperate efforts of the pilots to keep airborne only to see death rushing up at them. A feeling of great sadness descended on us when looking over that graveyard of young men's lives lost in the course of political aims. The area is treated by the locals as a memorial ground to the conflict and its dead. The taking of parts from the wreckage is decidedly frowned upon. The waste of men and material was laid out there before us.

It was back to the lodge to learn, unfortunately perhaps, that visibility had lifted enough for our plane to be on its way. Another tasty meal by Hattie, who then took us out to wave farewell as we became airborne. Our impression was of a rather lonely but gallant figure.

Back at Stanley it was a case of making the most of Susan's last few days. A long walk round the end of The Canache over the all-too-familiar tussac land brought us to Gypsy Cove in Port William, home to a large colony of Magellanic penguins. They were standing guard over their moulting chicks. We kept our distance. The whole area was just a mass of burrows, this species of penguin living underground. Behind them ran a wire fence, decorated with skull-and-crossbones signs, closing off the beach. It had not been cleared of Argentinian anti-personnel mines and probably never will be made safe. Large areas of the Islands are believed to be mined but with no records made by the Argentinians where exactly they laid their mines these suspect areas have simply been placed out of bounds to all, probably in perpetuity.

In the town we explored the limited number of dining-out prospects. The two hotels were reasonable but our favourite was Kay's. Her meals were so good and with her guest list ever changing there was always interesting company. For us staying there was a warm experience and a memorable feature of the whole trip.

Susan's departure day arrived and we went out in a hired car to Mount Pleasant Airport, thirty miles from Stanley. It has been built as an international airport, integral with the base for the armed forces whose presence is all-pervading. The cost of protecting these islands must be very significant indeed. What is the future for the Falklands? As on Gibraltar the people desperately want to remain part of Britain, retaining a deep antipathy towards their powerful neighbours. But with both Argentina and Spain there is a linkage which will not get less with the passing years. It must be possible to take advantage of the considerable benefits of this linkage without losing sovereignty. However this problem of distrust is so evident amongst the Falklanders and so deep in their souls that rational dialogue would seem to have no hope.

It was now back to business on board, Susan having gone. There was an adjustment involved in this for me as there was probably for the other two with a change in the routine they had got used to in my absence. However the overriding belief was the end was in sight and seemingly we could almost count the days to our homecoming. What we were not to know was that the return passage was to be longer and appreciably more exacting than it looked on the passage plan. These always look so beguilingly straightforward on paper, so simple and precise. And they always go adrift.

Transcending everything was the need to get to sea. We had been in the Falklands long enough. There was a sense of urgency to get ourselves shipshape and as they used to say, possibly still do, 'ready for sea in all respects'. Fraser was not saying very much but I knew he was fretting a little. He was in Stanley because the Islands featured in the passage plan, not because of any interest value they might have in themselves or a wish on his part to indulge in sightseeing. He was not a tourist by nature. He is a sailor first and foremost. For him there were two stages to the adventure. The first, the South American cruise with the Horn doubling, had been accomplished, and now the second beckoned, the ocean experience. I had become aware that because of the itinerary delays, there was a pressure on him with his personal circumstances at home, work and family, although he made no issue of it. Also I knew that Jeremy was wanting to get on with the final chapter of our saga, albeit he had a wider perspective through an interest in nature and wildlife. Although my own experience of the Falklands had been quite different I was at one with my companions in wanting to be homeward bound.

The countdown started the following night when there was a knock on the cabin doors whilst we were at supper. Phillip's voice came filtering through the grille. 'I have ten jerry cans with me. Do you want me to take them away and fill them while I have the Land Rover?' It was raining, cold and dark outside. He had done more than enough. 'Thanks all the same, Phillip, but there is no need. Fraser will take care of them.' Hollow laugh from Fraser but always to be the first he accordingly bounded out on deck to take the cans from him. Declining a drink, Philip vanished into the night. We now had both the water and fuel cans we needed, the major step in the logistics involved in our departure. It was typical of Fraser that whilst on deck, despite the unpleasant condition, he ran out another couple of shore lines, it now blowing very hard, bringing with it driving rain from the north-east. Coming from this direction it was forcing us off the piling to which we, with the load of *Cowrie* outside us, were moored. Dry and warm in the cabin, Jeremy and I leant our support to Fraser's efforts with appropriate words of encouragement, which we were sure he appreciated.

The indications were that the key to us getting away was going to be the weather and more especially the wind. To get the daily weather fax and synopsis I had been directed to FISHOPS, who were only too willing to oblige. One of its officers, Ray, ran off a copy for me of the daily weather information received from the meteorology office at the Mount Pleasant Airport. Each morning I would walk round the foreshore from The Canache to FIPASS, taking about a quarter of an hour, and then into the FISHOPS office. Ray would have copies of the printouts ready for me, on which we would have a discussion. All of this free of charge.

The weather map embraced the area into which we would be sailing, well out into the South Atlantic and clear of the Falklands local weather. We appeared to be entering a very unsettled spell, more so than usual according to Ray, with strong to very strong winds predominantly from a northerly direction. Just what we did not want.

In the meantime we were getting on with the things-to-do list. Jeremy and Fraser arranged stowage for all those newly acquired containers. Fuel cans into the cockpit and on the afterdeck, with the water cans under the saloon table and into the starboard unused quarter berth, requisitioned for the purpose. They all fitted in surprisingly well although there was a little concern that with the capacity of the cockpit so reduced there was nowhere for the water to go other than over the bridge deck into the cabin, should we take a solid sea over the quarter. The stores programme was completed but Jeremy ran into a problem with getting the propane gas bottles refilled. The one source he could find could only half fill them, which was to cause difficulty later in the passage. Provisions restocking was based on what we thought would be a very generous estimate of seventy days at sea to the Azores. All this was got on board and poor old *Marelle* was below her marks again.

Fraser in particular was keen that we started off with a clean underbody. We probably had grown a garden on the bottom since leaving Falmouth, although I was not too sure. From past experience I suspected the changing water temperature and likewise the salinity variations may have taken care of the weed and barnacle growth. There was one way we could be sure. At the end of The Canache was the local diving school. With an introduction effected by Carl its members were only too keen to get their wetsuits on, and armed with scrubbing brushes, they set about giving us a scrub-off. I took the opportunity to get them to check all the underwater fittings. They seemed to enjoy themselves at the same time and were pleased, I imagined, to be able to put something into the club funds. They indicated the bottom had been weedy, although not excessively so, but was now clean and fittings in good order. I had asked them to pay particular attention to the rudder and its heel fitting. They reported light bruising on the bottom of the trailing edge where we had grounded in Caleta Sara in Patagonia, but of no great moment. How anyone could enjoy immersion in murky, cold water I don't know, but they evidently did.

Although we continued to fret at being weather-bound, life was made more than bearable by a quite wonderful institution, a veritable home from home. Close by the FIPASS set-up was a small building, the Lighthouse Seamen's Centre, run by New Zealander Mike Hughes and his Danish wife Kirsten. Also known as the Mission to Deep Sea Fishermen, it more than lived up to its stated aim of 'caring for seamen'. With firm Christian beliefs, Mike and Kirsten had with them a small team of dedicated workers sharing the same religious convictions. Their aim was to afford to whomsoever walked through the door the benefits as well as the meaning of what their faith stood for, but without pressuring the beneficiaries with The Message. With delicious home cooking at very modest prices, television, small lending library, showers, self-service laundry and table tennis, it was a facility open to all seamen and fishermen, regardless of faith, race or colour. All were welcome. There was even a large bin of used clothing from which anyone could take any item. The bin was kept topped up by persons leaving unwanted articles. A charity shop but one with a difference. It was all free. We were to use the place every day, and it made a very big difference to our daily lot, as it did to those of the crews of ships in port, but even more so to the fishermen and fish labourers off the squid vessels. These men, South-East Asian, had a hard working life, poorly paid and frequently harshly treated. The Mission would have seemed like heaven to these virtual slave workers.

The squid fishing vessels were very much part of the Stanley scene, coming and going to discharge their catches into large storage mother-ships anchored in Port William or in the next large inlet further north, Berkeley Sound. At times they could be seen coming into Stanley Harbour to procure or renew their fishing licences. It is these that have transformed the Falklands economy. Commencing in 1987, the fishing licensing activity has tripled the GNP of the Islands, creating full employment.

The economy of course has always had a maritime linkage, being on the road to and from the Horn. This linkage was in the main to the advantage of the Islanders. As evidence of what was a highly profitable marine activity is the quite large number of hulks lying around the Islands, with a generous sprinkling of them rotting in Stanley Harbour.

In the great era of sail there was a steady stream of ships, knocked about in the Southern Ocean and in particular off the pitch of the Horn, desperately in need of repair to hulls and rigging, not to mention their crews. Lying downwind, the Falklands were the logical refuge to seek succour. Geographically it was the logical choice, but not financially. Stanley had an odious reputation for greed, exorbitant charges and outright exploitation of ships' captains and owners. The exploitation system began with a ship limping into Stanley. The insurance assessor would board the ship, examine her condition and call for a quotation for the repairs. He would then put on his repair yard hat and give an estimate grossly in excess of the insured value of the ship. He would next re-assume his insurance role and declare the ship a write-off, arranging the sale at a giveaway price to himself or an associated local company. The ship's cargo, fittings and timber, the latter almost priceless in the treeless Islands, would then be realisable assets of considerable value. The ship herself was turned into a storage hulk or used for other diverse activities such as a building block for a wharf or jetty at virtually no cost. There was nothing the hapless shipowner could do and another proud ship was consigned to the graveyard.

In Stanley there is a variety of condemned ships in various stages of decay. In Whalebone Cove, just round the corner from where we were in The Canache, lies *Lady Elizabeth*, iron barque, resting upright on the beach. Her mainyard is still crossed like a crucifix. There is an eeriness about her, having the appearance of a living ship, still sailing. She had traded for years to and fro from the Islands until, damaged on a rock, she was to follow the condemnation route. Moored in Stanley Harbour, she broke those moorings in 1936 in wild weather to ground in the cove, where she stands still proud and tall.

Off the town in shallow water lies the brig *Fleetwood*, built in Porthmadog in North Wales in 1874. Keeping her company in the harbour are the remains of another Welsh-built ship, the barque *Capricorn*, brought into Stanley after a fire off the Horn in 1881. Same story. An impossible repair bill.

In *Marelle* we had no repair work of any consequence, which was just as well, as being completely of teak she would have been a prime candidate in the system. In the course of a simple routine task I was to learn a little more about life. I had withdrawn the log (speedometer) to check it was clear of weed, using a small torch to see better what I was doing. This was promptly dropped down into the bilge where it vanished from sight. I resorted to a hand mirror in an attempt to see the errant torch. The mirror then followed the torch into the bilge, also to vanish. The gap down which they had slid was too small for me to get my hand down. Apart from removing the floorboards and lifting out the water tanks there was no way that I could see how to recover torch and mirror. With no one else on board I was able to give free and unfettered reign to my feelings before retiring to the Mission to collect myself. There Kirsten, sensing I seemed to be upset, asked what was wrong. 'Relax. My boy Adam, with a ten-year-old's hand, will have no problem in picking them out.' Great. In her car we went round and climbed on board *Marelle*. I showed them what was obviously the only access but young Adam did not want to risk getting his hand stuck. That was that. Kirsten asked if there was another way down. 'No,' I replied, 'that is the only way. There is no other solution.' 'Let me try,' she offered. After a close scrutiny she slid her arm down through a gap I hadn't even thought was a possibility and came up with the torch, then to be followed by the mirror. Adopting another approach altogether had resolved the problem. This left me musing about major world problems like the intractable situations in Palestine and Northern Ireland, going on for generations with no apparent solution. Perhaps another completely different approach to those adopted so far could be successful, if only the minds of those involved could be freed.

We had known about Mike and Kirsten before we arrived in Stanley. Whilst in Puerto Williams and in the course of conversation with Thies of *Wanderer III*, knowing he had been there for some time, I asked what facilities were on offer in Stanley. He made mention of the Hughes with particular reference to Mike's familiarity with the waterfront scene. 'How does one find this chap?' 'Don't worry, he will find you.'

As it happened when we finally arrived in Stanley, Mike was away on another island with his 75-foot converted Danish fishing trawler, *King David*, a big heavy ketch, which was having her, or I suppose his, bottom scrubbed. Shortly after our arrival the boat was back. A figure pulled over to *Marelle* in the trawler's tender to announce he was Mike Hughes and doing what Thies had said he would do. He added 'Now here is a real boat!', patting her topsides. She did not take offence and I immediately warmed to this discerning man.

In The Canache it was starting to become a full house. Mike had put *King David* alongside some piling opposite us, where she provided a lee for an Australian single-hander, Trevor in his *Iron Bark*, who had just arrived from having wintered in the Antarctic Peninsula. He had been through a particularly harsh time with almost no heating on board, everything freezing solid including all his food stocks. Coming in after him was another true ocean wanderer, *Joshua*, with a Canadian, Mark, and his wife Fraser, surprisingly from Cornwall and coincidentally with the same rather unusual first name as our Fraser. A tough girl. She had been troubled by a tooth at sea which Mark had extracted. Ahead of us lay *Express Crusader,* ex Naomi James, now owned by a friendly Welsh couple, Jim and Noelle. Very experienced long-distance sailors, they had also been down in the Antarctic and were getting themselves organised to sail on to the Balearics, where they had their permanent home. They were stuck in Stanley, locked in a bureaucratic struggle with the Chilean authorities in trying to recover some gear in bond in Puerto Montt and have it shipped to them. In the meantime Noelle was hand-making a new genoa. We were most impressed. Out-going shortly after we had arrived had been a Swedish yacht, with a husband-and-wife team, bound for Salvador, the original capital of Brazil. They would be encountering a very different way of life, going from one extreme to the other. The town is notorious for street crime, which doesn't exist in Stanley.

The vacant spot left by the Swedes was filled by *The Alderman* with Richard Wakeford and young crew. Theirs had been an interesting cruise. Richard had bought the boat in New Zealand, which he then proceeded to circumnavigate before crossing the Pacific to Chile; thence down to Antarctica and up to the Falklands. Their plan was to sail on to Mar del Plata and return to the Solent via the West Indies.

There were now three British-flagged vessels in one spot, being unique in our experience since leaving the Atlantic islands. *The Alderman* were a hospitable lot. A drinks party was given for the crews of the five boats now crammed into The Canache. It was an unexpected as well as generous occasion with no shortage of grog, bringing together a group who shared an overriding common interest in deep-sea sailing, but of a breed who normally keep to themselves. The total distance sailed by that gathering of ocean sailors would have been quite considerable. Included in the chatter was speculation on the whereabouts of Didier and Josette, our French friends from Mardel. They had been in Port Lockroy in the Peninsula with *Iron Bark*, sailing at the same time for Stanley. Being a bigger and faster boat than his, Trevor had been expecting to meet up with them again when he arrived but of them there was no sign. We were a little worried about them, particularly knowing about the design flaw in the centreplate casing. Drake Passage is not a stretch of water in which to experience hull weakness. Subsequently we were to hear they were safe and sound having diverted from their planned route.

We seemed the odd ones out, not having taken in Antarctica, but those present on that social occasion had a common experience drawing us all together. Cape Horn! The expression 'Cape Horners' has a special ring about it. It is a legacy from the great age of sail, being a term applied initially specifically to the American wooden full-rigged ships, known as 'clippers', built to service the development of the Californian coast and in particular the gold rush. These voyages, originating on the North American east coast, involved a double rounding of the Horn. The outward passage usually meant a laborious and dangerous beat to windward into the Pacific against the westerlies with the contingent risk of breaking gear and men. Homeward bound back into the Atlantic would have been an easier run but not always so with the not uncommon occurrence of easterlies, resulting in another hard-on-the-wind doubling of old Cape Stiff, the weather more often than not being bad. Under the charge of gung-ho captains and bucko mates these gloriously beautiful but delicate ships were driven to near destruction in very short time, the same treatment being meted out to their crews.

As this era moved into history square-riggers running their easting down from Australasia to round the Horn into the South Atlantic, and those who sailed in them, were given the title of Cape Horners. With the gradual demise of these ships the surviving masters in sail set up associations to keep alive the memory of those great days, meeting over dinner for the swapping of yarns. What yarns they would have been and what a tragedy it is that those priceless tales and the sea lore they contained were confined largely to word of mouth and never recorded. Treasures lost forever.

There is today an international Association of Cape Horners with a UK chapter applying strict rules of membership carried over from the early days. A requirement is that members have taken part in a 'non-stop passage (under sail) of at least 3,000 nautical miles, passing through 50 degrees south in both the Pacific (or Indian) and Atlantic Oceans.' Originally the true Cape Horner was a commercial square-rigged sailing vessel but those ships have now all gone. The modern version, the so called 'tall ships' used for sail training, are really hybrids. Equipped with large, powerful engines and even twin screws, they fit more into the category of power vessels with auxiliary sails, akin to the ships that bridged the evolutionary gap in the nineteenth century when sail was handing over to steam. Certainly the tall ship of today is unlikely to venture into the Southern Ocean. To keep the founding fathers' intentions alive the Association has extended membership to eligible yachts. Long-distance ocean-racing yachts such as participants in the Whitbread round the world race, for example, would qualify. However in our case as the latitude of The Canache, where we were all gathered, is 51°41′S this on its own meant we were not eligible to become full Members but would be accepted as Friends, a category of diverse types who have rounded the Horn, even including steamship captains and crews.

It is a whimsical thought that none of the pioneers of rounding Cape Horn would qualify as Members but at best only as Friends. And what a distinguished band of Friends they would make! We were in august company. It would include the Schouten brothers and Le Maire, the Nodal brothers, Anson and Byron, L'Hermite, Cook, Weddell, FitzRoy and Darwin. This is not even to mention Drake himself.

One could imagine these greats, especially Willem Schouten, the actual discoverer of Cape Horn and the first one recognised to have rounded it, being amused to know they could not call themselves 'Cape Horners'. Bizarrely the non-stop mileage stipulation would preclude them. For *Marelle* and her crew it was enough that we had made the Cape Horn connection and to have had that experience, with or without the title.

The denizens of The Canache shortly afterwards were thrown together again by courtesy of Mike from the Mission who took us off on an excursion up Mount Tumbledown. This overlooks Stanley and was the scene of a last stand by the Argentinians during the 1982 conflict. Leaving our transport at the bottom we trudged up the steep slopes under a bright sun and against a very strong wind. At the summit, where the young Argentinian soldiers had been entrenched, were the rusting remains of the field kitchens located in the shelter of the rock outcrops. On the other side of the ridge in a hollow in the rocks was an incredibly sad little memorial to the British soldiers who had been killed in the assault. A cross and plaque with names, ranks and numbers told the story. For the Argentinian fallen there was nothing. Any form of remembrance would have been totally unacceptable to the Falkland Islanders. Their bitterness ran deep.

We were told the British force, mainly Scots Guards, had marched more than eighty miles in particularly harsh conditions over extremely difficult country to drive the enemy off the heights. An overland feat which the defenders had thought impossible. How much that says for the fortitude, training and discipline of those young British troops. It was the end, Stanley being taken shortly after.

The wheel had done a complete turn. The story is told of two Royal Marines, part of the handful in the first days trying to hold Stanley against a large Argentinian force, lying behind the front fence of a house with their weapons cocked and ready. Out of the house comes its occupier, an elderly woman, who says 'Would you two young men like a cup of tea?'

Sitting on the rocks with Mike looking down the barren, brown slopes to the sweep of Stanley Harbour, we munched our sandwiches and thought about that war. Speaking as a dedicated Christian, Mike advanced the opinion 'It is unlikely there would be the same support now amongst the young in light of today's attitudes in society. But in any event I would not let my sons get involved and go to war.' I wondered about that. Even today, with such a free flow of people, worldwide communication and non-acceptance of what was once never questioned, have basic instincts changed? Are the young men and women today, once one gets below the surface, really all that different to those of 1982? I asked him 'But how much influence would you have over your boys when it came to the point, in a world where the young are taught to make their own intellectual way and be independent in thought and deed?' I did not get an answer.

It had been a good day, with a little more exposure to the Falklands. It was then back to our own small world in The Canache. Richard Davies came down with a little party to go sailing in *Cowrie*. Included in the group were the Brigadier and Fiona, the only female Squadron Leader I had ever met, and I could not escape from the thought that this appointment would have been to the decided benefit of the Service. They enquired about the water containers, giving me the opportunity to express first-hand our appreciation of their help. During our stay we had been the recipients of much in the way of kindly assistance. Richard Davies, apart from the letting us share his mooring facility, had been of considerable help to me personally, attending to an infected finger, savaged by an anchor way back in Niemann, as well as giving me a medical check-over.

In the meantime the requirement to get on our way was starting to press down on us. We were now into March with autumn looming. We needed to be out of the southern regions of the South Atlantic before the winter set in. Richard of *The Alderman* was also keen to get on his way. He came over in his dinghy with the latest weather fax from Chile (he of course had that facility on board) which looked reasonably encouraging.

However, with rain starting and an increasing wind, I called off sailing until I got the forecast update from FISHOPS, which would be more centred on our area. As usual Ray had my copy of the most recent weather map from Mount Pleasant. A Force 8 gale was coming in from the north-west but the synoptic chart suggested that if we could work north a hundred or so miles we would break out of the Falklands wind pattern to get into a high-pressure belt of lighter winds, before more nasty stuff came through.

Overnight, with luck, the wind would ease and the sea offshore quieten down a little. We were being too hopeful. Next morning at FISHOPS they told me the inter-islands supply ship *Tamar* had given up sailing for Punta Arenas and was sheltering in behind New Island. Furthermore they had given permission for a squid-vessel refuelling tanker to take refuge out of the weather in Berkeley Sound. We were to be stuck for another couple of days.

However there was life and movement in The Canache. Living in the reeds on the shore under our stern was a pair of steamer ducks. These extraordinarily aggressive birds will fight to the death with any intruder, dragging each other under water until one drowns. Our pair seemed to accept us but would come close by from time to time just to check on the situation. They were of great interest to Darwin, who describes them so well.

In these islands a great loggerheaded duck or goose which sometimes weighs twenty two pounds is very abundant. These birds were in former days called, from their extraordinary manner of paddling and splashing upon the water, race-horses: but now they are named, much more appropriately, steamers. Their wings are too small and weak to allow of flight, but by their aid, partly swimming and partly flapping the surface of the water, they move very quickly. The manner is something like that by which the common house-duck escapes when pursued by a dog: but I am nearly sure that the steamer moves its wings alternately, instead of both together, as in other birds. These clumsy, loggerheaded ducks make such a noise and splashing, that the effect is exceedingly curious.

We enjoyed the company of our loggerheads. They were fun.

A feature of the Islands is the lack of indigenous animals. The only four-legged mammal native to the Falklands was a large fox, of wolf proportions, which became extinct in the latter part of the nineteenth century due to predatory man. It was of special interest to Darwin who observed 'As far as I am aware, there is no other instance in any part of the world, of so small a mass of broken land, distant from a continent, possessing so large an aboriginal quadruped peculiar to itself.' The fox was remarked upon by all the early visitors; the first description recorded was by Captain Strong when he landed in 1690. It was left to Darwin to give it a scientific name, *Canis antarcticus*.

An authority on the Falklands, Ian Strange, has mused in his writings the question in the back of Darwin's mind: how did the animal come to be there in the first place? Fuegian canoes have been found on the Falklands shores. So perhaps its ancestors, Patagonian foxes, came over for the ride. This in its turn raises another question. Were Fuegian Indians the first people to discover the Falklands long before John Davis or the Spanish captain without a name? If so what happened to them? They would at least have felt at home in the climate.

There is a fox that can be seen today in the Islands, or so says the tourist literature. A South American fox was introduced in the 1930s but as in so many similar cases elsewhere in the world it only served to cause problems. Bird life was one sufferer.

Despite the never-ceasing wind, steady gale force from west-north-west, we nevertheless completed everything that had to be done to make our exit. As if willing this to happen, Fraser topped up fuel and water, Jeremy put on board the last of the stores, whilst I tidied up the ship's business. A call on Ken at Customs confirmed his cooperation. Although the departure formalities were completed which meant we should sail within twenty-four hours, he fully appreciated we might well be delayed for some time after that. 'Just give us a call as you clear the harbour.'

Next a farewell to Phillip and then to say goodbye to Kay. She of course had a freshly baked cake for us. 'To eat at sea!' she said sternly. Of all things, in the box there lay a little gnome. He was going to look after us. In her front garden she had quite a remarkable gnome layout which was very much her. Our little man was a very personal gift. On to the goodbyes to Carl and Dianne; thence to the Mission for tea with Mike and Kirsten, my last load of washing drying on a wildly rotating clothes line. Mike quite unexpectedly came out with 'If you don't want that long haul home I would love to sail *Marelle* back for you. Just meet my expenses and return air fare. I have the feeling coming on for another long sea passage.' He had I think a special regard for *Marelle*, referring again to her being 'a real boat'. 'I know one when I see one. I am a shipwright by trade.' I declined his suggestion but I must admit there had been times when such an offer would have been tempting. I left a small gift for Kirsten and at Mike's request made an entry in their visitors' book. This enabled me to put on record that the Mission had been a big factor in preserving our sanity. Jeremy and Fraser had also said their farewells with a present for the girls on the staff who had been so good to us. As a final gesture Mike said he would telephone Susan as he saw our rear end vanishing through The Narrows, when he would be sure we were finally off. He was of course to keep his word.

Back on board that night I thought 'this is all wishful thinking. We are not really on our way.' My journal records 'This infernal wind continues to inflict itself on us. No matter how I try to restrain them the halyards and running gear beat their bloody tattoo on the mast. I know tomorrow will be the same.' I was to be proved wrong.

Wednesday 8 March dawned to a perfect day. Very little wind and a bright sun streaming all over us. Warm enough for shirt sleeves. As had been arranged the day before with Richard, I walked round the end of The Canache to *The Alderman* to check the Chilean weather chart on his fax screen. He apologised for its quality, he having inadvertently run the boat's batteries down during the night, but the display was clear enough to tell us what we both wanted to see. Looked good with distinct prospects of westerlies, and moderate at that, north of the Islands. Right for us although it would put *The Alderman* on the wind for the South American coast. I said we would sail. Richard said he would be after us but would first have to go into Stanley to clear with Customs and Immigration.

The news had spread. As we singled up alongside *Cowrie*, our home for so long, with Fraser scrambling around on the foreshore letting go our shorelines, Mike paddled over in his boat to wish us in his words, which he meant, 'God speed'. Jim and Noelle in their dinghy from *Express Crusader* came alongside with a good-luck message and an offer to give us a pluck off our berth if needs be against the lightening wind. *Iron Bark* and *Joshua* teams were on deck to wave their farewells. We sailed at 1020.

CHAPTER NINE

SOUTH ATLANTIC HIGH

But oh, those Horse Latitudes! ...I had been plugging into the wind for the best part of 1000 miles, and I longed to pick up the SE Trades.
Sir Francis Chichester, *Gipsy Moth Circles the World*

Relaxing start – where are the westerlies? – mixture of good and bad weather – persistent north and east winds – variables – frustration – succession of gales – getting warmer – discarding Southern Ocean gear – at long last wind veering – chat with another friendly ship – hurrah! South-east trades – bird battles – star-struck again – Fraser's long-awaited fishing success – re-cross the Line

It was a perfect morning as we emerged from The Canache and headed across Stanley Harbour towards The Narrows. On the foreshore was a couple walking in shirts and shorts in a sun beaming down from a near cloudless blue sky. It felt strange that there was no wind. What was it all trying to tell us? Perhaps it wanted us to leave with a memory that the Islands were not just lowering, heavy rain clouds and tearing wind, sunless, bleak and cold. If it was trying to hold us back and seduce us into staying over to enjoy the best day we had known, it was a vain hope. As the square-rigger men would say, 'the Falmouth girls had hold of the tow rope.'

Despite the climate and marked limitations on the lifestyle, the Falklands had been, for me at least, a warm and friendly place. Susan and I had made a good friend in Kay, promising ourselves and her that we would be back.

Passing the Mission we waved to the girls whom we knew for sure would be watching, as would be Mike and Kirsten. I knew without any question Mike would be about to pick up the telephone and dial Susan. Adrie and Fraser's Sue would soon be in the picture. In the original plan we would have been in Stanley for ten days, which had grown into twenty-seven, well past the three weeks we had been allowed by Immigration, but as it became apparent they were not too concerned. After all, we had our own accommodation, travelling with us like the snail, as well as our own exit transport. However, it may have been that the earlier judgement we had passed on the Falklanders' attitude had been a little too harsh. All told we were fifty days adrift on the passage plan, but at least we could now say we were on the last lap.

Turning into the passage between Engineer Point and Navy Point, gateways to the harbour, we passed through The Narrows to head east down the reach of Port William. As we did so I called up Customs and Immigration reporting our departure, receiving a prompt acknowledgement and a cheery farewell. Still there was no wind. As we cleared the entrance and proceeded out into the ocean we were passed at high speed by a FISHOPS patrol boat on its way round to Berkeley Sound to do its business with the squid fleet. The waving from the crew of the patrol boat was our last link with Falklands life. We knew what our future was but did they know what was theirs? It was painfully obvious they and their fellow Falklanders very much wanted Britain but did Britain, want them?

By mid-afternoon with Cape Bougainville, another memorial to the romantic Frenchman, way off on our port beam we were well and truly ensconced once again in the South Atlantic. With a breeze filling in from the north we were comfortably holding the ordered course of 045° under 'all plain sail'. Beneath the rippling, glinting surface of the sea we could feel the lift of a long, slow swell. We set the watches and put Mr Franklin to work. It was time for tea and a slice of Kay's cake. Our mood was relaxed but deep down I felt a little grip of anxiety. A long, long way lay ahead and anything could happen. We were still in the Furious Fifties, that region of bad-tempered weather, it being only a matter of time before our present benevolent environment turned nasty.

WE LEAVE THE FALKLANDS

The 1750 log entry for Wednesday 8 March 2000 reads '51° 18'.8 S 57° 16'.5 W. Fine evening. Under full main and genoa. Losing the Falklands astern. Over against the land is a sail heading W of N. Must be *The Alderman* on passage for Mar del Plata.' We were not to see them again. A pity. Richard and his crew had added something to the community life of The Canache.

Dominant in our lives from now on would be the reading of the weather systems lying between the Falklands and the equator. Rather perversely perhaps I felt a satisfaction in knowing this would be by our own feel for the elements and knowledge of weather lore, doing it the time-honoured, natural way and not dependent on slick modern wizardry requiring the minimum of interpretative effort on the part of the user. Once again in drawing up the passage plan to determine the optimum route north, the invaluable *Ocean Passages for the World* was resorted to, giving as it does in detail the recommended tracks for sailing vessels at different times of the year. This gave two waypoints as the principal milestones on the route to the equator. First up was 35°S 30°W, on the latitude of the River Plate, calling for a north-easterly course. On this leg, one can expect a proportion of south-westerlies, but with the wind coming as likely as not from the north or north-west and plenty of it. Gales put in a depressingly frequent appearance in the wind roses on the Routeing Charts or Pilot Charts, their equivalent published by the US Navy. These charts are quite remarkable in the wealth of information they contain, there being one for each month of the year for all the oceans of the world. Based on a large number of observations over a number of years there are roses showing the direction and strength of the winds one can reasonably expect, lines of equal temperature and atmospheric pressure, ice limits, shipping routes and so on. Bearing in mind that the only constant in the performance of the elements is their variability, these charts are very useful. On this first leg the average wind strength was expected to be around Force 6. With 1,600 miles to cover we could be on the wind or close to it for much of the time so we were prepared for a hard passage. We were not to be disappointed. On the plus side we would get some help from the Southern Ocean Current which sweeps up past Staten Island, curving north-east at half a knot, albeit creating a wind-over-tide condition.

From this first milestone the course is more north-north-east up to the next waypoint at 10°S 25°W which is just a little south of the latitude of Recife on the coast of Brazil. This leg shows a big change in the weather patterns. It straddles the South Atlantic High, the permanent high-pressure system centred around 30°S with an average reading of 1020 millibars. The region in which it sits is known as the Variables, incorrectly and frequently referred to as the Horse Latitudes, which belong to the North Atlantic. These Variables can constitute a major headache for the sailing vessel bound north. Being in the southern hemisphere the winds are counterclockwise, which means the further west one is the greater likelihood of winds from the north or north-east. The name of the game is to work north and east, if the winds oblige, to get onto the north side of the high in order to pick up the easterlies as a prelude to entering the south-east trade wind belt. Having got there some joy starts to enter one's life. The Variables, characterised by calms and light to moderate winds from any direction, can be frustrating in the extreme to traverse.

By the time 10°S is reached the worst is over. The wind is now in an easterly quarter, course being altered to cross the Line between 25°W and 28°W in the period April to August, our time of the year. After the 10° parallel one is, or should be, well into the south-east trade winds belt, averaging the fresh end of Force 4, until north of the equator. Unfortunately the current is no longer any help, coming up from South Africa and swinging west at half a knot towards Brazil. However, we were to find first-hand that ocean winds don't always obey the rules. This certainly is the theme running through the accounts by small-boat voyagers when working up the South Atlantic. Before our trip I had read, amongst others, books by Chichester, Rose and Knox-Johnston about their experiences in those waters, the characteristics of their boats straddling those of *Marelle*. What befell them was of direct interest to us initially when drawing up our passage plan and subsequently when checking on our progression. Jeremy had plugged into his handheld GPS the en route positions noted by these three knights of the realm in their written accounts, as well as those by Naomi James for a further comparison. In the event our track was to follow more closely that of Rose than the others. A frequent complaint amongst these greats was the greater preponderance of headwinds than expected in the more southerly stages, that certainly being our experience. Well down in the Roaring Forties the frequency of westerlies we got was disappointingly low.

The situation however can be different. When thinking about what lay before us it had been encouraging to read the account in Richard Henry Dana's all-time classic *Two Years Before The Mast* of the glorious run, his words, by his ship *Alert* up through the length of the South Atlantic. This was in 1836. We pick the story up when they first sighted land having rounded the Horn, which they hadn't seen because of very poor visibility.

Friday ... there lay the land, fair upon the larboard beam, and slowly edging away upon the quarter ... The land was the island of Staten Land, just to the eastward of Cape Horn: and a more desolate-looking spot I never wish to set eyes upon – bare, broken, and girt with rocks and ice ... Yet, dismal as it was, it was a pleasant sight to us ... and with twenty-four hours of this breeze [we] might bid defiance to the Southern Ocean. It told us, too, our latitude and longitude better than any observation, and the captain now knew where we were, as well as if we were off the end of Long Wharf. We left the land gradually astern; and at sundown had the Atlantic Ocean clear before us.
Sunday ... when we were in lat. 50° 27′ S, lon. 62° 13′ W, having made four degrees of latitude in the last twenty-four hours. Being now to the northward of the Falkland Islands the ship was kept off, northeast, for the equator, and with her head for the equator, and Cape Horn over her taffrail, she went gloriously on; every heave of the sea leaving the Cape astern, and every hour bringing us nearer to home and to warm weather.

A week later 'At noon we were in lat. 36° 41′ S, lon. 38° 08′ W; having traversed the distance of two thousand miles, allowing for changes of course, in nine days. A thousand miles in four days and a half! This is equal to steam.'
There is a marvellous passage in the book in which Dana captures the beauty of a ship under sail:

One night whilst we were in these tropics, I went out to the end of the flying-jib boom upon some duty, and, having finished it, turned round, and lay over the boom for a long time, admiring the beauty of the sight before me ... the light trade wind was lightly and gently breathing from astern; the dark-blue sky was studded with tropical stars ... and the sails were spread out, wide and high ... so perfectly distended by the breeze. I was so lost in the sight that I forgot the presence of the man who came out with me, until he said (for he, too, rough old man-of-war's man as he was, had been gazing at the show), half to himself, still looking at the (sculptured) marble sails, 'How quietly they do their work!'

It was almost as though Dana had been writing about our own sublime experience in the tropics when sliding down the coast of Brazil. It was the same magic under the same tropical stars. Although my companion, Jeremy, albeit something of an old salt himself, did not measure up to being a rough old man-of-war's man, we also were together in tune with the beauty of our encompassing world and the splendour of the sky above. It is all so clear why ships, sailing ships, over the centuries have always been referred to as 'she'. The rounded form of their hulls with the subtle blending of one soft curve into another with no hard masculine lines. And above all the smooth, full-bodied shape of the sails pushing outwards like the bodice of a lovely woman. A ship has to be feminine.

In the days ahead in *Marelle* as we were struggling north I was to think back on this tale with wistful longing. But at least at any moment we knew where we were, unlike the captain of *Alert* who had not been provided with a chronometer. It was really not until the twentieth century that the cost had come down enough for shipowners to install this as the universal means of determining longitude. Lunar distance was the widely used method throughout the world's merchant fleet. This was something of a mathematical exercise, involving measuring with the sextant the angular distance between the moon and another heavenly body, star, planet or the sun when conveniently positioned. The distance so determined was compared with that which was tabulated against time in the Nautical Almanac to give precise Greenwich time. Knowing the local time of the lunar sight, the longitude could be derived. The method required considerable skill with the sextant and in general was not particularly accurate but this was not too important when a few miles out in the ship's position is not all that critical a factor on the broad expanse of the ocean.

A feature of the method was that by interpolation between the hour on either side of the moment when the lunar sight was taken, the actual time within a few seconds of the observation could be determined. Lunars could of course only be worked if conditions were favourable to give a clear view of the heavens. Conditions off the Horn were such that Dana's captain could not take his lunars, hence the great uncertainty about their longitude. He was having to rely solely on dead reckoning. Lunar distance was the system that allowed Joshua Slocum to navigate his way across the world and make reasonable landfalls, equipped only with his famous old alarm clock from which the minute hand was missing. He was very much a navigator of the old school, remarking 'The work of the lunarian, though seldom practised in these days of chronometers, is beautifully edifying, and there is nothing in the realm of navigation that lifts one's heart up more in adoration.' This was in 1898. It was not until about 1914 that lunar distances were dropped from the almanacs.

However, in more recent memory an American mathematician and physicist, John S. Letcher Jr, being also a small-boat sailor with an abiding interest in theoretical as well as practical astronomical navigation, resurrected the science of lunars.

In the course of a long passage in 1963, single-handed in his 20-foot yacht *Island Girl*, he began to have serious doubts about the accuracy of his chronometer. With no radio to get time signals he 'rediscovered lunar distance under … necessity.' Not having access to the old lunar distance tables he worked out a way to determine time and longitude incorporating moon distances but using the modern Nautical Almanac and standard sight reduction tables.

In deriving such a method be 'experienced one of the great intellectual triumphs of my life'. Subsequently he included his findings in a book, *Self-Contained Celestial Navigation*, published in 1977, preserving for latter-day students of navigation an insight into what lunar distances are all about. It is a book well worth reading even in this age of technology-driven seafaring.

A contemporary of Letcher's was Francis Chichester, much lauded as a navigational guru and deservedly so. Chichester in his book *Along the Clipper Way* muses on what he would have done if he had been the captain of Dana's ship *Alert* when off the pitch of the Horn and having no idea of his precise position. 'Horrified' at the complexities of the lunar distance calculations, Sir Francis pondered the problem. 'There must be an easier way,' he said to himself. 'Suddenly I thought of a simple solution,' and he proceeds to enlighten the reader.

Essentially what he came up with is that the navigator, lost at sea because he has lost the time, takes simultaneous sights of the sun and the moon, with the latter well to the east or west, and arrives at a position line fix in the normal way, using a best guess at Greenwich Mean Time. An hour or so later he repeats the exercise with another guessed time and joins the two fixes up. He then secures a meridian altitude from any body that is around to give the correct latitude, time for which need not be too precise. He transposes his known latitude onto the line joining up his sun–moon fixes and gets his correct longitude. In turn this gives him the actual time.

Although Chichester had reservations about the accuracy of his method he nevertheless was sufficiently pleased with himself to pronounce: 'The unfortunate thing about this method is that no one thought of it 300 years ago when it would have been a god-send to navigators.' He was never one to devalue himself.

It is axiomatic that two experts are unlikely to agree. It so happened that Letcher, having had his intellectual uplift over lunar distances, set about as the next step to find an easier mathematical exercise and succeeded with a method involving lunar altitudes rather than lunar distances. This was his second moment of triumph. He had 'discovered the principle of finding time or longitude by lunar altitudes', utilising position lines and the known relatively rapid motion of the moon.

His solution was similar to Chichester's idea but arrived at under very different circumstances. Letcher's was worked out bouncing about at sea in his little boat, whereas Chichester, one can surmise, thought his through from the comfort of his armchair, with no cause for practical verification. Letcher later read Chichester's description of his system and was not impressed. 'He [Chichester] does not recognise that at times the accuracy of the method can be so poor as to be entirely useless.' We lesser mortals have to leave the playing field to them and confine ourselves to the benches.

Today lunars would be a lost art, which is the way celestial navigation, complete with the chronometer, is going. Pocket calculators which, it is alleged, take the tedium out of looking up precomputed tables, and in more recent days the advent of computer technology, have delayed the demise of finding one's way round by reference to the heavens, but its days must be numbered. One can only ponder on how long the Nautical Almanac, published jointly by the Royal Greenwich Observatory and the US Naval Observatory, giving the position of those heavenly bodies suitable for navigation throughout the year, will continue to be available at an affordable price.

The following morning saw *Marelle* in a world of her own. The Falklands were way below the horizon south of us and the ocean stretched limitlessly before us. It was to be a long time before we were to see or have any contact again with the human world. Now began once again the settling-in process and adjustment to sea life. For Jeremy and Fraser this meant living with and slowly overcoming upset insides and the debilitating effect of seasickness. Neither complained but I knew they were feeling decidedly unwell. The recovery process, as usual, took a few days for Jeremy, but Fraser was not improving. He was not eating and had virtually bowed out of the galley roster. This went on for some days and I was becoming increasingly concerned. Fraser is easy to talk to and we discussed the problem. It was agreed it would help him overcome his indisposition if he were to integrate fully back into the ship's domestic routine. This he did. Through it all he had been playing his full part in watchkeeping duties, so it was a relief to see him once more taking his place in all that went on in our daily life.

The next couple of weeks were not easy for any of us with the wind firmly from a northerly direction, alternating between north-east and north-north-west. The rig we had settled on was genoa and mainsail with the storm jib on the inner forestay to improve the airflow over the mainsail as we reduced the size of the genoa when the wind got up. The wind speed was all over the place, varying between Force 6 and down to a 2. It was hard to accept we were in the Roaring Forties, after all the home of strong westerlies, in light of a typical log entry: '48° 36′.6 S 53° 07′.6 W Cloudy. Still sloppy head sea. Course 330°C. Force 2–3. Wind N.' But three days later it was 'Rough seas, wet and windy. 330°C Force 7–8. Wind NE.' Then to save us from any risk of the boredom we had a Force 1 from NNW, electing to motor-sail on a heading of 040°C to regain some easting, whilst having to accept the loss of precious fuel. It had been a very busy time with frequent sail changes but we were making progress, passing out of the Roaring Forties on Tuesday 21 March, coinciding with crossing the first major shipping lane, Rio de la Plata to Cape Town. There was nothing in sight. As a farewell gesture from the region we were handed out a north-north-west Force 8 gale to ensure we gave it the respect it felt it deserved. We reduced to trysail and storm jib. This is a snug rig with the centre of effort placed more inboard than would have been the case with a reefed genoa. She was going well, holding a reasonable course for the conditions, but it was rough work. Fraser captured the situation in his journal: 'It was a very bad night which reached its peak at about 0700 with the cockpit being continuously filled, threatening to break away the water and diesel cans.'

Leaving the Roaring Forties also marked our crossing the line shown on the Routeing Chart as the 'extreme iceberg limit'. We had not seen any sign of ice but it could have been around. Over against the South American coast the ice zone extends surprisingly far up, in fact to the north of the River Plate. Perhaps global warming has changed the picture, or were we lucky?

The long spells of contrary winds had pushed us too far to the west, the objective then being to regain easting in order to get nearer the first waypoint, 35°S 30°W, which Jeremy had whimsically named *Chichi* in honour of Sir Francis Chichester. This quest was helped by the wind backing into the west but steadily increasing, reaching by late morning severe gale Force 9. A high sea was running, superimposed on a big swell. The crests were breaking, being blown off and spread over the surface of the water like a white blanket. It was a quite remarkable sight, somewhat disturbing to one's peace of mind but nevertheless treating us to a raw display of warring elements, the wind fighting the sea. However, with the wind putting *Marelle* more comfortably on a broad reach she was taking it in her stride on a course which would put us nicely to the north of *Chichi*.

A day later we had no wind, but not for long. The capricious wind proceeded to box the compass to end up back in its favourite quarter, the north-east, and freshening. By the evening of 24 March it had worked itself up into another Force 9 touching storm Force 10 with a full supporting cast of a massive spume-streaked sea plus thunder and lightning laced with driving rain. It was building up into the worst experience of the whole passage north. By strange coincidence our latitude was that of Mar del Plata where we had met similar storm-force conditions four months before, constituting the worst experience in the whole of the passage south.

We were back under trysail and storm jib, sailing with the wind just forward of the beam, taking solid water over the port side, the breaking wave fronts smashing down onto the coachroof and into the cockpit. The foredeck and side decks were permanently submerged under rushing, boiling foaming water. The noise was a deep sustained roar, rising to a screeching whine as she lurched up to windward. We were making easting but at a price, holding a course at best of 115°C. It was bruising, slogging work and *Marelle* was taking a beating. Fraser records the scene: 'The rigging was vibrating and the noise below was frightful. Ben was on watch with Jeremy and me down below listening to the most terrible sounds of the sea hammering us. Just when I thought the boat was about to break up Jeremy said we had to do something before something happened to *Marelle*. It was chaos below with charts and books cascading onto the cabin sole.'

Up on deck it was bad enough but it would seem not as awful as it sounded down below. The cabin doors opened and Jeremy's head appeared. He was obviously most concerned and more agitated than I had ever seen him before. His equanimity normally reigns supreme. He made it clear that some action had to be taken. Although I had no doubts about her strength we needed to take the load off poor suffering *Marelle*. We dropped all sail, this proving to be a most difficult operation on a violently moving deck with heavy spray driving over us, but she was more comfortable. We were then lying to, a-hull, beam on to wind and sea, slowly fore-reaching but driving fast down to leeward. However, she was easier now we were no longer forging ahead under sail. We would have to live with the unpalatable fact we were losing hard-earned ground as we blew down on a course made good over the ground of south-south-east.

By next morning the wind was starting to blow itself out but the sea was still high and irregular. Fraser again picks up the story: 'Jeremy made the usual breakfast porridge only to see it take off, ricocheting around the galley to land up on the chart table. At lunch Ben's carefully prepared food also took off whereby he described in most colourful language what he would like to do with the South Atlantic etc, etc. Then a bucketful of sea water came down the galley hatch and that had the opposite effect to cooling him down.'

We were now entering the dreaded Variables and for the next ten days with the temperature steadily rising we were to experience winds from every quarter, ranging from west through south and back up to north-north-east. In general they were on the light side but swinging at times wildly from flat calm up to Force 7.

We were shedding our Southern Ocean cold-weather gear but oilskins and sea boots were mandatory whilst on watch in the persistently damp weather. The log is filled with comments such as 'Wind eased. Cloudy with drizzle' and 'Soggy night. Steady sailing' but come Saturday 1 April conditions began to change: '0625 31° 08'.1 S 31° 42'.1 W. Full main and genoa. Beautiful night's sailing. Course 055°C. Force 3. Wind N.' The cabin temperature that afternoon was up to 33°C and it was becoming uncomfortable trying to get any sleep. The thermometer is by the chart table within the entrance from the companionway and was reading appreciably lower than it would have done in the sleeping area. It was now a case of lying on one's sleeping bag with only a sheet over us compared to only a short time before, when snuggling down in the bag was a treat to look forward to whilst on watch in the southern regions.

An air flow through the cabin was badly needed, one obvious answer being to prop open the cabin skylight. Herein lay a problem. No matter what the sea state there was always the odd nasty little dollop that would land on the coachroof sending a douche of cold water down onto the occupier of the lee bunk. It was a choice of being cool and risking a sudden rude awakening or staying dry and sweating it out. We never did achieve consensus on this dilemma.

All this time we had been working north-east. We had missed waypoint *Chichi*, passing 200 miles north-west of it but four days later, Monday 3 April, was something of a red-letter day. At midday, bright and sunny, in a Force 4 from the west we had made up the lost easting

and were right on the passage plan track from *Chichi* to the next
waypoint, 10ºS 25ºW, plugged in by Jeremy as *Naomi*. We had passed to
the north of Uruguay and now had Brazil away over on our port beam. It
felt as though we were getting somewhere. According to the chart we
were crossing the shipping route from Rio de Janeiro to Cape Town, a
distance of 3,272 nautical miles. As usual there was nothing to be seen,
not a ship in sight. The South Atlantic remained our exclusive property.
Also, although we were not to know it, we were about to shake off the
Variables.

Our latitude at 1245 was 28° 44′.5 S with the wind backing steadily
from north-west through west to south. Late in the evening we gybed,
bringing the breeze, Force 3 or 4, onto the starboard quarter and what's
more laying *Naomi*, if that is the right expression. We were on our way.
The log records 'a good night'. On Tuesday 4 April at 0001 the log
mentions the wind had shifted to south-south-east with us in latitude 28°
06′.7 S. It was another momentous occasion because from that time on,
apart from a couple of days further up in the North Atlantic, the wind was
always to have easting in it and with reasonable weight in it except when
in the Doldrums. We were now definitely out of the Variables and could
start to look forward with eager anticipation to picking up the south-east
trade winds. Fraser in particular was impatient for this to happen as he
had been subjected to frequent perorations from Jeremy and me on the
delights of trade-wind sailing. It was to be hoped that like that other great
sailor, Commodore Anson, he was not going to be disappointed.

Small things have a huge dimension at sea in a small craft. The next
day the last of the Chilean-filled propane gas bottles gave out, the change
then being made to the first of the Falklands refills. We knew these were
only partially full so from now on we would be monitoring their
performance, the continued availability of gas being crucial to our way of
life. The other vital commodity of course was water.

Shortly afterwards one of the main water tanks ran dry, and into it we
decanted twenty-two gallons from our Falklands containers. Our water
was in fact lasting well, and so it should have done as we were
maintaining a very strict regime. All cooking was done in sea water,
apart from rice and pasta. For personal cleanliness we largely used baby
wipes and found them excellent value, leaving us quite refreshed after a
good wipe-down all over. They are alleged to harm the skin after
prolonged use but we did not seem to have any problems. Jeremy and I
shaved every day using electric razors whereas Fraser was bearded, for
which he only needed the attention from time to time of a pair of scissors.
I used sea water exclusively for tooth cleaning, drinking a fair amount of

it at the same time. I liked to think the salt replacement was beneficial, particularly during the transit of the tropical belts, as well as having oral health benefits. Washing our hair was something of a problem, particularly for me with more to worry about than the other two. I settled for first washing it in warm sea water, in which ordinary shampoo lathered reasonably well, finishing off with a fresh-water rinse. I didn't enquire too deeply into what methods the others employed, as I felt slightly guilty.

We were reasonably relaxed about our water situation. In addition to the main water tanks and the extra jerry cans, Jeremy had stuffed bottles of still mineral water into every conceivable nook and cranny. As a last reserve, apart from what might come down from heaven, we carried a manually operated watermaker. With continuous pumping by hand this could produce one gallon per hour, or so said the makers. Being small and portable its purpose in life was to be taken with us in the liferaft. In this unhappy event a watermaker could literally mean the difference between life and death, especially in the vast open spaces of the South Atlantic. Our watermaker was a generous personal gift from Adrie, on a 'use or return' basis. It was with some satisfaction I was able to give it back to her on our return.

Ocean voyagers of the likes of Bernard Moitessier and Robin Knox-Johnston seemingly had no difficulty in catching rain water, whereas Alec Rose never even made the attempt. In *Marelle* we had made provision for catching it and appointed Fraser as chief catchment officer. Although he made one or two sorties out on deck in rain squalls to catch the run-off from the mainsail at the boom gooseneck, it was an activity that did not feature prominently in our daily routine. Our hearts weren't in it. Rain gathering times were those not conducive to standing around in the open.

Our world was changing as we worked steadily north. Although the wind stayed faithfully from an easterly direction it was swinging about, alternating between first and second quadrants with squalls strangely more frequent than they had been in the Variables. Intermittently we were getting strong winds to keep us on our toes. Friday 7 April log entry reads '1205. 22° 25'.5 S 27° 31'.0 W. Wild morning. Big sea, occasional rain. Force 7 to 8. SE.' Next day it was Force 2 to 3 from east-north-east but our friendly wind did not let us down. It kept on coming. Later that evening it was 'steady sailing, under a clear sky. A star-drenched night.'

Although there are many times on a long ocean passage when I, for one, would prefer to be anywhere else but there, boredom did not enter into it. It is quite extraordinary the length of time that can pass just watching the inexorable movement of so much water, crisscrossed with the ever-changing complex patterns on its surface. Always present is the never-ceasing study of the cloud formations, trying to read the messages they contain about what lies ahead. Personally I can never relax completely at sea, living with an ever-present, small deep-down sense of anxiety. Slight perhaps but always there.

As proof perhaps that the sea is always changing, as we crossed the parallel of 20°S there was a dramatic change in sea colour from the grey, with which we had been so familiar for so long, to a sparkling, deep intense blue. An object with some weight like an empty metal can if dropped overboard could be seen for a long time in those clear, unpolluted waters as it commenced its long journey down to the mysteriously unknown sea bed. The chart gave the depth where we had crossed the parallel as 5,413 metres. One cannot even begin to imagine the world into which that can was entering as the depth became ever deeper. It is hard to believe that life goes on down there, but we are told it does.

At midday on 8 April we had the three islands comprising Islas Martin Vaz on our port beam at a distance of 90 miles. They were discovered in 1510 by the Portuguese sailor of that name. About 30 miles further to the west is the uninhabited Ilha da Trindade. This small island, only four miles long by two across, was discovered about the same time as its neighbour by another Portuguese, Tristão da Cunha. Trindade was in effect re-discovered in 1700 by Edmond Halley, the Astronomer Royal to be and of the comet fame, in the small Royal Navy 'pink' *Paramore*. On the island he found fresh water coming up from springs resulting from its volcanic formation. He claimed it in the name of King William III, leaving the Union flag flying to make the point. With a view to the island serving as a haven for shipwrecked sailors Halley landed some livestock in the shape of mixed-sex hogs and goats. He was a remarkable man, a young contemporary of Isaac Newton, making great contributions to science. Included in these was the construction of curves of equal magnetic variation, which are shown on charts today, being known as isogonic lines.

In thinking about the welfare of shipwrecked mariners Halley was long-sighted. Sailing vessels bound north usually keep to the east of the island group but *Ocean Passages for the World* suggests an alternative route passing to the west of them during the South Atlantic winter months. Taking into account the volume of traffic there was at the height of the sailing ship era, it was inevitable that ships, their longitude uncertain, would land on one or other of the islands. Today there is a light on Trindade but one wonders how many ships see it.

In 1895 there was a dispute between Brazil and Britain which was settled in favour of Brazil, it being considered da Cunha's discovery had prior claim over Halley's, despite his sticking a flag into it. Both countries at the time saw the island's potential as a telegraph and coal bunkering station similar to the Cape Verdes.

In more recent times several expeditions have been mounted to try to find treasure reputed to have been buried there by Captain William Kidd. This would possibly have been after Halley's visit, but Kidd would have had to be quick to get back to England in time for his execution in 1701. As far as is known no trace of the treasure has ever been found. However all was not lost. When his estate was wound up, some of the late Captain Kidd's fortune was used to purchase the property at Greenwich which now houses the National Maritime Museum.

In locating Trindade, its position and indeed even the island's very existence being in doubt, Halley would have found it necessary to use the method practised over the centuries of running along a parallel of latitude until the islands appeared over the horizon. No accurate way of finding longitude at sea had yet been found. However, Halley was to play a part in solving this riddle. In the early part of his voyaging he had devoted considerable time and effort to plotting the moon's somewhat erratic path and charting the positions of a large number of stars. On his subsequent appointment as Astronomer Royal he was to expand this programme. Like his fellow astronomers and mathematicians, he believed the key to unlocking the longitude conundrum lay in reading the heavenly clock, not in some manmade contraption like a mechanical clock. Halley, armed with the results of his research, agreed with his friend Isaac Newton's approach that the way to go was the 'lunar distance' to establish time, and hence obtain longitude, by measuring the distance between the known positions of the moon and stars or the sun. To this end an almanac was published showing the position of these bodies in the celestial sphere. Despite becoming a member of the Board of Longitude, heavily weighted in favour of the heavenly solution, Halley was sufficiently generous of spirit and open enough of mind to evaluate objectively Harrison's H-1 clock and to encourage the struggling watchmaker to perfect his epoch-making timepiece.

Halley was one of the great men of science and his work had helped to make possible the compilation of the Nautical Almanac as we know it today.

It was ironic that the 'lunarians', believing as they did so fervently in the celestial clock, were held back by the lack of a mechanical instrument sufficiently accurate to measure the heavenly distances to the required precision. All that was around was the quadrant invented by the worthy John Davis, which had been in use for the last century or more. It was simply not up to the job, particularly on the deck of a ship jumping around in a seaway. But the theoreticians were not to be held back for long.

The necessary device appeared, the reflecting quadrant, which was in effect an octant, having been invented simultaneously by an American and the better-known Englishman, John Hadley. Suddenly, after centuries when nothing had been on offer, there were now two methods available to the mariner to enable him to find his longitude. Heavenly and earthly. It was all go.

It is food for thought that an artisan, albeit a brilliant one to the point of being a genius, with his mechanical invention was eventually to worst the best brains in the land trying to measure time by astronomical methods. In the end, as the marine chronometer, Harrison's legacy, got cheaper and hence became more widely accessible to merchant shipping, it completely supplanted 'lunars'.

One could be excused for thinking that the answer to the time problem had to be in using the infallible 'great clock of the sky'. Apparently not, as even now in today's advanced state of scientific knowledge, to find our longitude to the accuracy demanded by modern usage we still have to use a fallible manmade object. The satellite.

Shortly after passing the islands we suddenly found we were no longer the sole occupants of this ocean.

During the afternoon watch Fraser and I were startled to hear a shout from Jeremy exclaiming that he could see what looked like the mast of a yacht, hull down, to the south of us. Neither of us at first could see what was exciting him and I had to get out the binoculars, even then having difficulty in picking it up. Jeremy has remarkably keen eyes, good even for a man half his age. 'I wonder if it is Goochy boy catching us up.' The reference was to a friend, Tony Gooch, one of the authors of the RCC Chile pilot, sailing his 42-foot aluminium boat *Taonui*. A redoubtable sailor, Tony, and one of the most modest. In the process of a circumnavigation he had been rounding the Horn, single-handed, when we were leaving the Falklands. I knew this because he had been in touch with Mike Hughes at the Mission, who in turn had kept me up to date. Tony is a twenty-first century sailor with all the communication equipment that goes with it. He had told Mike, also with the same gear, that he was intending to stop off in Stanley for a rest before continuing on to Falmouth. We learned later that on arrival in Stanley a sudden break in the weather persuaded him to take advantage of his luck and sail on, putting him close on our heels. Looking at the mast, however, it was very tall, rather too tall.

I called up the suspect on VHF, getting an immediate response. No, it was not Goochy boy but an English-sounding voice informed us that what we were looking at was the derrick of the oil drill ship *Robert F. Bauer* on passage from Peru to West Africa. Having had no success with their oil exploration endeavours in South America they were going to try their luck in Africa. As usual the captain handled the inter-ship communication.

'Can we help? Do you need anything?' came from Captain Brian Balfosur in warm and friendly tones. 'Thank you, yes, we would like cold beer and hot baths.'

'Sorry about the beer. We are a dry ship. But there is no problem with the hot baths.'

Taking into account the order of priority of these needs, we sailed on, asking if they would contact Falmouth MRCC with our position and ETA Azores, the third week in May. Confirming this done and wishing each other luck, she vanished over the eastern horizon. Once more for us it was 'the lonely sea and the sky'.

Although our awareness of the vast empty space around us had been reawakened with the departure of *Robert F. Bauer*, there did not appear to be an imperative to invoke the fishermen's prayer from ages past: 'O God! My boat is so small and Thy sea so wide. Have mercy.' Apart from certain deficiencies in the grog department and the inability to succumb to the seductive embrace of a hot bath, we were self-sufficient. In fact our future was more secure than that possibly facing Captain Balfosur and his men. They needed good luck and God speed more than we did. There was a certain measure of desperation in having to cross a whole ocean to pursue their means of livelihood. If, as could well be the outcome, they were not successful, what would be their own personal future prospects?

The memory of that cold beer near miss stayed with us. It had the same value as liquid gold. With the cabin temperature stuck at over 35°, there was still no possibility of keeping the skylight open. We could not crack the fore hatch either because of constant water on the foredeck. The only through-draught came from the two Dorade ventilators in the heads compartment but by the time the air from them reached us on our bunks it felt superheated. Relief, however, was not far off.

Two days later we entered the south-east trades. The wind veered south of east, settling down to a comfortable Force 4, occasionally lifting itself to a 5. With the breeze now abaft the beam we could prop open the skylight. Although the temperature remained high, the air flow down below made a dramatic difference. However, we still had to keep a weather eye open for rain squalls disturbing our slumbers. All was well if the watch on deck was alive and alert and took early enough action to close the skylight. If he was too tardy the occupant of the downside bunk would not have need of a wet wipe that day for his ablutions.

Even though we were sailing with the wind and sea now further aft the occasional rogue lump of unfriendly cold water would still land discouragingly on the coachroof. One such occurrence was when Jeremy was deeply asleep, lying on his side on the lee bunk. I was sitting on the other uphill bunk, reading, when there was the all-too-familiar ominous thump. Down came a stream of water straight into Jeremy's invitingly receptive ear. He was suddenly very wide awake. I laughed. A mistake. His reaction was expressed in a way I had not experienced before. Quite unlike him, I thought.

It was good and more relaxed sailing, now we were in the trades, but nowhere near the idyllic experience we had enjoyed when heading down the coast of Brazil. I think Fraser was a little sceptical of all that and remained somewhat reserved about the alleged delights of trade-wind sailing. However, as before, it did no harm to our state of mind and general morale, knowing we were highly unlikely to be on the receiving end of anything worse than a Force 6, and gales virtually unknown.

On the fourteenth of the month we landed on *Naomi*, 10°S, and after making an allowance for the west going current headed due north for the next target of 00° 25°W. As we had made northing the current had been playing an increasingly important role. Up to *Naomi* we had been in what is known as the South Subtropical Current, which sweeps across the upper part of the South Atlantic before turning south-west down the coast of Brazil. It then calls itself, not surprisingly, the Brazil Current. On our way south in the previous year this had been of considerable advantage but on the way north it had done nothing for us, just adding to our leeway. North of *Naomi*, from about 6°S, the flow now known as South Equatorial Current became of greater significance. It would be trying to push us to the north of Brazil, up into the West Indies. From ten or twelve miles per day its rate builds to over thirty in the western part of the ocean, being a most important factor in determining where to cross the Equator.

The weather being generally benign and the sailing more pleasant, all seemed set fair for our final dash to the Line. It was then disaster overtook us. Our porridge went mouldy! It was discovered on opening a new packet. Mass hysteria swept through the boat. In the overall world order a small enough event, but in our world a catastrophe, 10 on the Richter scale. We had been having it every morning for breakfast for as long as we could remember. It was looked forward to with enormous pleasure. The watch on deck would look down into the galley with high expectation, to watch the duty cook preparing the dish with all the rites of a religious ceremony. The watch below would be lying on his bunk with the same degree of anticipation, now fully awake, to await the great moment. Now it was all over. The oats, for some reason best known to the makers, Quaker Oats, were packed in cardboard boxes without any internal protective liner. Sea air had permeated through the cardboard and fermentation of the contents had set in. Jeremy and Fraser turned their noses up at eating any more of the oats, reverting to muesli, but I continued to have my morning porridge, although the sheer sublime delight of previous breakfasts had gone.

However, our state of woe was relieved a few days later by intervention from the natural world. Fraser put it most graphically: 'Joined in the evening by a fearless and friendly little bird, a noddy, which reminded me of Dennis the Menace because of the way his feathers stuck out in every direction. He took up possession of the danbuoy float until 0600 next morning. The following night we had the Battle of the Boom when two more noddies joined the first on the main boom. A major territorial fight carried on most of the night.' They seemed to be locked in permanent conflict. We were sailing in calm conditions at the time under boomed-out genoa and staysail with the mainsail down on the boom. It was comic to watch them fall off the boom into the water still fighting, only to fly back to their original perch with no interruption to the conflict. Strangely enough, although the action looked fearsome, they didn't seem to do any damage to each other. These little birds with their street-urchin behaviour were great favourites with each of us and it was with regret we saw them finally fly off, still bickering. They had brightened our lives.

That same day was noteworthy for another event. Jeremy baked a batch of bread. We had run out of the Falklands loaves and had run down our cake and biscuit stocks. Fraser and I watched with intense interest the master baker at work, voting his efforts an unparalleled success. Fresh bread at sea is a treat out of this world. The versatility displayed in our home bakery was impressive, embracing not only bread and flapjacks but that remarkable concoction, Australian damper.

Fraser, however, was not to be outdone as regards providing. In addition to his other duties he had been appointed chief fisherman. He had at one time been a commercial fisherman and had expressed an interest in putting this skill to good effect on passage by introducing some variety in our fare. He had brought an impressive array of lines, reels and lures but we seemed to be operating on a different frequency to the fish. That is until just short of the Line when we witnessed an excited Fraser hauling in one of his lines, which had been more or less permanently streaming astern. At the moment of triumph the fish got off the line and escaped the pot. Or so said Fraser. We had to accept his word because his back filled the foreground, denying us a view of the action. Next day we were treated to a similar performance. Same excitement, same confident hauling-in of line, same talk about fresh fish for supper, same disappointment. However this time there was a difference. We were proudly shown the head of a large fish. The rest of it was not with us, Fraser explaining be had been gazumped by a shark. Some of our confidence in him as a fisherman had ebbed away a little, but his time was yet to come.

Our fisherman could claim to be in good, or rather illustrious, company. Conor O'Brien, when sailing these waters in his renowned boat *Saoirse* in 1923 in the course of his great round the world voyage, records: 'the third hand [was] foolishly trailing a line over the stern in quest of fish. I say foolishly, because I find that he trailed that line for about 6,700 miles and caught four fish on it; that is one to every 1,675 miles, or less frequently than once a fortnight.' It has to be admitted that our man, in the outcome, did better than that.

After *Naomi*, as we closed the gap with the Line, the wind progressively dropped away, but this was expected. The last of the wind roses, centred on 03°S, showed a distinct tendency towards lighter winds, but still holding an average direction of south-east. This was luxury though. The comparison with the early days of the passage when we had struggled against persistent headwinds and repeated gales was so great, but the difficulties of sailing in the higher latitudes were fading in our memories. Apart from the intrusion of rain squalls, which continued to put in sporadic appearances, it was benign sailing with comments in the log varying from 'Fast sailing in ideal conditions' to 'Very light winds. Put up spinnaker' or one with a difference: 'Wind light and unsettled. Sharks!'

The calmer conditions encouraged attention to domestic tasks. The heads were becoming harder to operate and a strip-down could no longer be deferred, matters coming to a head, as one might say, when constipation occurred in the system. Nothing was moving. The rule in the boat is whoever blocks the heads unblocks them. Jeremy was the last one to use them and although the blockage was not of his making he stiffened his upper lip and gallantly got down to the job. The problem was soon apparent. Heavy scaling in the pipework had almost completely choked the flow of effluent. The pipes had to come out to be subjected to a beating out on the deck. An extraordinary amount of scale cascaded out. It was the accumulation of years, highlighting a shortcoming in the refit before we had sailed south. I had renewed the working parts in the Henderson diaphragm pump but had failed to examine the piping thoroughly enough.

The heads were afforded a major role in our domestic scene as, apart from their basic function, they allowed ourselves to be ourselves. With the heads door shut one could sit in complete privacy and 'commune with nature' quite undisturbed. This was the only part of the boat where this was possible. It was here that we could escape from each other. Perhaps sometime in the future I might put in there a little library.

The engine was also demanding its share of attention. We had a routine of running it every third day for battery charging, but came the time when it refused to start. The diagnosis suggested once again it was suffering from fuel starvation. The combined filter and water separator was choked with sediment, completely stopping any flow of fuel. Where had we picked up a load of contaminated diesel? A complete change of filters plus a shot of biocide cured the problem. We were to have no further difficulty, the Volvo once more running as sweet as a nut.

Once again we were deriving so much enjoyment from the tropical night sky, rain squalls permitting, the heavens star-studded with such a brilliant, dazzling display. The southern collection was leaving us, with old friends from the northern celestial sphere coming up to keep us company. The Southern Cross with its attendant Rigil Kentaurus and the very bright Canopus had taken their curtain call. Down had gone the Magellan Clouds. Faint but distinctive, they had been known to navigators before Magellan went south. They were our last link with that luminary who had played a starring role in the part of the world we had got to know so well when we in turn had gone south. Orion and Sirius, the jewel of the night, were back. The Great Bear, Big Dipper or Plough, whatever you like to call it, coming up with the likes of Cassiopeia and the familiar Pleiades, told us home was getting nearer. *Marelle* snored on and we were relaxed.

At 2357 on Thursday 20 April our position was 00° 00′ 25° 26′ W. A moment later we re-entered home waters, the North Atlantic.

CHAPTER TEN

NORTH ATLANTIC: THE HOME RUN

Many thousand miles behind us,
Many thousand miles before;
Mother ocean heaves to waft us
To a well remembered shore.

Sea shanty *Rolling Home*

Carry a breeze – much easier Doldrums transit – language exercise with
Spanish trawler – north east trades come in – wet going on the wind –
relief at crossing the trade-wind belt – Horse Latitudes – wind stays in
north-east – where are the westerlies? – give up on the Azores – plug on
– meet British and French yachts – friendly Dutch ship – repetition of
South Atlantic experience – persistent headwinds – slow, tedious passage
– occasional gale – very helpful German ship – transfer at sea – now
have glut of fresh bread – no wind off the Bishop – in touch with
Coastguard – inform us of welcome-home party – final flourish with
spinnaker run to Lizard – THEY are on Pendennis Point – champagne
reception – all over – home to bed

None of us was sorry to have left the South Atlantic behind, both literally
and mentally. It had been a long and trying passage, the most difficult of
the whole voyage. The actual crossing of the equator was importantly
symbolic even though it is nothing more than a line on paper drawn by
cartographers. It does though have an almost physical presence, making
an impact on the senses no matter how many times it is crossed,
particularly when in a small boat. It was a first for Fraser, Jeremy's
second and the third for me.

Crossing it however did see a change in the weather, the wind backing
north of east and getting lighter. At about 01°N we felt we had entered
the Doldrums, but they were to let us off lightly this time, to prove
infinitely less frustrating and despair-making. We continued to carry the
light breeze most of the day and even throughout the night, which was a
little surprising. But the more remarkable feature was the wind stayed
steady from the east-north-east. We would run the engine to carry us
through the infrequent no-wind patches but the hours when it was needed
were appreciably less than we had anticipated. Just as well perhaps as we
had used the engine more down in the South Atlantic than we had
expected. Also of course as the passage north was taking longer than
planned we were putting up extra engine hours for battery charging.

Fraser had been sceptical about the accuracy of our descriptions of trade-wind sailing and was becoming even more so now about the horror stories we had related about our south-going transit of the Doldrums. 'What's all the fuss then about these Doldrums? It seems to me they could be a lot worse.' We had to agree with him when it came to this passage north. It was in relative terms working out to be something of a dream ticket. A typical log entry would read 'Quiet, steady sailing, hot and sunny with long swell and calm sea. Wind Force 1 to 2. ENE.' Although the thermometer was still reading 35°C it was bearable in the cabin as we could keep the skylight propped open. We were getting the inevitable rain squalls but this time they did not harass us to anywhere near the same extent as on the way south. They had the same blood-curdling look about them but seemed inclined to avoid our company, lurking around on the horizon. We kept telling ourselves that when they did come over us we should seize the opportunity to improve the togetherness factor and take a rain-water shower. Working against this laudable objective was that it was so cold standing out in those squalls. Moreover there may have been a dignity, or lack of it, factor amongst the older members of the ship's company. The male figure is not always the most attractive of sights when dancing around unadorned.

We were trying to hold as near as possible to a northerly course, to put ourselves in the best jumping-off position for the slant across the north-east trades. We did not want to make westing until it was forced on us. We were expecting to meet them at about 05°N. Further to the east of where we had crossed the Line, the wind roses showed a marked lack of wind. Consequently we did not want to get too far east either, although this would have been to our advantage later. It was all one big compromise, but our tactics seemed to be working out. Crossing the equator close to 25°W had been near the mark.

The big thing was we were still carrying a breeze, but it was beginning to edge further north of east, resulting in the best course we could comfortably hold being no better than north-north-west.

We were now roughly midway between South America and Africa, Brazil and Sierra Leone. The nearest land was Penedos de São Pedro e São Paulo, an isolated small group of rocks otherwise known as Saints Peter and Paul, lying 220 miles to the west of us. They are a strange geological phenonomen suddenly popping up from an adjacent ocean depth of 3,650 metres. *Ocean Passages* issues due warning: 'Great care should be taken, and a good lookout kept, when in the vicinity of St. Paul rocks, as they are steep to and are not usually visible above 10 miles even in clear weather.' In our longitude they were not a problem to us but had been of concern to Bill Tilman, who relates that when on passage in his *Mischief* from the Cape Verdes to the River Plate he was too far to the west and was 'praying for a wind that would let us sail a point free so that we should not be set down towards St. Paul's Rocks.' He was to end up crossing the equator at 28°W, certainly too far west.

It is worthy of note that *Beagle*, also on her way from the Cape Verdes, took a lock at the islands, probably for Darwin's benefit, heaving to for a morning so he could get ashore in pursuit of his insatiable curiosity. FitzRoy was not quite so happy being in such close proximity to a very 'isolated danger', the depths being far too great to anchor. Apparently there is an anchorage shown on the large-scale Admiralty chart but with more hope than conviction. The geology of the rocks fascinated Darwin who remarked in typical Darwinian prose that their 'mineralogical constitution is not simple' but of greater interest perhaps, at least to us, is 'We found on St. Paul's only two kinds of birds – the booby and the noddy. Both are of a tame and stupid disposition.' Rather unkind to our much loved little bird but one had to admit its performance on board us did not suggest a creature of the highest intelligence.

On board *Marelle* we were soon to be reminded we did not, apart from Peter and Paul, have the ocean to ourselves. Two days after the equator crossing Fraser, who was on watch, sighted ship's lights on the port bow holding a collision course. The switching on of our tricolor masthead light triggered off a chat show. As in what we had come to accept as the norm, her captain was on the radio informing us he was Jesus. He wanted to know if we spoke Spanish and on my replying '*un poquito*', a very little, he laughed. He went on to spell out his ship's name, *Rosu Tercero*, adding that she was travelling at 9.5 knots on a course of 060°, presumably True. His request was for us to '*cambiar el rumbo*' when we would then run parallel with them. All of this was in Spanish, taxing me to the hilt, but with a little guesswork and quick looks at the dictionary, I was able to cope. Just.

On my reply we were a sailing vessel and the course alteration he wanted was '*no posible*' it was 'Okay! Okay!' They would alter course to clear us. It transpired she was a fishing vessel, although in the Spanish way not displaying the lights of one, out of Vigo and now working from Brazil. Jesus, for some reason, wanted to know more about me personally. I thought he would have known that already! How old was I? When I replied '*Tengo setenta y cinco anos*' there was a long pause and then Jesus said 'My God! That is older than my father!' I was not sure quite where that put me in the celestial pecking order. His grandad perhaps? Grandad of all grandads! Successively other members of the crew came on the radio to practise their English. So much so it was becoming difficult to close down transmission until someone asked if one said 'Good night' or 'Good evening' when saying farewell at that time of night, it being about 2100. With that she turned back onto her course and was swallowed up by the night.

The day after this exchange, which had been fun, we entered the north-east trades with the wind strength hovering around a Force 4. A little further south than expected but all to the good. It is of course not a precise line of demarcation when changing from one weather system to another but the trade-wind belts have a character of their own. Impressive big cloud formations and a steady wind from a more or less fixed direction. The sea now running more strongly, another characteristic of a trade-wind, and forward of the beam, meant we were starting to take water over the weather bow. Once more the lee scuppers were full of water. With a reef in the main and reduced genoa we settled down to the hard wearisome slog across these trades, a prospect we had not been relishing with much enthusiasm. This was where a boat of the size of Chichester's *Gipsy Moth IV*, with a waterline of 39½ feet, would have been able to handle the conditions so much better and make faster time. Our waterline on *Marelle* at only 27 feet meant we lacked the power to push through the seas, built up over long distances under these permanently blowing fresh winds. Consequently we had to sail off the wind, with sheets started, in order to keep boat speed up and equally importantly make life tolerable for ourselves. Even so as we worked north we maintained a course made good well to the east of his. But it would seem Chichester was not happy with the Illingworth design of his boat, whereas I was with *Marelle*'s. James McGruer had known what he was doing. The old girl was doing well but it was hard, wet going and taking its toll of boat and crew. We could expect to live with this way of life until we got up to about 25°N, which would be about the bottom fringe, at this time of the year, of the northern Variables or Horse Latitudes as they are popularly known.

Up to entering the trades we had been getting assistance from the Equatorial Counter Current, which runs east at a reasonable pace of half a knot. This was helpful in gaining us easting but now we were in the grip of the North Equatorial Current, which, starting out in life as the Canary Current, flows south-west from Africa and then turns to sweep over towards the Caribbean, where we didn't want to go. It was tempting to compare our lot crossing the trades with the 'milk run' from the Atlantic islands, principally the Canaries, over to the West Indies. This passage is with the trades comfortably astern and enjoying as well the benefit of the ocean current flowing west in harmony with the wind. A blissfully unexacting experience.

But we had to keep matters in perspective. Doing an audit of the blessings that had been bestowed on us, it had to be recognised we had been favoured with a remarkably easy transit of the Doldrums. These should really be more correctly referred to as the Equatorial Trough, as they are a low pressure system. They are best crossed in the earlier part of the year so we had been fortunate in that regard. They normally occupy a width of 200 to 300 miles with the centre line of the zone lying in about 04°N, moving to some extent seasonally with the sun. For us they were south and at their minimum width. All of this, coupled with being blessed with a friendly little wind for much of the time, had resulted in an easy Doldrums for us.

Up till now we had not seen much in the way of marine life, apart from birds. My main viewing was of a whale, possibly a killer, or even a large shark, crossing our wake well astern and completely ignoring us. However, as we entered the trades Fraser was treated to 'a tremendous display of long-snouted spinner dolphins which lasted for approximately forty-five minutes, leaping six or seven abreast in unison six feet clear of the sea, still continuing their swimming motions whilst in mid air. There must have been eighty to a hundred of them all around us.'

Near the end of his watch Fraser, as I was getting ready to relieve him, reported he had ship's lights away to the south. He had taken the correct action of switching on the tricolor but we were not in danger of our paths crossing. We were at that moment in the centre of a little web of shipping lanes. The North Atlantic was quite different to the South with regard to the chance of meeting ships at sea. We had the Curacao to Lagos and Bunny track crossing that of New York to Cape Town and Rio de la Plata to Bishop Rock. The latter of 5,880 miles. This brought home to us the distance we still had to cover, the Bishop being our expected landfall.

Although it was rather late at night I decided to call up Fraser's ship. It was some time since we had last got a message to our families. That had been when we had met the friendly *Robert F. Bauer* down in the South Atlantic. It was more than time we let them know we were still around. On calling her up there was an immediate response. Yes, they were quite happy to send on any messages. Communication was a little difficult as the master's English, although adequate, was not strong. However he was only too pleased to help. They were bound for Panama and seemed a shade surprised at meeting a yacht. I wondered because of the language limitations if a message ever would get through. I need not have worried.

To: MRCC, UK
FM: Mexican Reefer / 3FVQ3
24 April 00
MSG Relay FROM S/V MARELLE / MCFY3
Quote
    WE ARE ALL (FAMILY) ON BOARD AND ALL FINE. NOW
    PROCEEDING TO FALKLAND ISLAND. PSN 23 / UTC 0350 N
    02615 W
Unquote
MASTER

The folks at home were relieved to learn our ship's company was still complete with no one as yet having had to walk the plank. However there was a little consternation at the news we had decided to give it all away and were heading back to the Falklands but it was decided to await 'our next'. In all my communication with ships at sea I had noted particularly the speed of acknowledgement of my call. It was very evident there was always someone alive and alert on the bridge contrary to the popular idea that ships are a bit lax in this regard with the ship put on autohelm and left to her own devices, with no one on the bridge apart from the occasional presence of the ship's cook. That was far from the case with the ships we spoke. The bridge was always fully manned, with the captain on immediate call.

As if to mark the occasion of our contact with civilisation, Jeremy baked a soda bread. Perfect, our morale rising like the loaf.

The entry into the trades inspired frenetic activity in another department, fisheries. Our chief fisherman, confounding his critics, landed a big dorado which was 'filleted, in the pan and eaten. All within ten minutes.' On previous trips flying fish had featured on the menu but this time, although they were frequently found in the morning lying on deck, they did not find their way into the pan. It had been the same when we were coming south, when they seemed to be more prolific. My team did not seem to fancy them. Perhaps because of their small size they were beneath the dignity of our now-redeemed head fisherman to gut and clean. He was now a big fish man.

We had not expected to enjoy the cut across the trade winds and we were not to be disappointed, despite the near certainty that good daily runs were guaranteed. It was all very predictable, but surprisingly the weather was of dreary aspect and not like the normally agreeable trade-wind weather. The going was wet from spray licking over the weather bow and from the constant onslaught of the seas against the boat's topsides. It was the sea that was the limiting factor, not the wind. Even in the settled conditions of the trades there were variations in the combination of wind with sea, which required ongoing attention to sail trim in order to maintain boat speed, without over-driving her. Our different temperaments came out during this period. I was more content to let *Marelle* run on without much interference for quite lengthy spells, but I knew from my bunk when Fraser was on watch. The sheet winches would not be at rest for long. He liked to make the most of the conditions and was tireless in getting peak performance. As it was for our common good, I could not complain about all the frenetic activity, even be it the middle of the night.

With Mr Franklin doing all the steering, playing with sail trim contributed to taking the tedium out of the watch. We sailed much of the time with one reef in the main, with the storm jib as usual on the inner forestay and varying sail drive by adjusting the genoa on its roller furling gear. This of course was so much easier than having to change headsails, which would have involved working on a deck running water continuously and in a constant shower-bath of driving spray. The decision in Punta Arenas to put up with the problems in getting the furling gear repaired was well and truly vindicated. We probably would have gained in these conditions by replacing the storm jib with the larger staysail earlier in the piece, as some of the time we were under-sailing *Marelle,* but we were content not to push her too hard. After all we were not racing and our physical comfort was not something to brush aside lightly.

Once again I noticed how surprisingly irregular were the seas. They did not have an order to them, with the wave fronts at different angles to the high swell on which they rode. Strong winds emanating from under lusty rain squalls probably exacerbated the situation, leaving added confusion behind them as they hurtled across the sea surface. Approaching the latitude of the Cape Verdes the wind was veering and increasing, the seas piling up in unison. With the wind now east-north-east we were able to head up on a more northerly course and arrest the remorseless westing we had been making. In fact we had been doing pretty well in keeping this down and were to end up no further than 37°W, whereas I had been expecting 40°W or even more. It was gratifying we were keeping further to the east than Chichester had been, even with his bigger and more powerful boat.

The big advantage of the trade winds lying ahead of the beam was to allow the watchman to prop himself up in a corner of the cockpit under the shelter of the sprayhood. It was a smug feeling to watch the spray driving hard over poor old Mr Franklin beavering away and taking everything that burst over us. It also meant we could leave the cabin doors open, unlike when running downwind before the trades. Certainly that kind of sailing is not all 'beer and skittles'. We were now in the same trades belt we had been in on the way south and could remember the drawbacks such as the stuffiness with the doors closed and the incessant rolling and nothing staying put. There is always something not quite right in this sailing business, it would seem.

On 2 May we were abreast the Cape Verdes with our old anchorage of São Vicente 500 miles to the east. Seemed a very long time ago. The seas were now the biggest we had met since the South Atlantic. Despite two reefs in the main we were sailing fast in the fresh breeze and for a change under a bright sun. This was more like it. It was one of those days that remain in one's memory, but what made it particularly memorable was the head of our Fisheries Department excelling himself. Three dorado in rapid succession and what's more the timing was perfect. The duty cook was on the point of preparing supper. One fresh fish each straight out of the pan! The critics had nothing to say or rather, as our man recorded, 'That made them eat their words about my fishing ability!'

We were now in more robust waters, feeling the full prime of the trades and the flowing Canaries Current sweeping us south-westwards at twelve miles a day, fortunately wind and current being with each other. The Routeing Chart contains an interesting insert showing the likelihood of 'Winds of Beaufort Force 7 and higher.' Although the incidence for our area was still only one per cent, the wind roses showed for the first time the chance of winds up to gale force. However, encouragingly, it adds 'No hurricanes have been recorded'. I could recall my concern about hurricanes breeding when we were near the Cape Verdes before.

One of the contingencies I always had in the back of my mind was the disaster of losing *Marelle*. Fire, hitting a whale, anything. The ultimate disaster would of course be the death of one or more of us but next in line was the boat sinking. What would happen to us? We carried a six-man Forties liferaft and a 406 mHz Pains Wessex SOS EPIRB, registered with Falmouth Coastguard. The latter device would be the means of communicating our distress to the outside world but it had to be recognised that all manmade devices, however good, are fallible. In the event of taking to the liferaft where was our nearest bolt hole should a rescuer not appear on the scene? In the South Atlantic there was the problem of the vast distances of empty sea and little in the way of shipping. In the southern regions in the path of the prevailing westerlies a liferaft, south of the latitude of Cape Town, would simply blow into oblivion. Highly unlikely, but it was something I thought about, albeit somewhat unproductively. This was where Jeremy's philosophical attitude was relevant. If there is nothing to be done about something why waste time worrying about it? But he was not me, or the skipper. Further up that ocean we would be at the mercy of the conflicting currents and winds and where we would have landed up was highly uncertain. Further north the prospects were more favourable, with wind and current combining to sweep us up to the north coast of South America.

However my mind was eased when we got into the North Atlantic as a greater harmony between wind and current alleviated the problem. In the trades it was only a matter of staying alive until inevitably we arrived in the West Indies. Further north in the westerlies it would be a landing on the coast of Europe somewhere, but there would be a reasonable expectancy of meeting a ship. I could start to relax.

On board life was changing as we got to the north of the Cape Verdes. The wind was losing strength, the temperature was dropping and we were beginning to think about our arrival in the Azores. Bets were being placed on the date for Horta. There was a spread, reflecting perhaps on our natures. Jeremy 17 May, Fraser 19 and myself 24. It was to be an exercise in futility, but we were not to know that. Winning the bet became important if only for self-gratification, so the midday plotting of our position was of universal interest. When I had done this I would make a report in what had become a standard code. COG, SOG and DOG. Course, speed and distance over ground respectively, the latter being of particular interest.

With the going becoming a little more sedate Mr Franklin was not being subjected to the same frequency of sluicing deluges but we still had to be careful in the cockpit. It was easy to drop one's guard and be lazy about going through the performance of getting fully kitted up with oilskins and boots before going on watch. I have an entry 'Called up to Fraser to check whether it was wet up in the cockpit to be advised there was only a bit of spray but nothing to worry about. I took a risk and took over the watch without the full protective regalia. Fraser vanished, the cabin doors closed behind him and on me descended a large lump of solid sea.' I don't know if he heard my commentary on the situation but if he had, nothing came up from the depths of the warm dry cabin. Getting ready to go on watch had personal characteristics about it. A shared one was an immediate response to being shaken, otherwise there was a difference. Fraser on being called was remarkably quick in leaping into his foul-weather gear and out on deck. Jeremy never seemed to need a shake to relieve me. Whether he had some internal body mechanism that told him what was the time or whether he had an alarm clock buried in his sleeping bag with him I never discovered. He also did not waste any time when getting dressed. My performance did not match theirs. No matter what I did to improve it by meticulously laying out my gear ready for quick donning, it always took me ages longer to get organised than the other two. I would then compound the problem with a study of the barograph trace, followed by a quick look at the GPS and glance at the chart. Fraser had infinite patience and never once complained.

On 7 May we passed out of the trades and entered the Variables. The 0315 log write-up reads '23° 53´.7 N 36° 38´.1 W. Wind died in last hour of watch. Course 015° C. Wind Force 0 to 1. About N.'

The northern Variables are more popularly known as the Horse Latitudes, there being two versions of the story behind the expression. One has it that sailing ships out of Britain frequently made such slow progress in the variable regions that they ran out food and water for the livestock and in particular for horses, destined for the colonies in America, which had to be thrown overboard. The other is more esoteric but more probable, relating to the disposing overboard of a 'dead horse'. When a seaman signed on for a voyage he was given a month's wages in advance, probably spent in one long debauch. This period during which he worked off the advance was known as a dead horse. At the end of the first month at sea, which in all likelihood would be when getting down into the Variables, the custom was to make an effigy of a horse and drop it over the side, thus marking the working off by the seamen of their dead horses. In turn this led to the phrase 'to flog a dead horse', the inference being there was no future in trying to get more work out of a sailor during the period he was 'working off his dead horse'. From then on the boot was on the other leg, the seaman having the threat hanging over him of his pay being stopped if he did not co-operate.

The climax of the dead horse ceremony was for the crew to sing:

> *Now, old horse your time has come.*
> *And, we say so, for we know so!*
> *Altho' many a race you've won,*
> *Oh! poor old man,*
> *You're going now to say good-bye*
> *And we say so, for we know so!*
> *Poor old horse, you're going to die.*

Whatever the origin of its name, the region, like its southern counterpart, is characterised by light varying winds interspersed with calms with cloud and rain, but quite long fair periods with nothing much happening. Frustration is the keynote. This is the North Atlantic High, a permanent high pressure system centred on 30° north. We were expecting our share of frustration but its immediate manifestation was from an unexpected direction. It was discovered at breakfast that the remaining boxes of porridge were also spoiled. These had been held back in reserve. Coming from another retailer and bought at a different time to those condemned in the South Atlantic, we had high hopes of their edibility. Not so. They had suffered from the same penetration of damp. There was a round-table discussion. Jeremy and Fraser said they would finish off the remaining muesli and then turn to rice pudding for breakfast. I said I would stick grimly to the oats. The prospect of rice pudding was by far the greater of two ills. Cold rice pudding was a great favourite of Jeremy's and to a lesser extent Fraser's. A taste which I had no intention of trying to acquire. However to take our minds off this very serious situation our fisherman-in-chief, flushed with his earlier success, got the bit between his teeth and caught another dorado.

By next morning there was no doubt about it. We were well and truly in the Horse Latitudes. What wind there was, however, had remained fair but had hauled nearer south. We tried the spinnaker but it was having difficulty staying full as the boat rolled the wind out of it, the apparent wind now being very low. What was worse, there not being enough wind to satisfy Mr Franklin, we had to hand-steer. The foot of the spinnaker was falling in and sawing across the headstay, ending up by chafing through the tape along the foot. Jeremy did a good repair job, demonstrating again his flair for marlinespike seamanship, but we fell back on the alternative twin headsail rig. This was better, with the sails being under the control of their booms. With the breeze dying altogether we gave *Marelle* a leg-on with the engine. The rationale was we were only using the fuel that had been reserved for the Doldrums and not needed. It was noted however that we were not getting the usual boat speed commensurate with the engine revolutions, suggesting there could be heavy bottom fouling.

Whilst on watch that afternoon I was treated to a most spectacular display of dolphin power similar to that which Fraser had been privileged to witness. Ahead was a long line of rippling water approaching us like a small wave. It rapidly got closer to reveal serried ranks of dolphins in large numbers, diving to skim just under the surface then to leap clear of the water in perfect unison as though they were following some aquatic metronome. Opening ranks to pass us on either side, they re-formed to continue heading south. They obviously knew where they were going and were wasting no time about it, completely ignoring us.

There is an old piece of sailors' wisdom on weather portents which authoritatively states: 'When the sea-hog jumps, stand by your pumps.' In the language of the sea the sea-hog refers specifically to the porpoise. To the uninitiated the distinction between the porpoise and the dolphin is blurred but there is actually one particular difference in characteristics, apart from the porpoise in general being smaller, which is explained by Carwardine: 'Preferring to keep to themselves, porpoises are typically shy creatures and rarely perform the acrobatic feats of dolphins.'

Whatever breed of sea-hog it was that I was watching jump was an academic point, as there was certainly no need, in the weather we had to call all hands to man the pumps. It would appear some of the old shellbacks' doggerel can have a degree of unreliability not unknown to today's weather men.

The more relaxed sea conditions were conducive to the restoration of the happy hour, the only problem being we were running out of liquor. Fraser and Jeremy were whisky men but they had exhausted their stocks and the tide was receding in my last bottle of gin. It was then Jeremy fossicking around in a cupboard found a half bottle of rum. I had quietly put this on one side for a rainy day but the general opinion was that the rainy day had arrived despite the bright sunshine outside. The short-lived regeneration of the happy hour was another casualty of our slow passage. With hindsight we should not have been put off by the high prices in Stanley and should have laid in healthier stocks in case of medical emergencies.

I was reminded of the Francis Chichester lament in answer to a question put to him on completion of his circumnavigation. 'When were your spirits at their lowest ebb?' to which he thought the obvious answer seemed to be 'when the gin gave out.'

To my chagrin when clearing out the boat after our return I unearthed two bottles of Argentinian red wine under one of the quarter berths. The contents were still very palatable. I didn't let on to the others.

The Routeing Chart was starting to look like a map of the London Underground with a crisscrossing of shipping lanes now featuring prominently. We had just passed over the Trinidad to Gibralter track when in the late afternoon we sighted a ship crossing our stern. The voice sounded faintly Russian when we called her up. Yes, they would contact Falmouth Coastguard with pleasure, advising they would do this by telex. This seemed to be the commonly preferred medium.

FROM MASTER *SIERRA LEYRE* / 3FKO7
TO FALMOUTH COASTGUARD
    THE MAY 9TH AT 1727 GMT IN POSITION 26 56.8 N 47.9W
    SKIPPER SAILING BOAT *MARELLE* CALL SIGN MCFY3
    FROM FALKLAND TO AZORES, ASKED TO SEND YOU
    MSG THEY ARE OK.
    EXPECTED ETA HORTA 10 DAYS FROM NOW. PLS NOTIFY
    RELATIVES
    THKS N RGDS / MASTER

The invariable response we got from ships at sea was extremely friendly and wanting to be helpful. It may be that we provided a break from routine. They never failed to contact Falmouth Coastguard, who in turn were meticulous in getting in touch with Susan. Perhaps in an age of sophisticated communications we were looked on as an exotic relic from the past which should be humoured. I liked to think though that it confirmed that 'the brotherhood of the sea' was still very much alive amongst mariners of all nations.

Although the transit of the Variables was tedious we were getting wind, albeit it had embarked on a programme of veering steadily over the next few days round the clock. This meant dropping the twin headsail rig and reverting to full main and genoa, with the wind now on the port bow. It was quite strange having to adjust to the boat heeling the other way. For a very long time now we had become accustomed to the wind being somewhere in the east. We were now north of the latitude of the Canaries and the prospects were favourable for the run to Horta, this optimistic view being encouraged by the wind seemingly settled in the north-west and moreover at reasonable strength. Unfortunately the breeze had got itchy feet and could not let well alone. Moving through north it was back to the north-east but I assured the team we were passing out of the northern limit of the Horse Latitudes and could look forward to the prevailing south-westerlies lying just ahead of us. These would give us a comfortable ride to the island of Faial and Horta. Moreover we were in the Azores Current. Although flowing south-east this would still give us a helpful lift over to the east. The team believed me, despite having heard optimistic noises like this before which had come to nought. We were now four hundred miles south-west of Faial with the wind stuck firmly in the east at a gentle Force 3. We had experienced a relatively easy ride through the Variables so we couldn't really complain if our course was more northerly than we would have liked.

The 15 May log entry read 'Lovely sunny day. Light wind.' It would have been perfect if we had had the wherewithal for a happy hour. A day later the wind again got restless and backed north of east, putting Horta three hundred miles up to windward. Not promising, and it was starting to look as though Flores would be a more convenient landfall. I, for one, did not see much attraction in a beat to windward to make Horta. Ilha das Flores lies about 130 miles north-west of Faial and was now situated more in line with our track. Reading the RCC pilot the small harbour of Porto das Lajes, on the south-eastern tip, looked inviting. I was happy about a change in plan. There were however two problems. One was it is exposed to the north-east and as such wide open to the wind we were encountering. The other was a lack of gas supplies, apart from Camping Gaz which we did not carry. To refill our propane bottles we would have to get them to Horta. Diesel, water and a stores top-up would be straightforward. I quite liked the idea. It was also acceptable to the others. The fact that my credibility over the westerlies had taken a dent did not seem to have sown the seeds of mutiny.

Fraser, in particular, had been looking forward to a break in Horta although torn between this and the urge to get home. Horta after all is one of the major staging posts on the Atlantic circuit and has rather an exotic reputation. Jeremy had a different reason for wanting to get there. There was the possibility, albeit rather unlikely, that Adrie might be waiting impatiently there for us. She had talked about it before we left but in view of the uncertainty of our arrival it was improbable she would have gone there on a blind date as it were. She was as aware as anyone of the vagaries of sailing schedules.

Jeremy was not sure about the situation, but it was something we could check on when we did eventually get to Flores. Between most islands in the archipelago there are flight connections, including one from Flores to Horta. Having been to Horta, before I was not too fussed about missing it, particularly as it could well be full of boats en route from the West Indies to Europe. I, for one, did not fancy being squeezed in between other boats, rafted up six or more deep as I had seen them before. It would be hard to adjust, after so long 'in a world of our own'. Or so I told myself.

The wind was not cooperating, now having firmly taken up residence in the north-east. The best course we could now make good over the ground was north. On 18 May we were on the latitude of Porto das Lajes and ninety miles over to the west. The choice was either to beat that distance back to Flores or carry on for home. There was a division in the camp. Fraser had swallowed his disappointment about not seeing something of the islands and was now keen to keep going. This was also my choice. Jeremy still had his concern about the marital ramifications of leaving Adrie stranded in Horta but it was recognised that there should be little in the way of a problem in getting a message to her via a passing ship.

Over the last three days we had seen as many ships as we had met in all the time we had been at sea up till then. It was obviously a busy part of the ocean and from past experience we could rely on the next ship we met being willing to be a communication link with the Horta harbour authorities and thence to Adrie. Ultimately of course it was my decision, which I knew would be accepted. As the next step in the decision-making process we needed to do an audit on our stores position. I stated, I hoped with conviction, that based on an earlier experience we should get home in about ten days. On that occasion *Marelle* had brought me back to Falmouth from Ponta Delgada on São Miguel, admittedly further east in the group, in not much more than nine days and that was without trying too hard. Happily we did not know that this time it was going to take us twice as long. Once again my trusting companions accepted another of my confident prognostications. Water we were happy about. Diesel was low but we would have enough for battery charging plus a little to spare. Jeremy did a provisions stock-take and confirmed we were alright but the choice would be somewhat restricted. The problem was gas. We were on our last bottle and any day that would run out. Once again I cursed the poor recharging facilities in Stanley. However as a fall-back Jeremy had put on board his Primus stove. For this we had plenty of methylated spirits and paraffin. We could thus manage, albeit with some inconvenience. In the light of this scenario we sailed on, the younger members of the crew being prepared to forgo the fleshpots of Porto das Lajes.

Later that afternoon we had two sailing vessels on our port bow, coming from the west and on the wind, heading apparently in the direction of Flores. They were closing us and would pass ahead. The first one up was a French catamaran, motor-sailing under mainsail only. She was followed by a British yacht, *Wave Dancer*, with two on board, hailing from Devon. Their point of departure had been Bermuda and they complained with feeling about the absence of the westerlies. As a consequence they had used their engine more than expected and were now short of fuel but calculated they had just enough to get them to Flores. Their planned destination was Horta and then home. They seemed to have other problems on their plate, including being nearly out of gas and their main radio not working, which meant they were having to use their handheld VHF, the performance of which was not the best. They needed to make the Azores and I explained our situation. There was no problem, said the voice, the owner of which was Roger Stoyle. They would telephone Susan when they arrived in Porto das Lajes. This was good, as she would get in touch with Adrie wherever she was to be found. Jeremy relaxed somewhat. Subsequently we learned that in fact Adrie had not gone anywhere and was safely at home. *Wave Dancer*, we also learned later, on reaching Porto das Lajes did what they said they would do and called Susan. However they did not like the harbour conditions because of the north-easterly piling in and had plugged on to Horta, presumably after picking up fuel. If we had beaten up to Flores we would have faced the same situation.

No sooner had our Devonian friends disappeared to the east over our starboard quarter than a large Dutch container vessel came over the horizon north-west of us. She altered course to close us to enquire if we were safe and sound. We assured her we were and on mentioning we were 75 days out of Stanley they were both impressed and amused. To them on their tight schedules and quick passages this was something out of another world. Yes, they were only too pleased to pass on any messages to Falmouth.

To: MRCC FALMOUTH
FM: M.V. *SEA MASTER* / XYKJ
    HAVE JUST PASSED MSG FROM THE SAILING V/I *MARELLE* IN 44006N / 03306W ON UTC 181945. REGISTERED WITH MRCC FALMOUTH, SAILED FROM STANLEY HARBOUR FM FALKLAND IS ON 8TH MARCH. REQUEST US TO GIVE POSITION REPORT TO YOU AND WOULD LIKE TO PASS FLWG TO THEIR FAMILY
    QUOTE:
    ALL GOING WELL AND ETA IN NEXT 12 DAY, WILL NOT CALL TO AZORES
    UNQUOTE:
    B. RGDS
    MASTER

We were nearly there. Only 1,300 miles to cover on a rhumb line track, but thought had to be given to the actual route to follow. For our time of the year the predominant winds should be between south-west and north-west and of moderate strength. The wind roses also confirmed that in the run up to the Azores from the south-west we should have been getting such a wind. The persistent easterlies we were experiencing should not have happened. They hardly featured on the wind charts. North-west of the islands, where we were now positioned, strong winds principally from the south-west could reasonably be expected. The percentage of winds Force 7 and above has risen to ten percent and gale Force 8 symbols are sprinkled amongst the wind roses like confetti at a wedding. It is noteworthy that in *Ocean Passages* the further west one is the better when passing the Azores. For June it recommends as far over as 250 miles west of Flores to get the better winds. We were not as far as that but we were certainly north-west and that should be helpful. All of this was lending credence to my confident predictions. The indications were that we should aim to gain as much northing as we could and as early as we could, to get up into the sailing ship route sweeping north of the Azores into the Channel. We should be aiming for a prescribed waypoint at 45°N 25°W. Heading north also gave us a better cut across the Azores Current flowing strongly south-east. Achieving the waypoint ensures that one then stays in the east running North Atlantic Current, adding twelve miles a day, and safeguards against getting caught up in its offshoot trying to carry the unwary south-east towards the coast of Spain. Despite all the laid-down wisdom there is always the risk of a spell of easterlies inconveniently setting in. This was another reason to get north.

The route planning was straightforward enough but as had so often happened in the past the hard school of reality was to teach us once again that planning is not a precise art. For the next few days we remained in the grip of the Azores High, giving us light winds persistently coming from the north. Thereafter it was to be a very mixed bag of winds, varying between protracted calm and full gales anywhere from north-west to south-east. Throughout it all a grey dampness prevailed, the chill factor causing us to break out our southern latitude foul-weather gear again. We kept asking ourselves about the northern summer. Where had it gone?

On the heels of *Sea Master* we had a large ship, lightly loaded and high out of the water, closing us on a collision bearing. Looming large on our port side, she was soon heading directly for us. The picture was looking alarming so I called her up to be greeted with 'Don't worry, we see you. We are altering course.' This she did, passing close across our stern, revealing she was Greek. A small group was assembled on the bridge wing waving cheerily. Sounding her siren in salute, she swung back onto her course and was soon lost over the horizon, leaving us once more alone and longing for home. She was the sixth ship, plus two yachts, we had seen in the last few days. It was quite remarkable compared to further south when for the whole length of the South Atlantic we had met only one ship.

Expecting we could have two or even three more weeks at sea, we instituted some food rationing. Jeremy had made it clear that although our stocks were adequate in bulk they were out of balance. To get some order into our ongoing diet he set up a ready-use locker containing the day's rations, from which the duty cook drew for each meal. Also because we had so little gas remaining he rationed us to two hot drinks each per day. It was particularly unfortunate that because of the gas situation he could no longer bake any bread. This was a big hardship, especially as he had adequate stocks of the necessary ingredients. Fraser reveals all on the food situation. 'Bartering is the name of the game. I am giving up my daily ration of two Ryvitas, Ben is giving up his tinned fruit in exchange for them and we are not sure about Jeremy. We only have two tins of rice left and to take over from them we are to have the two remaining treacle puds for breakfast. Cold in order to conserve gas. Ben will carry on eating the rancid porridge provided he is allowed the remaining spoonfuls of golden syrup to disguise the taste. After that it is curried carrots. Meanwhile Jeremy creates a lovely Scotch broth with noodles on his Primus as a trial run. A welcome change after two weeks of corned beef.'

The last gas bottle expired and Jeremy commenced a series of trials with his Primus. It fitted well into the fiddles on top of the swinging stove but the pot or whatever utensil was on it had to be held as the whole assembly tended to overbalance when one's attention was elsewhere. But it worked, and well at that, providing one did not try to be too ambitious, particularly as when it was rough it became a two-man operation. The Primus does have a supporting framework in which it can swing, the whole assembly being mountable on the bulkhead, but believing it highly unlikely we would not be able to use the gas stove we had decided to leave that rather bulky accessory behind. Rather short-sighted as it turned out.

The days went past and somehow so did the miles despite the widely varying conditions and a wind that refused to settle down. Log entries tell the story. 'Tuesday 23 May 0620 44° 48'.1 N 28° 06'.1 W. Wind and sea increasing. Still raining. Course 070°C. Wind Force 6 to 7. SW.' But a day later as we approached our waypoint: '1800 45° 10'.8 N 25° 5'.1 W. Sun coming out. Whales on surface near by. Course 060°C. Wind Force 2. EAST!' Where were those westerlies, supposedly so true and strong? They should have put in a better showing by now. But far from it. On 25 May, the following morning, the log records at 0930 a full gale from the north-east, with us hove to under storm jib on a heading of 120°C. The blow was blocking us and made us all feel low. No one was saying very much.

The recurring easterlies had forced us north of track so much so that at one time the nearest point of land we could lay was south-west Ireland. I was beginning to think about Kinsale as a staging point. The possibility was always present that at that time of the year once easterly weather set in it could be with us for some time. This was an observation that Fraser would gloomily make on occasions. I was keeping an eye on the barograph but so far with no indication of a high developing. In the event the capricious wind freed and the Irish option ceased to be relevant.

Now we were getting nearer to civilisation Jeremy tried his radio but reception being indifferent we reverted to our isolated world. The fragment of news we had picked up confirmed that nothing serious seemed to have happened during our long period of no news. When viewed from a distance and not subjected to a daily bombardment from the media and strident 'political party broadcasts' it was so evident how little changes on the political scene. The same problems keep coming around and around. Free of this incessant attack on our senses we continued our reading off watch, the others more so than I, but of particular pleasure to me was Kipling's *The Jungle Book*. Some harmless violence maybe if one stretched a point, but what a relief from the obsession with sex in literature today. If it had not been for our circumstance I would not have had the enjoyment of reading that enduring gem.

Apart from difficulties with the weather we had been enjoying a trouble-free run over the last few weeks, but that happy situation changed. From down below I heard Jeremy handing the mainsail, for which I could think of no good reason. Shortly after he called out to say it had torn along the foot and he was putting in the first reef to contain it. That temporary remedy was not to last long before splits appeared elsewhere, leading to complete failure. This was not totally unexpected. The sail was not new when we had left but had been overhauled by my sailmaker and pronounced fit to travel. However it had been given an extremely hard time, particularly in the high ultraviolet levels of the tropics, which had exacerbated the effects of the flogging it had taken in the Doldrums and to a lesser extent in the Variables. These had been the killers, not heavy weather. The surprising feature was the sail had been through strong winds and up to its sudden failure looked in reasonable condition. We changed over to the spare main, one of the original from *Marelle*'s racing days. This also had been checked over by the sailmaker and had passed its MOT. Unfortunately what I had not done was to subject it to a full sea trial which would have revealed it did not set well. It had a decided crease running vertically down it, due, as it transpired, to shrinkage of the luff bolt rope. However although Mr Ratsey would not have approved, it did the job and got us home, not too much being expected of it. We had being experiencing gales at intervals during the last part of the passage up from Flores and when they hit the normal procedure was to shift down to storm jib and the well-used trysail rather than closely reefed main. It was a snug rig with the boom safely under control whatever the wind direction. If the wind was inconveniently too far aft a change could be made to boomed-out staysail. We had got used to handling Force 8 conditions. Life was uncomfortable whilst they lasted but they were pushing us along.

All this while I had been thinking about our food situation. We were not going to starve although the stocks were getting down and I would have liked to have a little more in reserve. Accordingly without discussing it with the others I decided if a suitable opportunity presented itself I would put pride on one side and with cap in hand ask a passing ship, assuming we were to encounter another one, to top up our reserves. I was not too sure about how the other two would feel about holding out the begging bowl, particularly Jeremy, who might take it personally as a reflection on his stores management. However, for better or worse, I had taken the decision so when Fraser, early next morning, called down to say he could see the upperworks of a large ship crossing astern of us I called her up. After exchanging greetings her captain informed us she was the German-owned container ship MV *Teval* bound for Hamburg. He said his name was Heinz Reese and could he help? In reply I said who we were and asked if they could get a message to our families adding that we were well but were short of some food items. His response was they were only too willing to satisfy both requirements. He then took charge. They were altering course and would be with us in fourteen minutes. They would stop upwind to give us a lee. Would we please position ourselves close under his starboard quarter for the transfer? His Chief Officer had been detailed off to take charge of the heaving-line party on the afterdeck. Communication then to be direct with the Chief Officer. All precise and organised. We were lucky with our choice of ship.

Teval arrived on the dot, presented her beam to us and stopped. We then closed her under engine with Jeremy manning the radio and Fraser on the foredeck. On *Teval*'s afterdeck was assembled a small crowd of grinning South-East Asians, could have been Koreans, heaving lines at the ready. They kept gesticulating I should get in closer but I was nervous about that. Tucked up under the high lee side of a large ship in a seaway is not the best of places in which to be hanging about. With unerring accuracy a line came over to be smartly gathered in by Fraser. Over on it came a large sack tied off at the neck. Taking the bag off. Fraser let the line go and I sheared off, thankful to have collected safely our goodies and to have got clear unscathed. That was that. No it wasn't. Much shouting of 'More! More!' The Chief Officer told Jeremy the transfer had only just started. Once more we got back under her looming stern and line after line came over with those big bags attached. Fraser was doing a remarkable job, holding the lines with one hand, undoing the bags with the other in time to gather in the next line as it sailed over the bow. He needed three hands as it would have been too risky to have tied off the lines. Meanwhile I was having to hold *Marelle* in position with little room for error. It was all a little tense but that was no excuse for me most unhelpfully to call out to Fraser to 'Buck up!' as another line landed which he could not possibly have attended to immediately. I deserved the filthy look he directed at me. The last bag came over. Fraser let the lines go free whilst Jeremy took the wheel and got us clear. I went on to the radio to thank Captain Reese and give him the details of what we would like him to send off to Falmouth. It had been an intensely interesting and successful evolution. It was also one which our donors had enjoyed judging by the enormous grins on the crew's faces. The captain as a final gesture volunteered his personal weather prediction. The persistent light easterlies we had been having he said would be replaced by a fair wind and plenty of it. They restarted their engines and with final farewells *Teval* resumed her course and continued on her way. Our message home was to be duly sent by fax.

It was now present opening time. The bags contained all we had agreed with the captain plus more. Rice, potatoes, vegetables, fruit, cheese and what was more an extraordinary number of loaves of bread of all different kinds. Then to our great surprise and pleasure a carton of German beer. Our happy hour was about to be resurrected. Captain Reese had asked if he should send over milk and eggs but after some discussion with him we had decided against these. We had plenty of the former and thought it would be pushing our luck with the eggs.

Suddenly we started living again. At breakfast it was no longer a case of making a decision on whether to have one's single Ryvita or save it to make a feast of two of them at lunch. Now it was 'What bread would you like? White or wholemeal, raisin or rye, sliced or thick-cut?' We could now live with the loss of our porridge. Also the belief that it has libido, enhancing properties was possibly not now important for some of the crew in view of the time we had been at sea. After our return home I wrote to the chairman of the company owning *Teval* to express our appreciation of the great kindness shown by Captain Reese and offering to pay for the stores transferred, but heard no more.

The captain was correct with his synopsis. Overnight the wind started to pick up and next morning extending through the following day we drove before a full gale from the south under our standard trysail and storm jib heavy-weather rig, complemented by a rag of closely reefed genoa. She was balanced and going well, albeit the conditions were rough and uncomfortable, but who cared? We were on track, making good time.

Jeremy's radio was now being put to good use. Not to hear the politicians wrangling but something meaningful. The Shipping Forecast. We had entered sea area west Sole. Moreover it was telling us what we wanted to hear.

The wind slowly decreased and, finally deciding to do what it was supposed to have done way back, settled into the west and was to stay between south-west and north-west until we got into home waters. Under leaden skies and immersed in misty dampness we arrived on the evening of 4 June in the Inshore Traffic Zone off the Bishop Rock, which guards the southern extremity of the Isles of Scilly. Whereupon the breeze left us. Our fuel position was critical. Wanting to ensure we had enough to get us onto our mooring in Falmouth Harbour, should the wind be unhelpful, we remained windless and motionless overnight, going up and down with the tide. In these waters, however, we were secure in the knowledge it was only a matter of sitting it out until the wind came back. I will let Fraser have a final commentary from his journal: 'Jeremy signs off as head chef with a grand spaghetti Bolognese. We are getting dab hands at preparing cooking and serving some quite tasty meals with one hand, while holding the Primus with the other and balancing at the same time. We hear Falmouth Coastguard. What a fabulous sound that good old Cornish voice! Changed watches and clocks to BST.'

It was now time for us to call up the Coastguard to report our arrival in home waters. Back they came with the request we keep them informed on our progress. They then broke the news which we had not really anticipated. A reception party had been organised to welcome us home and they, the Coastguard, would keep it up to date on our position and our likely time of arrival. What a service! Who would deny we have the best coastguard in the world? Everything comes to an end, including calms, and at breakfast next morning a gentle breeze came in from the north-west, only managing a Force 1 to 2, but we were moving. It was spinnaker time for the last fling. With that friendly breeze steadily building *Marelle* was going beautifully, taking us, as Jeremy with deep sentiment phrased it, 'down the wonderfully green and pleasant looking Cornish coast.' She had brought us home.

At intervals we called up the Coastguard, keeping them fully briefed as we crossed Mount's Bay and closed Lizard Point. They confirmed they were maintaining contact with the reception party who would be in position on Pendennis Point for the big welcome home. This vantage spot, immediately below the Coastguard station itself, at the entrance to the harbour, is where that self-same group had seen us off so many months before.

BACK TO THE LIZARD

Still carrying the spinnaker, pulling like the proverbial horse, we were off the Lizard at 1800. Dropping the spinnaker, we entered the home strait under main and genoa. With the flood tide under us we headed for The Manacles buoy making seven knots over the ground. I gave a further progress report to the Coastguard who told me to 'stand by'. On the radio came a voice I knew only too well.

'You don't know who this is, do you?'

'I can't imagine, but will be with you soon, luv.' There was a chorus of 'Ooh ahs' from the female staff in the background. The Coastguard had called Susan into their holy of holies, the operations control room.

'Falmouth Coastguard. This is *Marelle*. Can you give us a contact channel or telephone number please for Customs?'

'*Marelle*. Coastguard. Don't worry. We will call them for you and come back to you.'

A few minutes later, '*Marelle*. Coastguard. Have spoken with Customs. No problem. Just give them a call on their phone in Plymouth sometime after you get in.' That is Her Majesty's Coastguard for you!

Escorting us in were two boats belonging to friends of Fraser, *Forty Love* and *Maid of Islay*. The *Maid* had escorted us out of Falmouth when we had passed through those waters when setting out for the south over nine months before. We could only assume that her skipper and crew had been home for meals and to get their washing done in the intervening period.

At 2015 we could make out against the setting sun the little group of wives and friends on the Point, waving for all they were worth. It was a beautiful evening. Everything was just perfect. It was engine on for the run up the inner harbour against the evening breeze, asking *Maid of Islay* if she would stay with us in case we ran out of fuel over those last few metres. But we didn't. I had not wanted to incur any delay in our getting ashore by having to beat up harbour against the light headwind. On our way up to our buoy, off the Royal Cornwall Yacht Club, we passed *Taonui* on a visitor's buoy. Standing in her cockpit were Tony and his wife Coryn, all smiles. Tony could afford to grin. He had beaten us home. He jumped into his dinghy to help us secure to our buoy and then hand up a can of cold beer for each of us.

There was a strange feeling of being disconnected from the landscape around us, having for so long been isolated in a featureless, unbounded seascape. It was an unreal experience, after ninety days at sea, to set foot on the bottom rung of the steps leading up to the lawn in front of the club house and attempt the climb with our legs, devoid of strength, wobbling uncontrollably under us. Staggering on to the grass with warm, helping arms on either side, the champagne corks were popped. It was all over. Objectives achieved. It was home to bed, the dream consummated. We had rounded Cape Horn.

APPENDIX ONE

FEEDING THE INNER MAN

Adrie Burnett

'So, what does he have for breakfast?'

'Tea, cereal, eggs, two bits of toast, butter, jam, juice, coffee, milk, sugar.'

Thus began our plans to store ship for our husbands' voyage to Cape Horn.

'Right, we'll multiply by seven days and again by thirty-two weeks and by two men … that makes:

448 tea bags
16 lbs sugar
32 jars of coffee
224 litres milk
64 litres fruit juice
20 boxes cereal
48 jars jam, honey etc.
36 dozen eggs
80 lbs bread flour'

This would never do. We'd filled the boat twice over and we'd only done breakfast!

'Do you think they'd settle for porridge some mornings? A two-kilo bag of porridge oats will make breakfast for two men for twenty days. The strong plastic bag will stow in awkward corners …' Porridge turned out to be so popular that they had to restock in the Falklands where unfortunately they bought Quaker Oats in cardboard boxes with no inner bag. The boxes soon went soggy and the oats sour. Jeremy and Fraser refused but Ben kept right on eating them. On their return Ben wrote to the Quaker Oats people to complain. Somewhat mystified about the problem, the company nevertheless apologised and sent a couple of vouchers by way of compensation.

By the time Susan and I had planned what our menfolk might eat during a week and had multiplied by thirty-two weeks, and had allowed for the fact that for some of the time there would be three on board, we had some idea of how much was needed. A staggering amount!

Ben wanted to stock up as much as possible here in Falmouth because replacing tinned food on passage might not be easy. For this reason we divided what was required into 'non-perishables' such as tinned foods, pasta, rice, milk powder etc. and 'perishables' comprising fresh fruit, vegetables, eggs etc. To decide on which brand of tinned foods, we issued each other with samples to be tried and graded at home. A lot of tinned meat is pretty awful and quite a few samples got the thumbs down. Then Susan came up with a list of recipes needing, for instance, one tin of beef stew, one tin Scotch broth, one tin peas, one teaspoon of chilli powder and dried thyme. Ben practised these at home until the results reached perfection! As long as we provided the necessary ingredients all would be well. Jeremy is a more experimental 'let's see what we've got' cook, leading to mixed and interesting results. Fraser's speciality was fish cakes using tinned salmon and instant mashed potato. These he apparently turned out good-humouredly in the most trying circumstances.

Food takes on an exaggerated importance during long passages. On their return the one complaint was lack of variety. I readily agreed but am not sure how it could have been improved. Of the tinned meat and fish we sampled, only about ten made the grade. The boat had spices and dried herbs but of course very little fresh food once they were well offshore. These limitations, plus the sad fact that none of our men has featured on *Ready, Steady, Cook*, goes some way towards explaining the lack of variety.

To stow the boat for maximum utilisation of space I drew out the interior layout, measured the various compartments, noted where the stringers ran and where the spaces between the frames would take a four-inch tin on its side or a seven-inch one. Generally tins of the same sort. e.g. meats or rice pudding, were stored together. There was a convenient cubic space underneath a seat which became the *five day variety store*, the idea being that this would be used up first and then restocked from the main stores for the next four or five days. It worked pretty well and prevented a lot of upheaval digging out a can of baked beans from underneath a sleeping body.

The fo'c'sle bunk was not needed so became available for bulk storage. Large plastic containers of sugar, coffee, powdered milk, cocoa etc. fitted here. I had made an extra-large lee cloth from an old sail which fastened down on the outboard edge as well, thus preventing the load from leaping about. Sails etc. could still be piled on top.

We asked Paul Heiney, author of the *Ham and Pork* book, for a source of dry, cured ham that would last through tropical weather. He recommended Richard Woodall of Waberthwaite, Cumbria, who duly supplied a whole ham on the bone. This swung about in its pillowcase in the fo'c'sle and was chopped at as required. However, somewhere south of the Doldrums, maggots were discovered making themselves at home. That bit was cut away and the ham moved to the sterndeck in the fresh air where it kept well. They, our men that is, finished it off the Brazilian coast. It needed soaking in fresh water which was of course a problem. Consequently the ham was always a little salty.

Ben is unhappy when deprived of butter. A search began for the tinned variety readily available in places like West Africa where refrigeration cannot be guaranteed. Try as I might I could not get any here. Finally I rang our son's fiancée who was working at the Royal Geographical Society. Explaining my frustrated efforts, Juliet said 'How many pallets do you want?' One duly arrived and Ben was happy.

Of course, butter needs fresh bread and Jeremy made both yeast and soda bread successfully, weather permitting. Ryvita was the alternative.

To go with this we gave them four red Edam cheeses in the hope that these would keep better than the plastic-wrapped variety. The heat and humidity did finally get to them but they lasted until Mar del Plata.

Most modern passage-making boats have galleys equipped with fridges, freezers and microwaves and carry enough fuel to keep these running. *Marelle* is not one of these. Furthermore her ability to communicate was minimal. They had to be self-sufficient. Consequently we supplied mostly tinned food for when fresh food ran out. Dried goods require fresh water which might have been a problem. Inspired by visions of shipwrecked sailors on lonely islands, we carefully labelled the tins with indelible pens before removing their wrappers and storing them. On their island they may not have been able to open the tins but at least they would know what they were missing!

Here is a list of the main foodstuffs supplied:

Dry cured ham	7 kg
Tinned vegetables	240
Tinned meat/fish	330
Baked beans	72
Tinned fruit	60
Tinned rice pudding	96
Tinned soup	110
Tinned butter	11 kg
Dried fruit	5 kg
Powdered potato	4 kg
Spaghetti	16 kg
Cup-a-soups	54
Milk powder	10 kg

Sugar	4 kg
Rice	16 kg
Instant coffee	2.5 kg
Cooking oil	6 litres
Jam/honey	5 kg
Flour	16 kg
Oatmeal	8 kg
UHT milk	24 litres
Juice	16 litres
Edam cheeses	4
Tea bags	1000

Fresh food for the first three weeks to the Canaries included:

Bread	5 loaves
Butter/margarine	4 kg (stored in a cool box)
Vacuum-packed ham/bacon	2 kg
Cheddar cheese	1.5 kg
Eggs	3 dozen

and as many cabbages, potatoes, french beans, onions, carrots, bananas, oranges etc. as we could still squeeze in.

On their return they had left some tins of corned beef, tomatoes and rice pudding but not much more. And some day, when *Marelle* gets a refit, someone is going to find a Christmas pudding I put in there and wonder how long it has been there!

APPENDIX TWO

BIRDS AND OTHER WILDLIFE

Jeremy Burnett

The first thing that I should say is that I am not an expert but, as I am sure all voyagers will agree, the sea can be boring at times and, as time passes, what is to be seen in the way of nature becomes increasingly a means of entertainment and education. Thus as our trip went on we tried to identify what we saw and to relate this to the area in which we were sailing, and to what we had read in books about previous voyages along our route.

It seemed to me, as an amateur observer, that the further south we went the more interesting things became. This may be because the southern ocean had a novelty to it that could not be said of more northerly latitudes, but also by then we were used to life at sea and were more observant of what was around us.

We made no special preparations for wildlife observation. I had read some books and was looking forward to seeing albatrosses, steamer ducks and penguins, and hoping to see whales. We had on board *Seabirds*, an identification guide by Peter Harrison. This is extremely comprehensive and amazingly detailed. The Chile pilot also had an interesting section on flora and fauna. I kept a daily journal and noted down everything I saw; some of the identifications are probably dubious. It is very difficult, without expert guidance, to be always sure of what you are looking at. It wasn't until we got home that I was able to ask people about some things and confirm what they were.

Falmouth to Cape Verdes
The first note I have about birds says that in West Biscay I saw Cory's shearwaters. Then west of the Portuguese coast a whale was seen spouting; I remember thinking that the spout was more feeble than expected. North of the Canaries we passed a turtle flapping along, and there were many dolphins. South of the Canaries we met up with our first flying fish. These explode from the surface and using their tails for propulsion skim for considerable distances. Occasionally one would land on deck, and in the morning there were usually one or two in the scuppers.

Cape Verde to Mar del Plata

Apart from the ever-present flying fish the equatorial area seemed pretty empty. By 10 November as we neared the Brazilian coast at about 15°S there were no more and on the subsequent voyage north we saw the first of them again at 13°S. However, their departure was compensated for by the appearance of our first albatrosses. Some were black-browed and one magnificent bird we put down as a royal. Between about 20°S and Mar del Plata the black-browed became more and more common.

Mar del Plata to Punta Arenas

Mar del Plata itself was remarkable only for a large and smelly colony of southern sea lions that lived in an area near the fishing harbour. They are much bigger than the sleek Californian variety; the males have lion-like ruffs and are huge animals. Further south when coasting we could tell when there was a sea lion colony ashore from the smell that wafted some miles out to sea.

Before arriving at Mar del Plata and soon after we departed I had been seeing a bird I could not identify. It looked like a large guillemot as it swam around. It dived on our approach and made a strange mooing sound. At last the penny dropped and we realised that these were Magellanic penguins. One is so used to seeing pictures of penguins standing up that the fact they are wide-ranging sea birds initially fails to register. It was on this coast that penguins were first given their name by early British explorers.

As we sailed south birds became more plentiful, especially albatrosses and petrels, including the very small storm petrels. The most common variety was probably the Cape petrel. On one occasion a vast raft of many types of bird was seen inshore. Some were wheeling and diving and the whole scene appeared one of confusion. There was obviously a major food source present. I believe this may have been stirred up by a whale.

The Golfo Nuevo

RHEA

On this piece of coast is a major breeding area for southern right whales; there are also dolphins and orca (killer whales). As we were eager to press on we did not stop here and it was only when we were further south that we finally saw a whale breach. We did however stop for a couple of nights at Puerto Santa Elena, a beautiful deserted bay. Early in the morning a group of rheas walked across above the beach. These are ostrich-like birds that inhabit the pampas. Also ashore were a few guanacos. These are the largest terrestrial animals of Patagonia, like a small llama, and roam the plains in groups. In the bay were grebes and oystercatchers, and we were pleased to see our first steamer ducks. These are large flightless birds that can move at a great rate across the water by flapping their wings, thus they were named 'steamer' after the early paddle steamers. Ashore in a lagoon behind the beach were black-necked swans, the sacred bird of the Aonikenk Indians.

Punta Arenas to The Falklands

After our stop at Punta Arenas we continued west and south through the Chilean *Canales*. The shores closed in around us well covered with trees and greenery. The trees are mostly southern beech, but there are many other plants such as wild fuchsia. At the water's edge we started to see snow-white kelp geese. In the water there were black and white Commerson's dolphins. Over the mountains we saw large raptors, possibly condors. Black-browed albatrosses were common, as were terns. Turning east towards the Beagle Channel there were plenty of steamer ducks and small islands covered in trees with small beaches and clumps of flowers. On the beach at Caleta Olla a Patagonian fox chewed at our shorelines, no doubt attracted to the beach by the rubbish left behind by previous visitors. At Puerto Williams there was a group of ruffed ibises that flew over every morning; these are conversational birds that sound as if they are having a chat as they fly along. Also here were ashy-headed geese.

There is a sizeable fishing industry in this area mostly catching spider crabs and sea urchins. Mussels used to be the staple diet of the local canoe Indians but this fishery is largely closed due to the presence of toxic red algae, *marea roja*.

Between Le Maire Straits and the Falkland Islands we had some of the most spectacular bird displays of the whole trip. Every evening a huge gathering seemed to take place for our benefit. Wandering, royal and black-browed albatrosses circled the boat as well as petrels, prions, fulmars and shearwaters, seemingly of many types. It was a spectacular display.

The Falklands

The islands have a reputation for wonderful wildlife and we were not disappointed on this score. Apart from the shorefront colonies of upland geese that are persecuted by the local vegetable growers there are many steamer ducks in the harbour. These are violently territorial, allowing no stranger to enter their patch. We were able to take a trip to a penguin rookery, with a local guide, where there were king and gentoo penguins; at other sites there are also rockhoppers. The rookeries are noisy and smelly. Our guide later brought us a 3lb brown trout he had caught in the local river. The islands are keen to develop wildlife and fishing tourism but at present the local economy depends largely on the commercial squid fishery carried on by Japanese and Korean boats, who pay licence fees.

Falklands to Falmouth

Heading north we passed through the same bird zones as we had on the way south. But as we were further off the mainland shore some things were different. We were followed by albatrosses and at one stage we thought the same wandering albatross stayed for three days. On 6 April at 23° 43′ S we saw the last one. On the 8th we identified a masked booby. By the 12th the southern ocean birds had gone but we were seeing boobies, terns and storm petrels. On 17 April a brown noddy briefly took up residence.

BROWN NODDY

25 April was a landmark day when we caught our first fish. On subsequent days we caught more. South-west of the Cape Verdes on calm days we started to see a wide variety of jellyfish. Standing in the pulpit and looking down into the clear ocean there were all sorts of fantastic shapes floating as though in space, some with long trailing tentacles, others more rigid looking. One particular variety floated on the surface, indeed sailed, as it had a transparent pink-rimmed 'sail' rigged over its purple body. The sail stuck up and blew the whole thing downwind. The body was about nine inches long and the sail was shaped like a Cornish pasty. These were later identified for me as Velella velella.

West of the Azores there were Cory's shearwaters, terns and dolphins in large numbers. Between the Azores and the Western Approaches I saw several types of dolphins as well as what I think were pilot whales.

On 2 June, 235 miles out from Falmouth, there were gannets that made us realise we had not far to go. There were also Manx shearwaters, my favourite bird.

Overall the impression had been of a fantastic diversity of all types of wildlife. I realised how little I knew about it, and became keen to know more. I would recommend that anyone going on a voyage should consider the opportunities there will be for observation and prepare themselves accordingly.

APPENDIX THREE

BREAD ON BOARD

Jeremy Burnett

On a long passage, after the supplies of shore-bought bread have been finished, nothing smells or tastes better than a freshly baked loaf.

We found that the loaves we stocked up with before leaving lasted a couple of weeks, the actual eatability time depending on factors such as storage, latitude and one's attitude to mould! After a bit, when surface mould appeared, this could be trimmed off and the core toasted. I had read that 'double baked' bread had greater endurance but this is not easy to obtain. I did get the baker in Stanley to do some but cannot say that it showed much improvement over the normal.

The answer therefore is to bake one's own. I tried three methods:
1.   Bread-mix packets
2.   Straightforward plain flour and dried yeast
3.   Soda bread

Bread mix is fine and produces good results but it has some storage problems as the paper packets are vulnerable to damp. The advantage of plain flour, as I see it, is that this will probably be carried for other uses anyway so it simplifies life to carry only the one variety. Sachets of dried yeast seem to travel well and eliminate the need for measurement. I used the recipe on the yeast packets and found I did not need to do any weighing. Once the recipe is established a mug can be used to measure out ingredients by volume. Don't forget the salt! Fat can be margarine, olive oil or lard. Improvisation may be necessary as the voyage proceeds.

Baking required a little practice. As the ocean did not often seem to be flat the manipulation of the oven could be tricky. I would recommend that anyone contemplating a voyage should pay careful attention to the cooker gimballing arrangements. With the standard cooker when the oven door is open its weight will cause the cooker to tilt inwards, and if there is not a ledge on the oven shelf any tray inside will slide out! This can be overcome by fixing a weight to the bottom of the cooker so that the weight of the door will not tilt it. Oven doors should also have ledges.

In the breadmaking process, after mixing and kneading the dough has to be left to rise or 'prove'. This has to be done in a 'warm place'. It may well be that there is not one handy. No problem in the tropics, but in high latitudes one has to be conjured up. When we make bread at home I find that the bottom oven of the Aga, with the door open, does this very well so in *Marelle* I developed a variation to suit. The oven would be lit and allowed to warm up for a few minutes; when warm the gas would be turned off, the tin of dough put in, and the door closed. The insulation of the oven kept it warm enough to make the dough rise which could take forty-five minutes or longer. Once the dough had risen then the oven could be relit for baking.

This is simple to write, but in this procedure there are hidden dangers. Open the oven door and the previously explained problem can occur with the loaf ending up on the sole. Also, if the tin gets a sharp knock while being moved this may cause the risen loaf to collapse, meaning the 'proving' has to be done again. Enough to make any baker head for the Ryvita packet. To overcome this I would usually ask Fraser to hold the cooker steady while the oven was relit. Baking took around thirty-five minutes and the results were always worth the effort.

Soda bread is in some ways an easier proposition. It is made with baking powder and soda instead of yeast. I was given a recipe by friends in America. It also cuts out the 'proving' part of the operation, going straight from kneading to baking; it is thus economic on time and gas. It can also have raisins and other stuff added. My recipe called for buttermilk which we achieved by mixing a bit of vinegar into our powdered milk mix. As those who have sailed in Ireland will know, soda bread is delicious.

No discussion of on-board baking would be complete without a mention of flapjacks. These were unquestionably the most popular product to come from the oven. A simple recipe came from an on-board cookbook. Oats, golden syrup and brown sugar mixed up, put in a tray and baked. After cooling put in a tin for storage. The tin lived on a shelf in the saloon. Somehow there was never as much in the tin in the morning as there had been the evening before.

On-board baking can contribute greatly to the pleasure of a voyage and help to sustain crew morale in hard times. It is not difficult, and with a little practice before setting off success will be assured.

APPENDIX FOUR

SURVIVAL AT SEA

In an extended voyage embracing two oceans from one temperate zone, across the tropics to the other zone and back, it is inescapable a measure of bad weather will be encountered. We had our share. Normal Force 8 blows, if you can refer to a full gale as normal, hit us on several occasions in the more northerly latitudes of the North Atlantic and again further south in the South Atlantic regions. These blows were taxing enough but did not cause us too much difficulty apart from discomfort. What did stretch us were the two severe gales in the south, with one estimated to be reaching storm Force 10 on the Beaufort scale. That is a lot of wind and severally tests boat and crew. The more intense blow was handled by running before the seas and we felt safe, albeit losing a lot of ground in the process. *Marelle* tracked well with her long, deep keel down into the more stable water flowing beneath the turbulent, broken surface of the seas.

Much has been written of course about storm tactics, with comments on the various options that have been exercised in coping with extreme conditions in small craft in open waters. The conclusion that inevitably one comes to is that it is a doubtful exercise in trying to draw up 'recommended procedures for handling heavy weather', which the experts attempt to do. The infinite variations in weather conditions and wave formations are matched only by the equally infinite combinations of boat size, design and type. To attempt to get some corelation between all these variables would not seem to be too meaningful.

Over the years I had read various opinions on the subject but I think one that really impressed me was the view advanced by Bernard Moitessier, developed in turn from the influence of Vito Dumas, that indomitable Argentinian single-hander. Essentially it seemed they were talking about lessening the relative speed of very big seas, by running unhindered before them in order to reduce the force of the breaking waves hitting the boat and which were kept just on the quarter. Speed was the vital ingredient.

Their beliefs, based on actual experience in very severe conditions and extremely dangerous seas, would seem to run counter to the popular idea of streaming drogues or long lengths of warp to slow the boat down. In holding the stern at right angles to the wave fronts these devices are supposed to prevent broaching which could lead to a capsize. At the same time whilst holding the boat back they are expected to reduce the chances of the bows digging in and the boat turning end for end or pitchpoling. That may be the right thinking perhaps for lightweight multihulls travelling at express-train speeds but is it relevant for the more pedestrian, non-extreme monohull? Moitessier certainly did not think so.

The argument then works round to using a sea anchor off the bow. Until the advent of the parachute version this extraordinarily unhandy piece of gear had largely gone out of favour. All are agreed that the loads on the boat due to the parachute, as well as sea anchors in general, are very great indeed. Can it be right to subject the boat and her deck fittings to such high loadings? I personally have serious doubts. Alec Rose, it would appear, had similar misgivings. He records an occasion, earlier in his sailing experience, when streaming a sea anchor off the bow the seas were kept just forward of the beam but he noted the 'terrific' strain on the boat and warp. He further commented that with a sea anchor deployed in some of the weather encountered during his circumnavigation, he suspected that if the gear had not ended up being carried away, the boat was likely to have been damaged by the impact of wave crests.

Apart from the massive strains imposed by devices aimed at restricting the boat's natural free play, that is drogues and sea anchors, there is the great difficulty with their deployment and recovery, not to mention the storage problem. Sea anchors are not economical on space in a small boat.

Trying to rig and stream a large, complicated piece of gear such as the parachute sea anchor in a seaway, possibly at night, would tax even the strongest of crews, let alone say a single-hander. Drogues would be somewhat easier but again the prospect is a daunting one, should it be deemed necessary to weight down the outer end with something like an anchor and chain. Working on the cramped afterdeck of a small boat in a big running seaway is not a task to be contemplated with any feeling of equanimity.

In *Marelle* we were equipped to stream a form of drogue, carrying two car tyres for the purpose, with three 100-metre warps plus lengths of chain as needs be to weigh the whole assembly down. The tyres, fitted with chain support strops, had been artistically frapped with old rope by Adrie to stop them marking topsides, ours or anyone else's, as their other purpose in life was to act as a robust fender alongside other craft and hostile harbour walls. We had used them for this end but never found it necessary to deploy them as a drogue or even consider doing so. It is conceivable they would have been useful if we had been threatened with a lee shore but that would have to be a special circumstance with *Marelle* disabled and unable to claw offshore. It can be justifiably argued that in open waters, drogues or particularly sea anchors, of whatever design, can be useful in reducing the drift of the boat, when lying to in heavy weather, if wind and wave are inconveniently driving her in the wrong direction, but I feel the downside more than outweighs any benefit.

Then there is lying a-hull, letting the boat give to seas thereby reducing the force of the water striking the hull. For a boat of the characteristics of *Lively Lady* Alec Rose felt this was the preferred method, and he should know. Uncomfortable but safe unless caught by a giant rogue wave, which would be disastrous whatever storm tactic had been adopted. In the same category is the time honoured practice of heaving to with the smallest of sail areas for the boat to maintain some headway, giving to the waves with the sea just forward of the beam. The leeway will be considerable but that in itself is a good thing as it reduces the water impact. But here again it all depends on the type of boat. Modern designs are infamously not good at heaving to whereas older designs are usually more compliant. *Marelle* with her long deep keel and narrow to moderate beam is so inclined. She would lie to, quite relaxed under storm jib set on the inner forestay and trysail sheeted well in. With the storm jib set this way the centre of effort of the sail plan is nearer to the centre of lateral resistance, balancing the rig and keeping the bows up more into the wind than if the jib had been in the more usual position at the stemhead. We used the trysail a lot and this practice threw up a handling problem. We should have had a separate track for the sail. I thought I could get away without fitting one on the mast but this was a mistake. Having to feed the trysail into the mainsail track through a gate was laborious and at times rather risky. Moreover it really needed two people.

I felt that for *Marelle*, being of conventional design, albeit now considered old-fashioned, the long-established techniques embracing heaving to, lying a-hull or running before the sea were the most appropriate to adopt. We used these methods in severe weather and they served us well.

It is food for thought that in the 1979 Fastnet tragedy of the twenty-four boats abandoned nineteen were later recovered still afloat. Many of them had their hatches left wide open as the crews had taken to the liferafts. This would suggest that the boat, free to take up a natural position and give to the elements, is ultimately at her safest.

Support for the school of thought that a boat is safer in heavy weather if allowed to give to the seas comes from a somewhat unusual source. A graphic illustration of the probable salvation of a boat by letting her have freedom of movement is contained in an account by Tim Severin of coping with a full gale, encountered between Iceland and Greenland, in his 36-foot curragh *Brendan*. In this vessel, constructed in the traditional way on the west coast of Ireland, of leather stretched over a wooden framework, Severin was attempting to prove that Irish monks in medieval times successfully navigated the North Atlantic in such unlikely craft, ending up with one of their number discovering North America many centuries before Columbus.

Brendan had been running before the gale, rising to severe gale 9, and was in serious trouble of life-threatening proportions. Flooding, as a result of repeated poopings, was about to sink them. In the crew was a Faeroes islander with considerable experience of handling small craft in those stormy waters. On being asked if he thought they would be safer riding to a sea anchor his reply was unequivocal. Their best hope of survival was to continue running, allowing the curragh to slither or in effect slalom down the fronts of the waves. As the Færoes seaman put it, 'If we have sea anchor, *Brendan* cannot move.' With the seas hitting the bow they would be in bigger trouble from flooding and damage. Severin and his redoubtable crew were able to rig up leather screens to keep most of the water out of the open after end of the vessel and, despite continuing to be pooped at times, they ran on in comparative safety.

Under the heading of *Survival at Sea* comes the question of survival in the liferaft and in retrospect it may have been that a little more thought could have gone into planning for this eventuality. Of particular relevance was the South Atlantic. It was only when we were down in that ocean that we fully appreciated what an enormous empty waste it occupies. If we had found ourselves in the liferaft adrift in that expanse we could have been there for a very long time. The whole question was of much greater magnitude than for its northern neighbour.

In the eastern part of the South Atlantic near the west coast of South Africa the Beuguela Current flows in a northerly direction to become the South Equatorial Current and turn westwards. This is also the path of the south-east trades. A liferaft in these waters would eventually end up in the Caribbean. It has nowhere else to go.

If however one had the misfortune to be adrift further west and between the parallels of 10°S and 40°S the liferaft could get caught in the counterclockwise current and end up going round and round for ever. When Jeremy and I were heading towards Brazil we noticed a dark object lying low and motionless in the water. It was not impossible for it to have been a liferaft so we went over to investigate. It was a ship's mooring buoy which presumably had broken its moorings, quite probably having started its cruise from a West African port. It was heavily fouled with marine growth and looked as though it had been in the water for a very long time. At the time we were in the South Subtropical Current, and that buoy could still be out there in that great ocean, sweeping endlessly round in an enormous circle.

Our liferaft contains only a limited quantity of life support items. To bolster these there was, ready to hand in the stern locker in the cockpit, a 'grab bag'. In this was a miscellany of basics to improve the life style of the unfortunates in the liferaft. Biscuits, glucose sweets, orange juice, string, tin opener, towel, signalling mirror, container into which to urinate, toilet roll etc, etc. As a companion to this was another grab bag full of emergency flares. Adding to all of this was the portable manual watermaker. On the assumption we would eventually be rescued we each made up a personal satchel containing passport, cash and credit cards. With me went the handheld VHF radio in its waterproof bag.

With the South Atlantic in mind it would have been sensible to have made up a small stock of tinned food in a sealed flexible container, kept readily accessible but never touched until needed for the liferaft. The food stocks in the liferaft and grab bag certainly needed bolstering. To help with the catering, we should also I feel have given more attention to a more comprehensive pre-assembled small fishing kit with a selection of lures plus a telescopic fish spear. Additionally, although their performance is suspect, a solar still might have been a last-ditch backup to the watermaker. There were tucked away on board an emergency two gallons of water in a plastic container specifically to be taken with us. The liferaft was a six-man one so there was room for all this extra baggage with only three of us in it.

If the death of the boat was dramatically sudden there would obviously be no time for all of this gear to be collected up. However if there was time for an ordered entry into the raft it was to be hoped that most, if not all, of the emergency items, being already packed, could be taken.

Before we left Falmouth there was a general discussion with wives present on the subject of survival in the liferaft, and Adrie made the suggestion that we should have the means for propulsion and not be entirely at the mercy of wind and current. In other words a sail. The idea had obvious merit but was considered impracticable. Liferafts are not designed to be sailed and moreover are only expected to provide a short-term refuge. On reflection it was something we should have pursued. It should be possible to devise a simple telescopic mast with a sail attached which could be set up in the canopy opening. In the South Atlantic it could well be the difference between life and death by providing a means of breaking free from the grip of the prevailing currents.

Survival at Sea is a wide subject and may not relate only to saving one's physical self but may also concern the preservation of one's sanity. We involuntarily played a game in *Marelle* called 'Chase the Can'. In one locker there is always one can that has not been securely jammed in place. It lies silent until the occupant of the adjacent bunk has snuggled down into his sleeping bag. It is one of the natural laws that the can is always next to the sleeper's head. It lies silent until the moment of dropping off to sleep. The can then, as Fraser once put it, tangos from one side to the other. The bunk occupant first tries to ignore it but is finally beaten. Pulls the backrest squab off its Velcro, opens the locker door to try to locate the errant can. No sign of it. All seems secure. He moves things around a bit and then closes the door. All is silent. Puts the cushion back in place and settles down once more and zips up his bag. Tango starts again. The game goes on until the would-be sleeper is in a state of mind which, if he had been at home, would have meant calling in the men in white coats.

Navigational Notes
Although the risk of losing the services of the GPS to tell us at a glance where we were was very slight, it nevertheless was a possibility that had to be taken into account. Failure of the boat's electrical power would close down the installed GPS set and then a malfunctioning of the stand-by, handheld unit would mean we were lost at sea.

To provide for this contingency we carried two sextants, two different forms of sight reduction tables, plotting sheets, star charts and a quartz watch with a known rate of gain, plus my star globe.

If we had had to fall back on astro-navigation I would have used the method known as longitude by chronometer which at one time had been used in merchant shipping. Although the system involves not inconsiderable calculation and hence is susceptible to error, I prefer it to the modern short, quick and easy system which uses three volumes of *Sight Reduction Tables for Air Navigation.* Despite the title they have been used widely in marine navigation and are the basis of the RYA's Yachtmaster Ocean courses. The disadvantage is the system requires lines being drawn to a considerable degree of precision on charts, or more usually special plotting sheets, when laying off azimuths and position lines. The drawback is, when in a strongly flowing seaway, it is not easy to fight a bucking chart table to accomplish this drawing work.

In my experience it is easier to wedge oneself in a corner of the cabin with work book on knee and Norie's compact book of tables open on the bunk ready to hand.

For those interested in the methodology and mathematically so inclined, longitude by chronometer solves the spherical triangle PZX, the so-called navigational triangle described as though on the earth's surface, where P is the earth's pole nearest to the observer, Z is the observer's position below the zenith and X is the point on the earth immediately beneath the heavenly body. The included angle ZPX between the meridians of the body and the observer is the local hour angle LHA. The object of the exercise is to determine the LHA at the time of the observation. Then the difference between it and the Greenwich hour angle GHA of the body gives the longitude of the observer.

To calculate the LHA the cosine haversine formula is worked, the haversine being a device which, always being positive, ensures suitability of use with logarithms. The formula reads:

$$\text{hav LHA} = \frac{\text{havZX} - \text{hav(latitude} \pm \text{declination)}}{\cos \text{latitude.cos declination}}$$

The zenith distance (ZX) is the angular distance (subtended at the earth's centre) between the observer's zenith and the body, and is equal to 90° minus the altitude. The zenith is the point on the celestial sphere directly overhead. The declination is the angular distance of the body from the celestial equator. The latitude is of course that of the observer.

The formula looks daunting but in fact is straightforward in application, the necessary input being readily available from nautical tables such as Norie's or Burton's and the Nautical Almanac. Not so long ago these were indispensable volumes on the navigator's bookshelf over the chart table. The formula requires the DR (dead reckoning) latitude to be plugged into it and of course the calculated longitude is dependent on the DR latitude accuracy. The latitude is confirmed in due course by a meridian or ex-meridian altitude by sextant of any body that happens to be conveniently placed in the firmament, but usually this would be either the sun or a star.

It has to be said that although the method using the tables for air navigation is not as accurate as cos-hav, the degree of precision is within that which can be achieved with the sextant at sea.

In actual practice for us none of this had to be resorted to, as the GPS behaved itself and there was no need to fall back on what would be regarded by today's yachtsperson as a relic of quaint antiquity. But what would happen if their GPS fell down?

When considering the fallibility of electronically controlled equipment the memory of the tragic fate that overtook Peter Mulgrew comes before me. It had been through him, all those years ago, that I had been offered an opportunity to have the Cape Horn experience. He paid a return visit to Antarctica as the in-flight commentator in a DC 10, chartered from Air New Zealand, to take a group of sightseers for a flight over the continent. The plane was full. In very low visibility it crashed onto the slopes of Mount Erebus, killing all on board. The official reason given for the accident was incorrect data input into the plane's electronic navigational system. It could be said that this was not the fault of the equipment itself, but in earlier times the pilot would have used his natural senses and turned back to safety.

MARELLE

Reprinted from *Yachting Monthly* August 1965
Reviewed by Bill Mison

Third off the stocks since Deacons Boatyard at Bursledon, after many years of repair work, decided last year to start building, this deep fin keeler came from the drawing boards of cruise-racer designers McGruer of Clynder to the requirements of keen ocean racer Mrs Honor Spink. On their mettle, with such distinguished designers and experienced owner to please, Deacons have completed a craft of excellent material and craftsmanship.

Carvel planked in 7/8in finished teak, with 7/8in teak transom, on an all-afrormosia backbone, the stem, timbers and the one-piece stern post, horn timber, outreach and shaft chock all laminated, with 1½in Canadian rock elm intermediate frames, the lead ballast keel is secured with bronze bolts. All under-water fittings, rudder stock and pintle, and all floors are also in bronze. Beams are of larch, oak and spruce, carlins of laminated mahogany, cockpit and coachroof coamings of 7/8in teak, fore-and-afters of spruce, deck of 7/16in teak laid on 6mm proofed ply, and the 3/8in ply coachroof is glass fibre covered.

The mast heel butts into a 3.5ft long galvanised mild steel base secured on the coachroof, and the mast beam, pillars and hanging knees are of the same metal. Fastenings of copper-bronze and galvanised steel bolts, silicon-bronze screws and copper nails, standing rigging, bow and stern pulpits, guardrail stanchions and sockets in stainless steel complete a high specification.

Her sails, comprising main, three jibs, three genoas and two spinnakers, are by Bruce Banks and J.R. Williams, the alloy mast by Ian Proctor and the boom is spruce.the binnacle aft in the cockpit carries the wheel and a Danforth-White Constellation compass.

Below, with her waterline of only 27ft, the fine tapering bow lends well to the provision of ample stowage in the long forepeak for her very comprehensive racing wardrobe. This 12ft long compartment contains hanging cupboards to port and a draining locker to starboard of the space immediately below the forehatch, which has a Perspex panel, on the coachroof forward, a 30gal fresh-water tank, bonded store and, just forward of the saloon bulkhead portside, a toilet and shower compartment with nearly 6ft headroom, and a fridge and more lockerage to starboard.

The cable pipe elbow is on the coachroof portside and the chain pipe leads down through the toilet compartment to the chain locker below.

BEKEN OF COWES

Marelle 12 tons
Registered Number 307264. Southampton
McGruer – designed Burlesdon built ocean racer

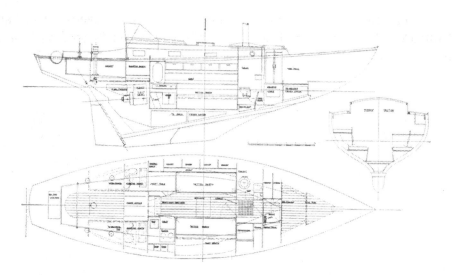

ON A 27FT WATERLINE, *MARELLE*'S LAYOUT ON DECK AND BELOW IS DESIGNED TO MEET HARD
RACING REQUIREMENTS

Abaft the forward bulkhead the 9ft long saloon, with over 6ft headroom, has a 6.25ft settee berth with a pilot berth above and stowage below starboardside and abaft the foot the galley space contains the gas cooker, sink and culinary stowage. Opposite the settee berth has shelves and lockers above and the chart table, with drawers and locker below, at the foot.

The saloon is well lighted with windows in the coamings and another Perspex panelled hatch on the coachroof just abaft the mast plate.

Between the galley and chart table the removable companionway ladder gives forward access to the engine and leads to the top of the engine compartment hatch, under the sliding coachroof hatch, with access to a 6.25ft quarter berth extending under the cockpit seats each side. A 14gal paraffin tank is sited under the starboard and another fresh water tank holding 70gal is located in the bilges.

The cockpit has sufficient seating for the watch and a six-man inflatable liferaft is housed in a semi-sunken stowage on the short aft deck. The spacios foredeck, side decks and the forehatch giving easy handreach of the sail stwage below combine with all other well-planned amenities to make working ship easy and safe.

The 15bhp Ailsa Craig AD2 diesel auxiliary is well sited for service access under the cockpit sole and drives a 14in by 7½in pitch three-bladed screw. Under power trials just over 6.5 knots was logged at 2,000rpm.

Under sail in a Force 3–4 south-easterly with her well-bedded tan Williams 11¼oz main and large genoa she was nicely stiff and on a broad reach 7 knots was indicated on her Brookes & Gatehouse log.

DATA

LOA	36.3ft
LWL	27.0ft
Beam	10.5ft
Draught	6.0ft
TM	12 tons
Ballast keel, lead	3.40 tons
Sails by Bruce Banks & J. R. Williams	
Main	335 sq ft
Weather genoa	404.5 sq ft
Light genoa	408 sq ft
Inter genoa	246 sq ft
Working jib	124.2 sq ft
Storm jib	52.1 sq ft
Trysail	111 sq ft
spinnaker	185 sq ft
Mast	Ian Proctor Metal Masts Ltd
Engine	15bhp Ailsa Craig AD2 diesel
Designers	McGruer & Co Ltd, Clynder, Dunbartonshire
Builders	Deacons Boatyard Ltd, Bursledon, Hants.
Owner	Mrs Honor Spink

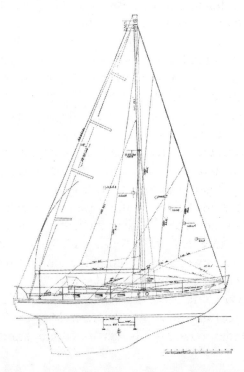